COPYRIGHT AND PUBLIC PERFORMANCE
OF MUSIC

COPYRIGHT
and
PUBLIC PERFORMANCE OF MUSIC

BY

STANLEY ROTHENBERG
A.B., LL.B., LL.D.

FRED B. ROTHMAN & CO.
Littleton, Colorado 80127

1987

Library of Congress Cataloging-in-Publication Data

Rothenberg, Stanley.
  Copyright and public performance of music.

  Reprint. Originally published: Hague : M. Nijhoff, 1954.
  Includes index.
  1. Copyright--Music. 2. Copyright--Performing rights. I. Title.
  K1457.2.R68 1987   346.04'82   87-23420
                           342.6482
  ISBN 0-8377-2535-6 (alk. paper)

 The paper used in this publication meets the minimum requirements of American National Standard for Information Sciences—Permanence of Paper for Printed Library Materials, ANSI Z39.48-1984.

COPYRIGHT
and
PUBLIC PERFORMANCE OF MUSIC

BY

STANLEY ROTHENBERG
A.B., LL.B., LL.D.

THE HAGUE
MARTINUS NIJHOFF
1954

Copyright 1954 by Martinus Nijhoff, The Hague, Holland
All rights reserved, including the right to translate or to reproduce this book or parts thereof in any form.

PRINTED IN THE NETHERLANDS

*TO BARUCH AND LENA ROTHENBERG
MY FATHER AND MOTHER*

ACKNOWLEDGMENTS

Grateful acknowledgment is made to: Mr. Herman Finkelstein, General Attorney, American Society of Composers, Authors and Publishers (ASCAP), and Mr. Robert J. Burton, Vice President and Counsel, and Mrs. Theodora Zavin, Attorney, Broadcast Music, Inc. (BMI), for their invaluable assistance; Mr C. A. Wiessing, Directeur, and Mr J. van Nus, Adjunct Directeur, Bureau voor Muziek-Auteursrecht (BUMA), for their endless co-operation; Miss An Vriend, BUMA, for her cheerful willingness to assist me; Mr. H. L. Walter, General Manager, Performing Right Society, Ltd. (PRS), Mr. Léon Malaplate, Directeur, Société Auteurs, Compositeurs et Éditeurs Musique (SACEM), and Mr. Marcel Henrion, Secretary, Fédération des Sociétés de Droits d'Execution, for their generous assistance; the Honorable Arthur Fisher, United States Register of Copyrights, for enriching my insight into the role of creators and distributors of intellectual property in a free world; Mr. Abraham Kaminstein, Chief of the Examining Division, Mr. William P. Siegfried, Assistant Register of Copyrights, Mr. George D. Cary, Principal Legal Advisor, and other members of the Copyright Office, for their expert guidance; Mr. John Schulman, of Hays, St. John, Abramson & Schulman, New York City, for his keen criticism; Professor Benjamin Kaplan, Harvard Law School, for his wise counsel; and in particular, to Professor Mr G. H. C. Bodenhausen, Utrecht University, for his inestimable help.

Further, gratitude is acknowledged for the support accorded me as a Fulbright Scholar by the United States Educational Foundation in the Netherlands.

Lastly, I appreciate the ceaseless co-operation and goodwill of Martinus Nijhoff, Publishers.

CONTENTS

INTRODUCTION 1

Part I. United States

I. AMERICAN COPYRIGHT AND COMMON LAW

 A. Distinction between common law protection and statutory copyright   5
  Common law prior to copyright statute (5). — Constitution authorizes copyright protection (5). — Congress exercises constitutional power (6). — Act does not displace common law (6). — Common law protection until publication or registration (7).

 B. Boundary between copyright and public domain.   8
  Statute requires copyright notice (8). — Authors and assigns entitled to copyright (9). — Publications abroad by foreign authors (10). — Deposit of copies; claim of copyright (11). — Manufacturing clause (11). — Duration of copyright (12). — Renewal notice? (14).

 C. Meaning of publication — especially concerning musical works   14
  Public performance; distribution of films (14). — Patterson v. Century Productions (15). — Sale and distribution of phonograph records (16). — The Miracle case (17). — Reconciling Miracle and Yacoubian (18). — Can records secure copyright? (19). — Circumventing the Miracle case (20).

 D. Conclusion.   21

II. PUBLIC PERFORMANCE OF MUSIC IN THE UNITED STATES

A. THE STATUTORY LAW 22
Nonprofit performances excluded (22). — Juke box exception (22). — Dramatico-musicals not limited (23).

B. PUBLIC PERFORMANCE FOR PROFIT AND THE COURTS 24
Receiving set in public (24). — Broadcasts are public (25). — Broadcasts are performances (25). — Commercial broadcasting (25). — Performing right is a separate right (26).

C. (ECONOMIC) NECESSITY IS THE MOTHER OF INVENTION 27
First society in France (27). — American societies (28).

D. AN ANATOMY OF ASCAP 29
I. *Birth* (29); II. *Contracts*: Present and future rights (30). — Non-dramatic rights (30). — Non-exclusive assignments; antitrust suits (31). — Blanket and per program licenses (32). — Network broadcasting (32). — Source licensing (33). — License fees subject to control (34); III. *Management and its Election*: Voting rights (34). — Nomination of directors (35); IV. *Royalties, or Raison d'Etre*: Publisher and writer royalty funds (35). — Royalty appeal procedure (36); V. *Relief Fund and Annual Dues* (36); VI. *Royalties Revisited*: Membership requirements (37). — Distribution of royalties (38). — Distribution on broadcasting performances (38). — Program analysis (39). — Foreign societies (39). — Performance values (40). — Withdrawal from society (40).

E. THE BMI STORY 40
I. *Background*: Radio opposes ASCAP (40); II. *Birth of BMI*: Radio and ASCAP settle dispute

(43); III. *Contracts*: Licences (44). — Exclusive assignments (44). — Film music (46). — Right to record (47). — Writer and publisher royalties (47). — Additional catalogs (48); IV. *Other Departments* (48); V. *Royalties*: Fixed amount per broadcast performance (50). — Unethical practices (50). — Writers receive $^1/_2$ as much as publishers (51). — Foreign rights (52). — Guarantee (53). — Analysis of broadcasting performances (53).

F. BMI AND ASCAP — DIFFERENCES AND SIMILARITIES 53
I. *Contracts*: Dramatic and non-dramatic rights (53). — Exclusive and non-exclusive assignments (54). — Disputes due to two licensors (54). — Government supervision of license fees (55). — Composition of ASCAP and BMI (56). — Motion picture performing rights (56); II. *Royalties*: Rates; distribution formulas (57). — Television performances (58). — Program analysis (58). — Non-exclusive rights (59). — Royalty appeal systems (59); III. *Withdrawal*: Withdrawal from membership (60). — BMI v. Taylor (61). — Dual membership (62); IV. *Operation*: Criticism of BMI (63). — Alleged favoritism (64). — Conclusion (64).

Part II. Britain, Netherlands, France

III. EUROPEAN COPYRIGHT

A. BERNE UNION 69
International Copyright Union (69). — National treatment (69). — Limitation on formalities (70). — Restrictions on nonmembers (71). — First publication in nonmember country (72). — Definition of publication (72). — Netherlands: sale is not publication (73). — The Gone With The Wind case (74). — England re publication (75). — Term of publication (76). — Distinction between published and unpublished works (77). — Universal Copyright Convention (77).

B. GREAT BRITAIN 78
England abolishes common law copyright (78). — First publication in U.S. (79). — Simultaneous publication (80). — Definition of publication (81). — Indefinite duration of protection (81). — Records and pre-1911 law (83). — Distribution of motion pictures (84). — Compulsory licensing (85). — Term of protection (86). — Absence of formalities (86). — Limitation on right to assign (87). — Criminal provisions (88). — Originality is not novelty (88). — Infringement must be substantial (88).

C. NETHERLANDS AND FRANCE 89
The moral right (89). — Netherlands: Act contains moral right (89). — France: recognition by jurisprudence (90). — U.S. and Britain: no moral right (90). — Nationals first published in U.S., etc. (91). — Films and records; performance of music (91). — France protects all authors (92). — Fair use; compulsory licenses; formalities (92). — Posthumous works and phonograph records (92).

IV. PUBLIC PERFORMANCE OF MUSIC IN EUROPE

A. THE STATUTORY LAW. 94
Profit requirement absent (94). — No jukebox exception (94). — Britain: copyright in records (95).

B. CASE LAW 95
Gramophone Co. v. Carwardine (95). — France: performance of records (95). — Britain and U.S. (96). — Netherlands (97). — Summary (98). — Right of broadcasting not specified (98). — Britain (99). — France (99). — Netherlands (99).

C. GREAT BRITAIN 100
I. *Performing Right Society, Ltd.*: a. Membership and Management (100). — b. Assignments (102). — c. Licenses (104). — d. Programs (105). — e.

Distribution (107). — f. Mechanical societies (110);
II. *Phonographic Performance Ltd.*: a. Recording
companies and Musicians' Union (110). — b.
Monopoly (112); III. *Recommended Tribunal* (112).

D. FRANCE 113
One society; no government supervision (113). —
SACEM; programs (113). — ASCAP royalties
(113). — Operas (114). — Broadcasting (114).

E. THE NETHERLANDS 115
a. Governmental control (115). — b. Membership
and management (116). — c. Assignments (118).
— d. Licenses (119). — e. Programs (119). — f.
Distribution (120). — g. Other activities (123).

F. CISAC 123

G. WITHDRAWAL FROM SOCIETIES 124

CONCLUSION 126

APPENDICES
   A. ASCAP DOMESTIC CONSENT DECREE. 128
   B. ASCAP FOREIGN CONSENT DECREE 138
   C. ASCAP MEMBERSHIP CONTRACT 143
   D. ASCAP ROYALTY DISTRIBUTION 147
   E. BMI CONSENT DECREE 148
   F. BMI CONTRACT FOR PUBLISHERS 154
   G. BMI CONTRACT FOR WRITERS 161
   H. BMI PUBLISHING DEPARTMENT CONTRACT 166

TABLE OF STATUTES AND CONVENTIONS CITED. 171

TABLE OF CASES CITED 173

TABLE OF WORKS CITED. 177

INDEX 180

INTRODUCTION

There have been many notable descriptions of music but perhaps one of the most apt from the viewpoint of law and commerce was Ian Hay's statement, "Music is about the most vulnerable piece of property that a man can bring into the world, especially today." With the increased use of music brought about by technological advances, such as radio, sound films and television, and the concomitant decrease in the sale of sheet music and phonograph records, the need for writers and publishers of music to share in the revenue from public performances became urgent. With this urgency the author's rights in the public performance of his music became the subject of much literature and litigation which continues to this day.

The purpose of this book is to present a clear picture of this much written and litigated about subject: the author's right in the public performance of his music. In order to do this we must indicate not only the nature of the right but also how it is exercised for it should be evident that with performances taking place throughout the world and in a multitude of ways, the exercise of the right by an individual author or publisher would present insurmountable problems. Furthermore, the nature of the performance right can only be fully appreciated by examination of the right in connection with various related rights granted in the composite right known by such names as, *copyright* (United States, Great Britain, etc.), *auteursrecht* (The Netherlands), *droit d'auteur* (France, etc.), and many more. In Chapters I and III these related rights will be discussed, though, of necessity, the treatment will be limited in scope. In addition, general problems involved in securing copyright protection will be considered.

Since the exercise of any of the rights encompassed within the copyright involves a number of commercial considerations, in studying the exercise of the performing right we must delve into the *business* of selling and using the music performing right. The business of licensing and enforcing performing rights is conducted by organizations known as performing right societies and it is almost axiomatic to say that a proper study of such institutions will yield a proper picture of the performing right. Thus Chapters II and IV consider the nature of the right and the societies which exercise it.

Due to the international nature of intellectual property, and of music in particular, it is necessary, for a sound appreciation of the performing right, to understand the law and practice of countries other than our own. It is with this purpose in mind that I have chosen several countries for examination and comparison (with variations in emphasis due to availability of material). Therefore Chapters I and II comprise Part I, which is devoted to copyright and performing rights in the United States, and Part II, Chapters III and IV, concerns these rights in three European countries, *viz.*, Great Britain, the Netherlands and France.

Part I
UNITED STATES

CHAPTER I

AMERICAN COPYRIGHT AND COMMON LAW

A. DISTINCTION BETWEEN COMMON LAW PROTECTION AND STATUTORY COPYRIGHT

Common law prior to copyright statute.

In Europe when one speaks of *copyright* one refers to statutory protection of literary and artistic creations. [1] It does not make any difference whether the work is published or in the form of a manuscript, not yet revealed to the public, although the place of publication may be relevent. [2] In the United States authors had rights in their *unpublished* works prior to the passage of any legislation by Congress providing for uniform nation-wide protection. [3] This can be traced to the common law of England, [4] existing prior to the American Revolution, which the individual states of the United States adopted, subject to some modifications, as their own common law.

Constitution authorizes copyright protection.

The Constitution of the United States, [5] the document which enumerates the powers given to the federal government, provides with respect to copyright:

> "The Congress shall have power ... to promote the Progress of Science and useful Arts, by securing for limited times to Authors ... the exclusive Right to their respective Writings." (Art. I, sect. 8).

---

[1] 4 UNESCO Copyright Bulletin nos. 1–2, p. 104 *et seq.* (1951), carries an analysis of all the European copyright statutes.

[2] The United Kingdom, for example, does not give protection to Commonwealth subjects if the work is first published in a country having no special link with the United Kingdom, *e.g.*, the United States. *Id.* at 171.

[3] Wheaton v. Peters, 8 Pet. 591 (U.S. 1834).

[4] Donaldson v. Beckett, 4 Burrows 2303 (K.B. 1769) and 4 Burrows 2408 (H.L. 1774), cited in Reeves, *Superman v. Captain Marvel or, Loss of Literary Property In Comic Strips*, ASCAP COPYRIGHT SYMPOSIUM NUMBER 5, p. 5 (1954).

[5] Adopted in 1787 and in effect since 1789.

Congress exercises constitutional power.

When Congress exercised this power it interpreted the Constitutional language quite liberally. [6] Thus we find almost every kind of literary and artistic creation listed in section 5 of the Copyright Act of 1909, which is the basic national law under which the United States presently operates (Title 17, U.S.C.):

"(a) Books, including composite and cyclopedic works, directories, gazetteers, and other compilations.
(b) Periodicals, including newspapers.
(c) Lectures, sermons, addresses (prepared for oral delivery).
(d) Dramatic or dramatico-musical compositions.
(e) Musical compositions.
(f) Maps.
(g) Works of art; models or designs for works of art.
(h) Reproductions of a work of art.
(i) Drawings or plastic works of a scientific or technical character.
(j) Photographs.
(k) Prints and pictorial illustrations, including prints or labels used for articles of merchandise.
(l) Motion-picture photoplays.
(m) Motion pictures other than photoplays."

In addition, section 5 stipulates that, "The above specifications shall not be held to limit the subject matter of copyright as defined in section 4," which simply restates the cryptic phraseology of the Constitution:

"The works for which copyright may be secured under this title [Act] shall include all the writings of an author."

Act does not displace common law.

One might expect that with the entrance of the federal government into the field of copyright, common law protection in the individual states would no longer exist or be necessary. However, the need for common law rights remained because the Copyright Act was not drafted to cover the entire area of copyright, as copyright is known in Europe. The Act does not come into operation until the work is published, [7] or registered as an

---

[6] Likewise the court in Burrow-Giles Lith. v. Sarony, 111 U.S. 53 (1884).

[7] Section 10: "Any person entitled thereto by this title may secure copyright for his work by publication thereof with the notice of copyright required by this title; and such notice shall be affixed to each copy thereof published or offered for sale in

DISTINCTION BETWEEN COMMON LAW AND COPYRIGHT 7

unpublished work (which is not permitted in all categories). [8] Thus the Act was simply intended to supplement the common law and, accordingly, section 2 states:

"Nothing in this title shall be construed to annul or limit the right of the author or proprietor of an unpublished work, at common law or in equity, to prevent the copying, publication, or use of such unpublished work without his consent, and to obtain damages therefor."

Common law protection until publication or registration.

The expression *publication* (see footnote 7) is generally considered to mean that the work has been reproduced and placed on sale, sold, or publicly distributed. [9] Therefore, a work which is

---

the United States by authority of the copyright proprietor, except in the case of books seeking ad interim protection under section 22 of this title."

Section 13: "After copyright has been secured by publication of the work with notice of copyright as provided in section 10 of this title, there shall be promptly deposited in the copyright office or in the mail addressed to the Register of Copyrights, Washington, District of Columbia, two complete copies of the best edition thereof then published ... No action or proceeding shall be maintained for infringement until the provisions of this title with respect to the deposit of copies and registration of such work shall have been complied with."

[8] Section 12: "Copyright may also be had of the works of an author, of which copies are not reproduced for sale, by the deposit, with claim of copyright, of one complete copy of such work if it be a lecture or similar production or a dramatic, musical, or dramatico-musical composition; of a title and description, with one print taken from each scene or act, if the work be a motion-picture photoplay; of a photographic print if the work be a photograph; of a title and description, with not less than two prints taken from different sections of a complete motion picture, if the work be a motion picture other than a photoplay; or a photograph or other identifying reproduction thereof, if it be a work of art or a plastic work or drawing. But the privilege of registration of copyright secured hereunder shall not exempt the copyright proprietor from the deposit of copies, under sections 13 and 14 of this title, where the work is later reproduced in copies for sale."

Section 14: "Should the copies called for by section 13 of this title not be promptly deposited as provided in this title, the Register of Copyrights may at any time after the publication of the work, upon actual notice, require the proprietor of the copyright to deposit them, and after the said demand shall have been made, in default of the deposit of copies of the work within three months from any part of the United States, except an outlying territorial possession of the United States, or within six months from any outlying territorial possession of the United States, or from any foreign country, the proprietor of the copyright shall be liable to a fine of $ 100 and to pay to the Library of Congress twice the amount of the retail price of the best edition of the work, and the copyright shall become void."

[9] Schulman, *Authors' Rights*, 7 COPYRIGHT PROBLEMS ANALYZED 23 (1952). However, since the Act is poorly drawn it has been necessary to construe some of the language differently than one normally would. For example, section 2 states that "the copyright ... shall endure ... from the date of first publication." Thus one must interpret the act of registering an unpublished work as a publication in order to bring the work within the intended period of protection of the Act prior to its public distribution or sale. If this is not done then two possible and unlikely alternatives are presented: (1) the registered unpublished work does not receive the benefits of the

unpublished and unregistered (either voluntarily or because it is unregistrable until published) is not protected by the federal copyright law. The owner of such a work is protected by the common law of each state [10] and this protection is quite broad. If it is a drama, the owner has, among other rights, the sole right to present it in a theatre or to license others to present it. [11] If it is a musical composition, he can, among other things, permit or refuse people the right to perform it. [12] It is immaterial whether the performance of music is for profit or not, whereas the Act extends protection only to performances of music which are for profit. This right is discussed in detail in Chapter II. Without enumerating all the possible uses of a literary or artistic work, it suffices to say that the creator has the complete right of reproduction and use [13] in the United States *until* he publishes [14] the work or registers it as an unpublished work. [15]

B. BOUNDARY BETWEEN COPYRIGHT AND PUBLIC DOMAIN

Statute requires copyright notice.

This common law right, which is usually referred to as a common law copyright [16] or literary property right, [17] is often described as a right of first publication. [18] However, publication is meant in a narrow sense and therefore the common law protection is greater than such a description indicates. When the work is published it falls into the public domain *unless* the formalities [19] specified in the

---

Act, (2) the work receives the protection of the Act until the stipulated periods, calculated from the date of first publication, expire, and therefore, conceivably, statutory protection forever. See Tannenbaum, *Practical Problems in Copyright,* 7 COPYRIGHT PROBLEMS ANALYZED 10 (1952).

[10] In the United Kingdom Parliament in 1911 brought unpublished works under the protection of the Copyright Act.

[11] Ferris v. Frohman, 233 U.S. 424 (1912).

[12] McCarthy & Fischer v. White, 259 Fed. 364 (S.D. N.Y. 1919).

[13] For the author to show an infringement of the Act the matter which is copied must be substantial or material in respect to the work from which it is copied. Caruthers v. R.K.O., 20 F. Supp. 906 (S.D. N.Y. 1937). Golding v. R.K.O., 77 USPQ 415 (Cal. App. 1948), however, gave protection to a common law owner although the matter copied was not substantial or material.

[14] Falk v. Gast, 54 Fed. 890 (2d Cir. 1893).

[15] Photodrama v. Social Uplift Film Corp., 220 Fed. 448 (2d Cir. 1915).

[16] Schulman, *Authors' Rights,* 7 COPYRIGHT PROBLEMS ANALYZED 19–20 (1952); Karp, *Copyright Litigation, id.* at 143, however, states: "The common law plagiarism action ... is sometimes erroneously referred to as a common law copyright action."

[17] Schulman, *supra* note 16.

[18] Pushman v. New York Graphic Society, Inc., 287 N.Y. 302 (1942).

[19] See note 7 *supra.*

Act are followed. [20] Thus the border line between the common law and statutory copyright (or the public domain) is passed at the instant the work is published, or registered (if the work is in the registrable category). Therefore, it appears possible for an author (with the assistance of his heirs) to retain rights in his work indefinitely by simply avoiding those uses which technically result in a publication. This, however, may be an abuse of a doctrine the purpose of which was to protect the author in his unpublished manuscript and which originated prior to broadcasting, recording and motion pictures.

After copyright is secured a new line of demarcation arises separating copyright protection and the public domain. Failure to observe the formality of placing notice of copyright on "each copy thereof published or offered for sale in the United States by authority of the copyright proprietor" results in a forfeiture of copyright, thereby placing the work into the public domain. [21] The type of notice to appear on each copy (whether to secure or retain copyright), and its location thereon, varies according to the class of work. [22] Copyright is thus secured, and retained, by the author or his assignee, upon observing the proper formalities.

Authors and assigns entitled to copyright.

Whereas the common law extends protection to all authors of unpublished works irrespective of their nationality and domicile, [23] section 9 of the Act states that copyright cannot be secured if the work is by an author who is a citizen or subject of a foreign nation except under certain conditions: (1) if the author is domiciled within the United States at the time of first publication, [24]

---

[20] Wheaton v. Peters, 8 Pet. 591 (U.S. 1834).

[21] Deward & Rich, Inc. v. Bristol Savings & Loan Corp., 120 F. 2d 537 (4th Cir. 1941).

[22] Section 19: "The notice of copyright required by section 10 of this title shall consist either of the word "Copyright" or of the abbreviation "Copr.," accompanied by the name of the copyright proprietor, and if the work be a printed literary, musical, or dramatic work, the notice shall include also the year in which the copyright was secured by publication. In the case, however, of copies of works specified in subsections (f) to (k), inclusive, of section 5 of this title, the notice may consist of the letter C enclosed within a circle, . . . accompanied by the initials, monogram, mark, or symbol of the copyright proprietor: *Provided*, That on some accessible portion of such copies or of the margin, back, permanent base, or pedestal, or of the substance on which such copies shall be mounted, his name shall appear."

[23] Schulman, *Authors' Rights*, 7 COPYRIGHT PROBLEMS ANALYZED 23 (1952).

[24] Therefore, he cannot secure copyright in an unpublished work via registration,

or (2) if the President of the United States *proclaims* that the foreign nation of which the author is a citizen or subject extends protection to United States citizens by means of treaty, law, etc., or that such foreign nation "is a party to an international agreement which provides for reciprocity in the granting of copyright, by the terms of which the United States may, at its pleasure, become a party thereto."

Publications abroad by foreign authors.

It is not certain whether a publication in a foreign country by a foreign author need carry a copyright notice to secure copyright. In *Heim v. Universal Pictures Co.*, 154 F. 2d 480 (2d Cir. 1946), the court held that it was not necessary, however, this is a departure from precedent [25] and former interpretations [26] of section 10 relating to the necessity of a notice on copies published abroad. [27] In view of the conflict the wisest course for foreign authors is to publish with notice when first publication takes place abroad. Furthermore, since notice of copyright may be necessary the publisher and author should be certain that it is in the name of the proper party, otherwise the work will not secure copyright. Although notice *may* not be necessary abroad, it *is* necessary when the work is republished in the United States and an incorrect notice will result in loss of copyright. [28] The contracts used by one Dutch music publisher, for example, provide for the assignment of the full and unrestricted right to publish the work, *i.e.*, to print copies and to trade and distribute them. [29] The

unless publication in this case is interpreted to include the act of registering. See note 9 *supra*.

[25] Basevi v. O'Toole Co., Inc., 26 F. Supp. 41 (S.D. N.Y. 1939).

[26] 2 LADAS, THE INTERNATIONAL PROTECTION OF LITERARY AND ARTISTIC PROPERTY 698 (1938), states: "It would seem difficult to give a safe interpretation of the Act in this respect. However, if the rule established in the first part of section 9 [now section 10] is to be given effect to, *i.e.*, the rule that a person "may secure copyright for his work by publication thereof with the notice of copyright required by the Act"; it would seem that no person is entitled to claim statutory copyright under the Act, unless, when first publishing the work abroad or in the United States, he has affixed the statutory notice. Thereafter, the notice need not appear on each copy of the work published outside the United States, since the second part of section 9 requires this only of "each copy thereof published or offered for sale in the United States."

[27] It should be borne in mind that a copyright question is authoritatively settled when decided by the Supreme Court, such as in the White-Smith and Washingtonian cases (*infra*) but the Heim and Yacoubian (*infra*) cases, to name a few, did not reach the Supreme Court.

[28] Leigh v. Barnhart, 96 F. Supp. 194 (D. N.J. 1951).

[29] Holland Music, Amsterdam, the Netherlands.

publisher, in this case, would not be entitled to secure copyright since he merely has an assignment of the publishing rights. Therefore, the notice should be in the name of the author, or the publisher should receive the right to secure copyright. The assignment can, nevertheless, provide that rights other than publishing rights, *e.g.*, mechanical and performing rights, are reserved to the author or authors' societies. In the case of Holland Music, which is a partnership of music writers H. Dunk and A. Zmigrod, if the published work was written by one of the partners, a copyright notice in the name of the publishing firm could not result in anyone being mislead and therefore would most likely be adequate. [30]

Deposit of copies; claim of copyright.

In addition to notice of copyright, the Act requires a deposit of copies with *claim of copyright* [31] "after copyright has been secured by publication." [32]

Manufacturing clause.

The well-known *manufacturing clause* is found in section 16, which requires printed books and periodicals protected under the Act [33] "except the original text of a book or periodical of foreign

---

[30] National Comics Publications, Inc. v. Fawcett Publications, Inc., 191 F. 2d 594 (2d Cir. 1951).

[31] The claim of copyright is in the form of an application blank supplied by the Copyright Office. The applications consist of two parts, one which the Copyright Office retains and one which is stamped and returned to the applicant as a certification of claim of copyright. This certificate does not constitute the copyright nor does it attest to the fact whether or not the applicant has a copyright. It only certifies that the applicant *claims* he has secured a copyright by following the necessary requirements of the Act and serves "as prima facie evidence of the facts stated therein" (section 209). The presumption gives way, of course, to proof of contrary facts.

[32] See note 7 *supra*. However, in Washingtonian Pub. Co. v. Pearson, 306 U.S. 30 (1939), although the plaintiff had failed to register his claim and to deposit copies prior to an infringement which took place fourteen months after publication, the court not only found that the copyright was still valid but also that the deposit and registration could take place *after* the infringement and not affect the plaintiff's right of action against the defendant. The copyright proprietor is, nevertheless, subject to the requirements of section 14 (see note 8 *supra*).

[33] Section 22: "In the case of a book or periodical first published abroad in the English language, the deposit in the Copyright Office, not later than six months after its publication abroad, of one complete copy of the foreign edition, with a request for the reservation of the copyright and a statement of the name and nationality of the author and of the copyright proprietor and of the date of publication of the said book or periodical, shall secure to the author or proprietor an ad interim copyright therein, which shall have all the force and effect given to copyright by

origin in a language or languages other than English" to be printed and bound in the United States except for a limited number of copies.[34] This requirement of American manufacture is not deemed to apply to sheet music.[35]

Duration of copyright.

The period of protection given by the Act, after which time the work enters the public domain, is dealt with in section 24, which provides:

> "The copyright secured by this title shall endure for twenty-eight years from the date of first publication... shall be entitled to a renewal and extension of the copyright in such work for the further term of twenty-eight years when application for such renewal and extension shall have been made to the copyright office and duly registered therein within one year prior to the expiration of the original term of copyright: *And provided further*, that in default of the registration of such application for renewal and extension, the copyright in any work shall determine at the expiration of twenty-eight years from first publication."

Thus the copyright is secured merely for a period of twenty-eight years from the date of first publication [36] and will be extended for another twenty-eight years only upon compliance with the formality of renewal. The section gives the right of renewal to the author [37] except in a few instances.[38] This pro-

---

this title, and shall endure until the expiration of five years after the date of first publication abroad." Apparently there is no protection until the registration.

Section 23: "Whenever within the period of such ad interim protection an authorized edition of such books or periodical shall be published within the United States, in accordance with the manufacturing provisions specified in section 16 of this title, and whenever the provisions of this title as to deposit of copies, registration, filing of affidavits, and printing of the copyright notice shall have been duly complied with, the copyright shall be extended to endure in such book or periodical for the term provided in this title."

[34] Section 16: "Said requirements shall not apply to works ... of foreign origin ... imported into the United States within five years after first publication in a foreign state or nation up to the number of fifteen hundred copies of each such book or periodical if said copies shall contain notice of copyright ... and if ad interim copyright in said work shall have been obtained pursuant to section 22 of this title prior to the importation into the United States."

[35] HOWELL, THE COPYRIGHT LAW 93 (3d ed. 1952).

[36] With regard to a copyrighted unpublished work see note 9 *supra*.

[37] "If still living, or the widow, widower, or children of the author, if the author be not living, or if such author, widow, widower, or children, be not living, then the author's executors or in the absence of a will, his next of kin." Section 24.

[38] If the work is published posthumously or if the copyright is in a composite work, *i.e.*, containing works of various authors, the right to renewal belongs to the proprietor.

vision is quite unusual in that it permits an author to assign or "sell" his copyright and yet retain the right of renewal.[39] In *Fred Fisher Music Co. v. M. Witmark and Sons*, 318 U.S. 643 (1943), the question came up: "Does the Act prevent the author from assigning his interest in the renewal copyright before he has secured it?" If the author could assign his renewal right at the same time he assigns the original copyright it would remove an economic safeguard the Act could otherwise provide. The Supreme Court, however, upheld the assignment of the contingent right, saying:

> "If an author cannot make an effective assignment of his renewal, it would be worthless to him when he is most in need. Nobody would pay an author for something he cannot sell. We cannot draw a principle of law from the familiar stories of garret-poverty of some men of literary genius. Even if we could do so, we cannot say that such men would regard with favor a rule of law preventing them from realizing on their assets when they are most in need of funds ... We do not have such assured knowledge about authorship, and particularly about song writing, or the psychology of gifted writers and composers, as to justify us as judges in importing into Congressional legislation a denial to authors of the freedom to dispose of their property possessed by others. While authors may have habits making for intermittent want, they may have no less a spirit of independence which would resent treatment of them as wards under guardianship of the law."[40]

The author's right of renewal is, however, only a contingent right because if he dies prior to the expiration of the twenty-eight years's term the right of renewal belongs to the other persons stipulated in the Act and his assignment, if he made one, is of no value. When the right of renewal becomes vested in one or more of the other stipulated persons and is exercised they have thereby "acquired a new and independent right in the copyright, free and clear of any rights, interests, or licenses."[41] Thus when interpreting the statutory phrase, "renewal and extension of the copy-

---

Also, if the copyright proprietor is "an employer for whom such work is made for hire" he is entitled to the renewal period. Section 24.

[39] "An assignment by the author of his copyright in general terms did not include conveyance of his renewal interest." Fred Fisher Music Co. v. M. Witmark and Sons, 318 U.S. 643 (1943).

[40] *Id.* at 657.

[41] Fitch v. Shubert, 20 F. Supp. 314, 315 (S.D. N.Y. 1937).

right", the stress should be placed on the word, renewal, since it is a new copyright rather than an extension of the original term of copyright. Care must be taken to submit the application for renewal before the twenty-eighth year has passed otherwise the work enters the public domain.

Renewal notice?

The Act does not state whether copies published after the copyright has been renewed must bear notice of the date of renewal. Howell suggests that the original notice be used together with notice of renewal, *e.g.*: "Copyright 1914 by John Doe. Copyright renewed 1942 by Richard Roe." [42] However, since there is no mention of a requirement of a renewal notice it is unlikely that a court would read one into the Act and thereby place a work into the public domain for lack of such a notice. [43]

C. MEANING OF PUBLICATION — ESPECIALLY CONCERNING MUSICAL WORKS

Public performance; distribution of films.

As stated previously publication is generally considered to mean that the work has been reproduced and placed on sale, sold, or publicly distributed. It is relatively easy to apply this rule to printed matter. Difficulty arises, however, when we have to deal with other methods of exploitation or making a work known to the public. The courts have said that a public performance of a drama [44] or musical composition [45] is not a publication. They have also said that material used on the radio need not be copyrighted because the broadcast of a work is not a publication. [46] In regard to the distribution of motion picture films to exhibitors on a contractual basis, Howell says:

> "When so distributed for the purpose of commercial exhibition, this constitutes publication; but not so where copies are sent out for restricted exhibition on a non-commercial basis prior to distribution for enjoyment by the general public." [47]

---

[42] HOWELL, THE COPYRIGHT LAW 118 (3d ed. 1952).
[43] See note 20 *supra* for the form of copyright notice.
[44] Ferris v. Frohman, 233 U.S. 424 (1912).
[45] McCarthy & Fisher v. White, 259 Fed. 364 (S.D. N.Y. 1919).
[46] Uproar Co. v. National Broadcasting Co., 8 F. Supp. 358 (D. Mass. 1934).
[47] HOWELL, THE COPYRIGHT LAW 66 (3d ed. 1952).

MEANING OF PUBLICATION — ESPECIALLY MUSIC

Tannenbaum, on the other hand, states:

"In the motion picture industry, the common practice is to lease motion pictures for exhibition only. This does not constitute a publication of the unpublished scenario or manuscript."[48]

Patterson v. Century Productions.

Howell and Tannenbaum each cite *Patterson v. Century Productions, Inc.*, 93 F. 2d 489 (2d Cir. 1937), which is not a model of clarity, as authority for their propositions. [49] By examining the court's opinion we can easily see the portions therein upon which each writer relies:

"A limited publication which falls short of dedication is not to be given the effect of general publication which does dedicate the work to the public. Public exhibition is not necessarily a general publication merely because the public generally is shown the work. The test of general publication is whether the exhibition of the work to the public is under such conditions as to show dedication without reservation of rights or only the right to view or inspect it without more. If conditions of publication are such that the only right is to look at the copy of the work exhibited, there is no general publication which makes the work thereafter a published work in the copyright sense.

"This motion picture was not distributed except for exhibition in the strictly limited non-commercial way above described. As the distribution was limited to exhibitions of the picture without charge, no one was given the right to use the copies sent out for any other purpose whatsoever. The positive films were merely loaned for that purpose which did not permit copying. There was, therefore, no publication."[49a]

If the question of publication were now to arise for the first time it would not be difficult to accept Howell's position, on the theory that the public distribution of a film is equivalent to the public distribution of a manuscript. And, since the latter is a publication [50] then the film distribution is likewise a publication. However, the question of publication has arisen before, *e.g.*, in a case in 1907 involving the public exhibition of a painting. The

---

[48] Tannenbaum, *Practical Problems in Copyright*, 7 COPYRIGHT PROBLEMS ANALYZED 10 (1952).
[49] The Patterson case involved a film showing wild animal scenes taken on an African hunting trip and did not discuss a scenario or manuscript.
[49a] Patterson v. Century Productions, Inc., 93 F. 2d 489, 492–493 (2d. Cir. 1937).
[50] White v. Kimmell, 193 F. 744 (9th Cir. 1952).

Supreme Court held that this was not a publication because the art gallery did not permit the public to copy paintings on exhibition and therefore the work did not have to carry a copyright notice. [51] The question has also been raised, as noted earlier, in connection with the public performance of musical and dramatic compositions. Thus, as far back as 1907, 1912 and 1919 the courts had to resolve the issue of publication. If public distribution of a film is equivalent to the public distribution of a manuscript then the public presentation of a drama, work of art or piece of music should also constitute a publication since each in its own way acts to present the work to the public. In order to have an unpublished musical composition performed on the radio there must be a distribution of records or of copies of the music and in order to have a film exhibited copies must be distributed. Furthermore, in the latter case the films are merely leased to the exhibitor. The courts, however, do not treat the public performance of music and plays or the public exhibition of paintings as a publication. The law should be consistent unless there is a sound reason for deviations. Therefore, the court's decision in 1937 should be viewed as confirming the three earlier decisions, despite its attempted distinction between commercial and noncommercial distributions. Since the distribution in question was noncommercial the court's reference to commercial distribution is mere dictum and does not establish a precedent. Moreover, even if the distribution of a film is a publication it is not clear whether the distribution and public performance of the accompanying sound track, containing, for example, unpublished music, is a publication of the music embodied therein. It is submitted that the rule applicable to the distribution and public performance of phonograph records should apply because of the similar nature of these two forms of the right of mechanical reproduction.

Sale and distribution of phonograph records.

In the field of phonograph recordings the recording of a musical composition and its subsequent public distribution was not deemed a publication which will enable the owner to acquire statutory copyright by affixing notice of copyright to each phonograph

---

[51] American Tobacco Co. v. Werckmeister, 207 U.S. 284 (1907).

record. [52] Therefore, it was thought that absence of a copyright notice would not place the musical composition into the public domain. *Yacoubian v. Carroll*, 74 U.S.P.Q. 257 (S.D.Cal. 1947), supported this traditional view by holding that the sale of phonograph recordings without copyright notice did not place a *copyrighted* musical composition, in which the author had secured copyright via registration, into the public domain. The court cited *White-Smith Music Publishing Co. v. Apollo Co.*, 209 U.S. 1 (1908), which held that the manufacture of phonograph records, embodying a musical composition, was not an infringement of the copyright owner's exclusive right to make *copies*. [53] Since records are not copies and since the publication requiring copyright notice is the sale or distribution of copies, the sale or distribution of records is not a publication requiring notice of copyright.

The Miracle case.

Despite over forty years' reliance by the music industry on the proposition that the distribution or sale of records does not constitute a publication of an unpublished musical composition protected by the common law, the court in *Shapiro, Bernstein & Co. v. Miracle Record Co.*, 91 F. Supp. 473,475 (N.D. Ill. 1950), considered the issue anew:

> "The evidence is that Lewis [author] abandoned his rights... to a copyright by permitting his composition to be produced on phonograph records and sold before copyright. It seems to me that production and sale of a phonograph record is fully as much a publication as production and sale of sheet music. I can see no practical distinction between the two. If one constitutes an abandonment, so should the other."

On Motion for New Trial

> "The brief argues that phonograph records are not copies of a musical composition, that public sale of records prior to copyright therefore does not destroy common law rights in the musical composition.
> "It seems to me that publication is a practical question and does not rest on any technical definition of the word "copy". Modern recording has made possible the preservation and re-

---

[52] McDonald, *Law of Broadcasting*, 7 COPYRIGHT PROBLEMS ANALYZED 46 (1952).
[53] This case resulted in an amendment to the Copyright Act giving the author the right of mechanical reproduction. (section 1e).

production of sound which theretofore had disappeared immediately upon its creation. When phonograph records of a musical composition are available for purchase in every city, town and hamlet, certainly the dissemination of the composition to the public is complete, and is as complete as by sale of a sheet music reproduction of the composition."

Reconciling Miracle and Yacoubian.

Thus the *Miracle* decision may be considered as contrary to the earlier *Yacoubian* case. [54] Whether other courts will follow the Miracle decision and whether a higher court will then uphold it remains to be seen. It is arguable that a factor lending support to the Miracle case is the compulsory license clause of the Act, dealing with phonograph records. [55] By not registering or publishing a musical composition so as to subject it to the Act, the owner retains the exclusive recording right under the common law, at least prior to the *Miracle* case. Therefore, the argument continues, this is contrary to the intent of the Act which gave composers and lyric writers the right of mechanical reproduction subject to compulsory licensing. On the other hand, however, although it is true that Congress was not creating an *exclusive* recording right in copyrighted musical compositions, it was legislating only as to copyrighted works and expressed no intention of altering the common law. If the legislature intended the limitations stated in the Act to affect rights in unpublished works, to carry the argument to its proper conclusion, the public performance of music would be a publication thereby forcing an author, who wished to rely on his common law rights, to secure copyright and thus prevent him from circumventing the profit limitation of the same

---

[54] McDonald, *Law of Broadcasting*, 7 COPYRIGHT PROBLEMS ANALYZED 46, 61 (1952), infers that the two cases are inconsistent. It will be shown that this is not a necessary conclusion.

[55] Despite the opening sentence of section 1 ("shall have the exclusive right") subsection e, which establishes the mechanical right, states: "And as a condition of extending the copyright control to such mechanical reproductions, that whenever the owner of a musical copyright has used or permitted or knowingly acquiesced in the use of the copyrighted work upon the parts of instruments serving to reproduce mechanically the musical work, any other person may make similar use of the copyrighted work upon the payment to the copyright proprietor of a royalty of two cents on each such part manufactured." Although the right of mechanical reproduction applies to the sound track of motion picture films (called the synchronization right), as well as to phonograph records, Jerome v. Twentieth Century-Fox Film Corp., 67 F. Supp. 736 (S.D. N.Y. 1946), held that the compulsory license does not extend to the film sound track. Unfortunately the right of mechanical reproduction only applies to works published and copyrighted after July 1, 1909.

section 1 (e) of the Act. Since such a restriction does not apply to the common law performing right in music it should not be read into the recording right under the common law, at least not on the basis of the compulsory licensing argument.

As a result of its rejection of established practice, the *Miracle* case may raise doubt as to the validity of copyright and common law rights in musical compositions which have been recorded. [56] The decision dealt with the question whether an unpublished work protected under the common law, which is recorded and given wide distribution, has had a publication so as to put it into the public domain. However, the question arises whether the distribution of records, after copyright has been secured, is a publication necessitating a copyright notice on each record. If such were held to be the corollary of the *Miracle* case then most recorded copyrighted music has been "dedicated" to the public. However, even if we accept the Miracle decision we need not reach this conclusion. The *Yacoubian* case concerned just such a situation. The musical composition was copyrighted as an unpublished work under section 12 and then recordings were made and publicly distributed. The court said that this did not terminate copyright protection. We can reconcile the two cases by holding that even if public distribution of records is a publication terminating common law protection, there is no need for the notice, which the Act states "shall be affixed to each copy", on recordings of copyrighted works because a record is not a *copy*. The question of termination of common law protection is not in issue since the work is protected by the Act and can lose its protection only when the author does not comply with the Act's requirements. Thus, the *Miracle* court can ignore the *copy* question in defining common law publication but must consider it when dealing with statutory forfeiture.

Can records secure copyright?

The question also arises whether a notice on recordings of an unpublished work protected under the common law is adequate

---

[56] In regard to the situation presented if the Miracle doctrine is followed, Burton, *Business Practices In The Copyright Field*, 7 COPYRIGHT PROBLEMS ANALYZED 103 (1952), writes: "If that happens, you will have the largest public domain this side of Venus because no one is paying the slightest attention to the theory that, if you release records before a work is published with a copyright notice, it is a dedication."

to *secure* copyright for the composition as a publication under section 10 of the Act. If the recording is not a publication in the statutory sense so as to forfeit copyright, then it follows [56a] that it is inadequate for securing copyright. Howell suggests the possibility of such a publication sufficing to secure copyright or necessitating a "deposit" in order to sue for infringement. [57] In regard to the *Yacoubian* case he states: "Inasmuch as the sale of such records constitutes publication of the musical compositions, it would seem necessary to deposit in the Copyright Office two copies of each composition as required by section 12; or two copies of each record if not otherwise published." Section 12 deals with the copyright in an unpublished work, such as in the *Yacoubian* case, and requires deposit "where the work is later reproduced in copies for sale." Thus, if *White-Smith* is still sound law then a phonograph record is not a copy and therefore no deposit is necessary. Commenting on the *Miracle* case, Howell writes: "Had the composer taken the precaution to put an appropriate notice on the records, he might have fared differently." The only reasonable interpretation of this suggestion is that the author might thereby have secured copyright. Therefore, the same problem arises that appeared in the *White-Smith* case: Are records copies? Sections 12—14 (see note 7, 8) appear to answer the question by requiring of publication that it produce *copies* in order to secure copyright. To hold otherwise might reverse the Yacoubian decision, since section 10 applies to both securing and retaining copyright, and throw the majority of recorded copyright music into the public domain. Thus we are forced to cling to the outmoded literal interpretation of the Act until it is corrected by legislation. Unfortunately this means that distributing records, despite proper notice of copyright affixed, may result in terminating common law rights, if we follow the *Miracle* case, without at the same time being adequate to secure copyright.

Circumventing the Miracle case.

Unpleasant as the *Miracle* decision may be for those authors who allowed recordings to be made prior to securing copyright and whose works are plagiarized within the jurisdiction of the

---
[56a] See sections 12—14.
[57] HOWELL, THE COPYRIGHT LAW 63 (3d ed. 1952).

Miracle court, it does not foreclose for them the possibility of registering future musical compositions as unpublished works, thereby coming within the *Yacoubian* rule and circumventing a recurrence of the gap produced by the *Miracle* case.

The *Miracle* case may cause a reconsideration of the question of publication in connection with the public presentation of music, films and dramas. Since the decision is based chiefly on the analogy of the sale of a phonograph record and a piece of sheet music, and the idea that the record preserves the sound which formerly disappeared, an important distinction can be made between records and public presentation. In the latter form of "publication" there is nothing material which the consumer can purchase because it is of the ephemeral sort referred to by the *Miracle* court.

This discussion should expose the weakness of having a statute which does not apply to unpublished works from the time of their creation but relies instead upon another body of law, *i.e.*, the common law, to fill the gap. Unfortunately, as shown, the gap may not always be filled.

D. CONCLUSION

Among the ways in which protection under the Copyright Act differs from common law protection, the following are perhaps, for our purpose, the most important:

(1) statutory protection requires publication, or registration, and observance of formalities;
(2) common law protection ends upon publication;
(3) the Copyright Office registration certificate is prima facie evidence of a valid copyright in the plaintiff;
(4) the statutory period of protection is a maximum of 56 years whereas the common law right can last, conceivably, forever;
(5) the common law right in a musical composition is not limited in respect of public performances or recordings;
(6) common law protection extends to nonresident aliens irrespective of nationality, domicile, and Presidential proclamations.

Chapter II

PUBLIC PERFORMANCE OF MUSIC IN THE UNITED STATES

A. THE STATUTORY LAW

Since the *common law* gives the author exclusive control over reproduction of an unpublished work, his permission is necessary for a public performance even though the performance is not for profit. Nevertheless, the public performance right in music was not included in the *copyright* until 1897. If, prior to that date, an author secured copyright in a musical composition he relinquished the right to control public performances. In the Copyright Act of 1909 the 1897 public performing right in music was altered so as to read:

> "To perform the copyrighted work publicly for profit if it be a musical composition." (sect. 1e).

Nonprofit performances excluded.

Thus a nonprofit public performance of music does not invade a right of the copyright owner. If, however, the work is of a dramatico-musical nature then the author is protected under clause 1 (d): "To perform or represent the copyrighted work publicly if it be a drama," and is not limited to performances for profit. The reason for the distinction is found in section 5 (see page 6) which classifies dramatic and dramatico-musical compositions together.[1]

Juke box exception.

The 1909 Act, in addition to adding the *profit* requirement, further circumscribed the public performing right in music by a subsequent paragraph in the same subsection:

> "The reproduction or rendition of a musical composition by or upon coin-operated machines shall not be deemed a public

---
[1] Herbert v. Shanley, 229 Fed. 340 (2d Cir. 1916).

performance for profit unless a fee is charged for admission to the place where such reproduction or rendition occurs." (sect. 1e).

An establishment in which a juke box (as these machines are popularly called) is maintained is usually not the type of place where a fee for admission is charged. Therefore, performances of copyrighted music in public by means of juke boxes are generally not *public performances for profit* under the Copyright Act.

Dramatico-musicals not limited.

As noted, the right of public performance given to the author of dramatic and dramatico-musical compositions is not limited to performances *for profit*. There does not appear to be a logical reason for distinguishing between such works and musical compositions (and nondramatic literary works). In the case of both categories the author should have the right to prohibit a public performance of his work. Furthermore, nonprofit public performances, which compete with public performances for profit, are no less damaging to the author than unauthorized public performances for profit.

Certainly no exception should be made in the case of the very profitable public performances by means of juke boxes. The anomalous situation is presented that if the proprietor of the establishment where a juke box is maintained supplies its music "free" he needs permission of the copyright owner, however, if the customer pays for the music directly, no permission is necessary. In *Herbert v. Shanley*, 242 U.S. 591, 594-595 (1917), the court said:

> "If the rights under the copyright are infringed only by a performance where money is taken at the door they are imperfectly protected ... The defendant's performances are not eleemosynary [devoted to charity]. They are part of a total for which the public pays ... If music did not pay it would be given up ... Whether it pays or not the purpose of employing it is profit and that is enough."

There is a dispute as to the reason for the exception in case of a juke box. Counsel for the writers say that it is attributable to an aim in 1909 to foster an infant industry — which is now quite grown up. The juke box interests, on the other hand, claim there were thousands of coin-operated machines, comparable to today's juke boxes, in existence in 1909. Whatever the reason may have been it seems only logical that, if a writer is entitled to payment when his work is used as background music in films or broadcasts, he should also be properly reimbursed from juke box performances, in which his music is the sole commodity the customer is purchasing.

B. PUBLIC PERFORMANCE FOR PROFIT AND THE COURTS

The right granted by the Copyright Act is to *publicly perform* for *profit*, therefore, let us examine how the courts have interpreted these three terms in order that we may better understand the right which is licensed by the performing right organizations in the United States.

Receiving set in public.

The Act, enacted before the advent of radio, does not mention the right of broadcasting. Nevertheless, the courts have protected composers by treating broadcasts of music as public performances for profit.[2] In *Buck v. Jewell-LaSalle Realty Co.*, 283 U.S. 191 (1931), it was held that bringing a radio broadcast into a hotel lobby by means of a loudspeaker arrangement was a *separate performance* by the hotel owner. In this case neither broadcaster nor hotel owner held a license from the American Society of Composers, Authors and Publishers (ASCAP), licensors of the music performing right. Therefore, to insure the same result when the broadcaster does comply with the law by securing permission to broadcast copyrighted music, *i.e.*, to avoid the possibility of an implied license to receivers of the broadcast (*e.g.*, the hotel keeper), the ASCAP licenses to radio and television broadcasters specifically provide:

> "Nothing herein contained shall be construed as authorizing LICENSEE to grant to others any right to reproduce or perform publicly for profit by any means, method or process whatsoever, any of the musical compositions licensed hereunder or as authorizing any receiver of any such broadcast rendition to

---

[2] Jerome H. Remick & Co. v. American Automobile Accessories Co., 5 F. 2d 411 (6th Cir. 1925): "The statute may be applied to new situations not anticipated by Congress, if, fairly construed, such situations come within its intent and meaning."

publicly perform or reproduce the same for profit, by any means, methods or process whatsoever."

Broadcasts are public.

Is a performance over radio a *public* performance? In the *Remick* case [3] the court stated:

"A performance, in our judgment, is no less public because the listeners are unable to communicate with one another, or are not assembled within an enclosure, or gathered together in some open stadium or park or other public place. Nor can a performance, in our judgment, be deemed private because each listener may enjoy it alone in the privacy of his home. Radio broadcasting is intended to, and in fact does, reach a very much larger number of the public at the moment of the rendition than any other medium of performance. The artist is consciously addressing a great, though unseen and widely scattered, audience, and is therefore participating in a public performance."

Broadcasts are performances.

Most courts have assumed that broadcasts are performances and have concerned themselves with the *public* and *profit* aspects of broadcasting. The *Remick* court, however, referred to a broadcast as a performance:

"Radio broadcasting... does reach a very much larger number of the public ... than any other medium of performance."

Finally, when is a public performance a public performance for *profit*? Mr. Justice Holmes gave us the answer in the most quoted American performing right case, Victor Herbert against Shanley's Restaurant (see page 23 *supra*).

Commercial broadcasting.

In order to understand the recent case of *Associated Music Publishers, Inc., v. Debs Memorial Radio Fund, Inc.*, 141 F. 2d 852 (2d Cir. 1944), one should be familiar with the following distinction between broadcasting in the United States and in Europe. In the United States most broadcasting stations are privately-owned commercial enterprises. The programs (whether they be concerts, dramas, etc.) are sponsored by business firms (*e.g.*, Coca Cola). The sponsor uses a portion of the program to

---

[3] *Id.* at 412.

advertise his particular product, for which he pays the broadcaster. Usually, however, the broadcasters cannot secure advertisers for all their programs, and these non-sponsored broadcasts are known by the anomalous term, sustainer, anomalous because these programs do not sustain, or support, anyone.

There are also some stations which are operated by nonprofit associations (*e.g.*, a university or municipality). These are somewhat similar in concept to the BBC or the Dutch stations at Hilversum.

Now to return to the recent case. The broadcast of copyrighted music on a sustainer program by a nonprofit radio station (Debs Memorial, which devoted only one-third of its broadcasting time to commercially sponsored programs), was held to be a performance for *profit*. The sustainer aspect of the program is consistent with the Holmes decision,[4] *i.e.*, though the music was not directly paid for, it is part of the total for which the advertiser (of other program) pays, since he wishes the station to be in full operation, with interesting programs, to attract listeners. In reference to the nonprofit nature of the station, the court said: "It is unimportant whether a profit went to Debs or its employes or to the advertisers." *Quaere*, however, whether the court's language is not too broad, for to consider a public performance as being for profit simply because the employes are being paid is to almost eliminate the profit requirement, since at most public performances some people are employed to assist the performance, whether they be musicians or ushers or janitors.

Performing right is a separate right.

It should also be noted that the right of public performance for profit is separate and distinct from the right to vend sheet music, sell recordings and synchronize the music to films. The exercise of these rights does not convey, or license, the right to publicly perform the musical composition for profit. [5]

Now, having some idea as to what is meant by the right of

---

[4] Herbert v. Shanley, 242 U.S. 591 (1917).
[5] Sheet music: Interstate Hotel of Nebraska v. Remick Music Corp., 157 F. 2d 744 (8th Cir. 1946); recordings: Irving Berlin, Inc. v. Daigle & Russo, 31 F. 2d 832 (5th Cir. 1929); film synchronization: Famous Music Corporation v. Melz, 28 F. Supp. 767 (W.D. La. 1939).

public performance for profit in the United States, we can go on to examine the organizations that license this music right.

C. (ECONOMIC) NECESSITY IS THE MOTHER OF INVENTION

Copyright proprietors throughout the world realized that it would be physically impossible for them, as individuals, to visit thousands of different establishments to see whether there were public performances of their copyrighted compositions. Even if they could check on each use of their work, the cost of enforcing their legal rights would be prohibitive. The collective action of copyright proprietors was necessary to make effective the public performance rights given by the law. According to the American Society of Composers, Authors and Publishers (ASCAP):

> "Prior to the formation of the Society there was no market among users [apart from the theatre] for performing rights of single numbers or for groups of numbers or even the numbers of entire catalogs of writers and publishers. The establishments with which the Society deals helped themselves to the same without trading or bartering for such rights. They never paid for any such rights, and there never was any price fixed for such rights, and there was no means of determining the value of such rights." [6]

It was thought that an organization with branches throughout the country could "police" public performances, and if any unauthorized performances were discovered the organization would seek to have the user take a license — if he did not, they could then press an infringement suit.

First society in France.

France recognized performing rights in 1791. Thereafter French authors of drama formed an organization to enforce their rights. The organization was later expanded to include all dramatic creators — composers as well as authors (Société des Auteurs et Compositeurs Dramatiques (S.A.C.D.), 1829). This resulted in leaving the rights in *non-dramatic* public performance of music (*petit droits*), as a practical matter, unprotected. Thus the Société des Auteurs, Compositeurs et Éditeurs de Musique (SACEM) was formed in 1851 to grant licenses and collect royalties for the non-dramatic public performances of its members' works in addition

---

[6] Defendant's Answer, p. 52, U.S. v. ASCAP, E78–388, S.D. N.Y. (1934).

to protecting the composers, authors, and publishers against piracies of any kind. SACEM served as a model for societies throughout the world, including the United States. Since it was relatively simple for copyright proprietors to discover unauthorized *dramatic* performances of musical compositions they did not find it necessary to invest music performing right societies with such rights. However, we do find in some countries, the French opinion, that better protection and exploitation of dramatic performances results from an industry-wide organization. Thus, for example, in the Netherlands, in addition to the performing right society (BUMA-Bureau voor Muziek-Auteursrechten), there has recently been formed SEBA (Bureau Theaterrechten van de Stichting tot Exploitatie en Bescherming van Auteursrechten), for the protection of dramatic performances of music and drama; but more about Europe later.

American societies.

From its birth in 1914 the American society, ASCAP, grew sufficiently strong so that by 1940 the broadcasting industry, feeling that radio was the "exploited" rather than a "villainous industrial exploiter," came forth with Broadcast Music, Inc., (BMI), to provide the broadcasters with their own reservoir of music. This was possible because the United States copyright law does not require a music performing right "intermediary" to secure permission from the Government in order to operate; such permission is necessary in some countries, *e.g.*, the Netherlands.

In fact, the United States has an antimonopoly law which has been used by the Government in an attempt to prevent noncompetition in the field of music performing rights, but more about this later, too.

In addition to ASCAP and BMI there are several small privately owned licensing groups, the largest of which is SESAC, Inc. (formerly, Society of European Stage Authors and Composers), formed in 1930, which receives about one million dollars [7] a year from performing right licenses as compared with over five million

---

[7] Hearings before Subcommittee on the Judiciary, House of Rep., 82nd Cong., 2nd session, on H.R. 5473, part 2, p. 228.

[8] Gross income of BMI and subsidiaries for the fiscal year ending July 31, 1952: $ 5,607,842. Broadcasting-Telecasting, October 27, 1952, p. 30.

[9] Gross income of ASCAP for 1952, total: $ 17,672,000; domestic: $ 16,343,000; foreign: $ 1,329,000. Variety, April 8, 1953, p.1.

dollars [8] and over seventeen million dollars [9] collected by BMI and ASCAP, respectively.

Now let us examine the two major American groups in detail.

D. AN ANATOMY OF ASCAP

I. Birth

Years ago, it was standard practice in the music industry for the writers to sell their compositions to publishers outright, or simply to provide for royalties on the sale of sheet music. [10] Due to this, an organization solely of writers (assuming they could have raised sufficient funds) would have been ineffective because it would have controlled so few copyrights that the commercial users would have ignored it and simply performed compositions out of the vast publisher catalogs. On the other hand, an organization solely of publishers faced the fact that there were many compositions which they did not control, *e.g.*, foreign works, and the likely prospect that users, through trade organizations, would deal directly with the writers so as to have a current supply of music. In this connection one should consider the broadcasters' BMI, subsequently formed.

Therefore, the only practical way to protect the rights given under the Copyright Act was by means of an organization of *writers and publishers* and consequently the American Society of Composers, Authors and Publishers (ASCAP) was formed.

ASCAP consists of composers (writers of music), authors (lyric writers), successors of deceased composers and authors (*i.e.*, their heirs), and publishers. It is a nonprofit association; by nonprofit is meant that after payment of expenses the revenue is distributed to the members. It was organized on February 13, 1914 by a group consisting of, according to deceased counsel Nathan Burken, ten leading writers and four prominent publishers [11]; whereas present attorney Herman Finkelstein writes: "Victor Herbert and eight other outstanding writers and publishers organized the American Society of Composers, Authors and Publishers." [12] In either event, its membership increased steadily, so that in 1953

---

[10] Klein, *Protective Societies for Authors and Creators*, 1953 COPYRIGHT PROBLEMS ANALYZED 33 (1953).

[11] Burkan in Defendant's Answer, p. 3, U.S. v. ASCAP, E 78-388, S.D.N.Y. (1934).

[12] Finkelstein, *Public Performance Rights in Music and Performance Right Societies*, 7 COPYRIGHT PROBLEMS ANALYZED 69 (1952).

ASCAP's membership totaled 3,000 writers and 550 publishers. The expression, "writer," as used in this book, means composer and/or lyric writer.

II. Contracts

Present and future rights.

Each member (writer and publisher alike) executes an assignment vesting in ASCAP the right to license until 1965 the *non-dramatic* public performance of the member's works: compositions already in existence and those yet to be created. [13] However, the grant was only until December 1953 (not yet extended in April, 1954), with regard to television, because the members dealing in musical shows (theatre) were wary of the distinction between dramatic and non-dramatic performances in this new medium.

Non-dramatic rights.

ASCAP has nothing to sell — no sheet music, no phonograph records, no "Broadway musicals," no musicians or vocalists — it simply licenses the *non-dramatic* performing rights of its members' works. These rights are also referred to as *petit droits* or "small" performing rights. The rights to all dramatic performances, whether they be via the theatre, television, films or radio, are reserved by the members. However, the distinction between dramatic and non-dramatic performances, as noted above, is not always an easy one to make. The ASCAP television licenses state it thus:

> "For the purposes of this agreement, a dramatic performance shall mean a performance of a musical composition on a television program in which there is a definite plot depicted by action and where the performance of a musical composition is woven into and carries forward the plot and its accompanying action. The use of dialogue to establish a mere program format, or the use of any non-dramatic device merely to introduce a performance of a composition shall not be deemed to make such a performance dramatic."

---

[13] "The general rule is that equity will enforce assignments of contingent interests and expectancies and of things having no present, actual or potential existence, but rest in mere possibility, if fairly made and not in contrary to public policy, not as a grant or present positive transfer, but as a contract to assign, which will entitle the assignee to specific performance as soon as the assignor has acquired the power to perform it." BALL, THE LAW OF COPYRIGHT AND LITERARY PROPERTY 553 (1944).

A similar distinction is made in radio, thus the presentation of an opera is not covered by the ASCAP license. As will be noted when dealing with BUMA and PRS, some European societies do not treat a radio broadcast of an opera as a dramatic, or "grand," performance.

Non-exclusive assignments; antitrust suits.

Television and radio, together, are responsible for over 75% of ASCAP's total revenue. [14] Nevertheless, there are many other commercial users who take out ASCAP's licenses, *e.g.*, dance halls, hotels, film producers, restaurants, department stores and "wired music" firms, such as MUZAK. [15] All the users can deal with the individual copyright proprietors if they wish because a member's assignment to ASCAP is, to this extent, *non-exclusive*. [16] However, for apparent practical reasons this is not done. This restriction is one of many placed on ASCAP by virtue of a consent decree and its amendment, which was entered into by the Society and the Government in settlement of suits under the antitrust laws, usually called the Sherman Act, mentioned earlier. [17] The purpose of this restriction, and of the others which were imposed upon ASCAP, was to permit a break in the Society's monopoly in music performing rights. Whatever one may think of the necessity of a monopoly in this field, as long as monopolies are illegal in the United States, with certain exceptions, it was not the Court's function to legalize ASCAP by "judicial legislation." Although the judge in the government's antitrust suit did not decide the question of ASCAP's legality, or illegality, in a civil suit, *Alden Rochelle, Inc. v. ASCAP*, 80 F. Supp. 888, 893, 895 (S.D.N.Y. 1948), brought under the Act, the court found:

> "Almost every part of the ASCAP structure, almost all of ASCAP's activities in licensing motion picture theatres, involve a violation of the anti-trust laws. Although each member

---

[14] 9 million dollars from radio; 5 million dollars from television. Variety, August 5, 1953, p. 1.

[15] Wired music: recorded music from a central studio is sent over private wires to restaurants and cafes. It is similar in idea to *radio disributie* in the Netherlands.

[16] Amended Consent Judgment, ASCAP, civil action No. 13–95, entered March 14, 1950, section IV.

[17] For a discussion of several state statutes aimed at regulating ASCAP, but which do not appear to affect the normal operation of the Society, see Finkelstein, *The Composer and the Public Interest — Regulation of Performing Right Societies*, 19 LAW AND CONTEMPORARY PROBLEMS 275 (1954).

of ASCAP is granted by the copyright law a monopoly in the copyrighted work, it is unlawful for the owners of a number of copyrighted works to combine their copyrights by any agreement or any arrangement, even if it is for the purpose of thereby better preserving their property rights."

"The reasonableness of the prices or the good intentions of the combining units would not absolve them from the charge that they have violated the anti-trust laws."

The antitrust laws are formally referred to as:

"The Act of Congress of July 2, 1890, entitled "Act to Protect Trade and Commerce Against Unlawful Restraints and Monopolies" and the acts amendatory thereof and supplemental thereto." [18]

Blanket and per program licenses.

Radio and television stations have their choice of blanket or per program licenses. Under both licenses the station may perform any work in the ASCAP catalog. The distinction between them is in computing the fee payable to ASCAP. Under a blanket license the station pays a percentage of the total revenue from the sale of "time" (*i.e.*, income from advertisers) plus a fixed sum for the music used on sustainer programs (*i.e.*, no advertising sponsor). Per program licensees pay a higher percentage of their advertising receipts than do the blanket licensees, however, they only pay as to income from programs utilizing ASCAP music. Listeners do not pay a radio tax for the privilege of using a receiving set since the cost of maintaining a broadcasting system is borne by the business firms which purchase "time" to present their commercial messages.

Network broadcasting.

Broadcasting in the United States differs from that in Europe in the following way, too: there are many stations located throughout the country. As of October, 1953, there were 315 commercial television stations and 2,497 commercial radio stations. [19] About half of them are affiliated with one or several networks, the remaining half being "independent" or "local." A "network" broadcast is one which does not originate with the stations presenting it, rather the stations affiliated with the

---

[18] Consent Decree, ASCAP, civil action No. 13-95, entered March 4, 1941, p. 2.
[19] Variety, December 30, 1953, p. 27.

network simply transmit the program as it is received, something again similar to *radio distributie* (see note 15), except that each affiliate operates in a different part of the country. The affiliated stations are generally separate and distinct companies; they simply have commercial arrangements whereby they purchase transmitting rights from the network company for a certain sum, similar to an arrangement between a cinema theatre and a film distributor. The qualification, "generally," is made because the Federal Communications Commission, which supervises broadcasting, permits a network to own and operate a few stations, from which the network program usually originates. The local, or independent, broadcast is one which originates with the station presenting it. With this as background material we can return to the ASCAP contracts.

All the radio networks and *most* of the local stations (*i.e.*, not affiliated with a network company) have blanket licenses. This is not so in television, where many of the independent stations have per program licenses, the effect of which will be seen later.

Source licensing.

The statement that the "music was cleared at the source," means that if a network company broadcasts a program using ASCAP music, the network's license suffices for all the affiliated stations in the United States carrying the program. Likewise, the individual restaurants do not need an ASCAP license as long as all the ASCAP music which they use comes from a "source-licensee," such as MUZAK, the wired music service.

The situation is slightly different in the case of cinema theatres, although the principles of balancing economic strength and simplifying the licensing process are still present. ASCAP is prohibited from "proceeding against any motion picture theatre exhibitor for copyright infringement relating to motion picture performance rights." It must negotiate with individual motion picture producers. The decree goes so far as to prohibit the members of ASCAP from granting synchronization, or recording, rights to any film producer unless the member, or ASCAP, grants corresponding film performing rights. [20] Thus the court has, in

---

[20] Amended Consent Judgment, ASCAP, civil action No. 13–95, entered March 14 1950, section V.

effect, merged the right of public performance with the right of mechanical reproduction. (European-made films will be considered in connection with the European societies.)

License fees subject to control.

When ASCAP and an applicant for a license cannot agree on a fee to be paid, the user may apply to the Federal Court for the Southern District of New York, which supervises the judgment against ASCAP, for the determination of a reasonable fee. Pending such determination the applicant may use works in the ASCAP catalog, whereupon ASCAP may ask the Court to fix an interim fee until there is a final rate determination. [21] This is, like the source licensing above, another of the restrictions placed on ASCAP by the consent decree.

III. *Management and its Election*

ASCAP is managed by a board of twenty-four directors, twelve of whom are writer members and twelve of whom are publisher members. Three of the writers and three of the publishers represent standard music (*i.e.*, "serious" or classical). Term of office is two years. A quorum consists of thirteen directors, with a two-thirds vote necessary to carry a motion. The officers of ASCAP are elected annually from among the directors by two-thirds of the entire Board of Directors, with the President limited to three consecutive one year terms. He is the chief executive officer of the Society having general supervision over business affairs. During the intervals between meetings of the Board of Directors the over-all supervisory power is in an Executive Committee, selected from among the Board members, by the Directors.

Voting rights.

The writer-Directors are elected by the writer members, and the publisher-Directors are chosen by the publisher members. Each writer has one vote for each $ 20, or major fractions thereof, in domestic royalties received from ASCAP during the previous calender year. The voting unit for publishers is $ 500. However, no publisher or writer has less than one vote. [21a] In the case of

---

[21] Amended Consent Judgment, ASCAP, civil action No. 13–95, entered March 14, 1950, section IX.

[21a] See Appendix D for non-participating membership.

posthumous membership, the successors (*i.e.*, heirs) have no voting rights.

Nomination of directors.

The candidates for the Board are selected by a Publisher Nominating Committee (three members, one of whom is a standard publisher) and a Writer Nominating Committee (six members, one of whom is a standard writer). The retiring Directors appoint the nominating committees, with the members of the Board not eligible to serve upon the committees. *All* members of the Board vote for the members of *each* nominating committee, with each Director automatically a candidate for re-election. Thereby the publisher and writer members each have an indirect voice in selecting the entire Board, and the automatic candidacy of the Directors probably reduces the amount of "politics" entering into the election of the nominating committees. In the case of the Writer Nominating Committee the six writers are selected one from each of six graduated classifications, *i.e.*, the maximum amount of domestic royalties distributed to a writer is the base and this is divided by six. The object of this method of selection is to ensure equal representation on the nominating committee of writers with various incomes. For example, if Irving Berlin earned $84,000 in domestic writer royalties from ASCAP, the six graduated classifications would be 0–$14,000, $14,001–28,000, etc.

In the case of a group of affiliated publishers, it cannot have more than one member on the Board of Directors. Nor can a Director participate in transactions between ASCAP and a licensee if the Director has a pecuniary interest (*e.g.*, the Director's publishing company may be a subsidiary of a film producing company), nor can a Director participate in the adjudiciation of any case in which he is personally interested. The foregoing material concerning management can be found in greater detail in the ASCAP Articles of Association (as in effect June 1, 1950).

IV. *Royalties, or Raison d'Etre*

Publisher and writer royalty funds.

All the royalties and license fees collected by ASCAP after deduction of operating expenses, sums payable to foreign affiliate societies and possible additions to a reserve fund (not exceeding 10% of the net amount available for distribution), are divided into *two equal funds*, one to be distributed among the publishers, and one to be distributed among the writers. [22]

The royalties are allotted by two committees, one consisting of the writer-Directors for the determination of the writer distribution, and one consisting of the publisher-Directors for the determination of the publisher royalties. [23] The membership of these two committees and of the Appeal Board (*infra*) certifies the importance of this aspect of ASCAP's operation. In short, the royalty is the *raison d'être* of ASCAP.

Royalty appeal procedure.

Any member dissatisfied with his royalties may, after any quarterly distribution, file a written protest with his classification committee. Should he be dissatisfied with its decision he may appeal the case to the Board of Appeals. This appellate body is chosen by the general membership in the same manner as are the Directors, who serve on the classification committees. The Appeal Board, consisting of three writers and three publishers (neither members nor affiliated with members of the Board), sits as a unicameral body, as opposed to the dichotomy on the classification level. Then, if the member or the classification committee is not satisfied with the decision, either one may appeal to a Panel, whose decision is final. The Panel consists of an Impartial Chairman (someone not a member of ASCAP) chosen by the Board of Directors, and two ASCAP members, one selected by the member and one chosen by the classification committe concerned. In case a member is reclassified the new classification is not retroactive but becomes effective with the next quarterly distribution. [24]

V. Relief Fund and Annual Dues

In the *Third Copyright Law Symposium* 389 (1940), sponsored by ASCAP, the Society states that it is dedicated to the principle:

"No man or woman in the United States who writes successful music, or anyone dependent upon him, shall ever want."

---

[22] Articles of Association of the American Society of Composers, Authors and Publishers, as in effect June 1, 1950, article XV.
[23] *Id.*, article XIV.
[24] *Ibid.*

Toward this end, the Articles of Association provide that the Board of Directors should annually put aside a portion of the revenue for such purposes.

For this task there are two Relief Committees, again a committee for publishers and a committee for writers. The committees look into urgent calls for help from members, or their widows, infant children or indigent parents. [25] ("Widow" is probably intended to include "widower," where necessary, since Article XXIII provides for the reverse situation: "When the masculine pronoun is used such reference shall be to both sexes.")

The annual dues for participating publishers are $ 50, and for participating writers (and successors of deceased writers) they are $ 10; $ 25 and $ 5 respectively for non-participating members. [26] The money received in payment of the annual dues, in addition to a part of the operational proceeds, as noted above, is designated for the use and benefit of the Relief Fund, unless it is otherwise directed by the Board of Directors.

VI. Royalties Revisited

Membership requirements.

To become a member of ASCAP a writer need only have one work regularly published. [27] He will thereafter receive performance royalties from ASCAP, even when his works are subsequently published by a non-ASCAP publisher, because the performing rights are now in ASCAP. If the writer's publisher is in ASCAP (publisher's membership requirement: he must be a regular publisher [28]), he, too, receives royalties for the performance of the composition, though out of the publisher fund. [28a]

When the writer is not a member of ASCAP (or BMI), but the publisher is a member of ASCAP, the Society generally acquires the performing rights by virtue of the writer's contract with the publisher and the publisher's assignment to ASCAP, resulting in the organization paying royalties to the publisher alone. These

---
[25] *Ibid.*

[26] Articles of Association of the American Society of Composers, Authors and Publishers, as in effect June 1, 1950, article III.

[27] Amended Consent Judgment. ASCAP, civil action No. 13-95, entered March 14, 1950, section XV.

[28] *Ibid.*

[28a] See Appendix D, however, for the effect of nonprofessionalism and few performances on membership rights including royalties.

payments are not any larger than when the writer is a member, even though the organization does not pay a royalty to the non-member writer. The ASCAP writer members as a group benefit in such a case, and this is reversed when the writer is in ASCAP and the publisher is not. Thus, there is this economic pressure to join one of the performing right organizations (and in the case of publishers to join both ASCAP and BMI, the rival organization, via separate corporations).

Certainly a writer does not wish to share his performance fees with the publisher simply because the latter is not affiliated with the writer's particular licensing group. The same situation presents itself when the publisher is affiliated and the writer is not, since in both cases the member is not receiving a larger royalty due to the non-affiliation of the other party. Furthermore the nonmember, as a practical matter, does not have the necessary bargaining power to persuade the affiliated party to part with a share of his performing royalties.

Distribution of royalties.

Due to ASCAP's involved formulas, and constant revisions thereof, for the distribution of royalties (for which see the Appendix D), no attempt has been made to spell out to the last digit the mathematics now in use.

Distribution on broadcasting performances.

Although ASCAP receives revenue from licensees, *e.g.*, night clubs, hotels and restaurants, in addition to radio and television, performances therein are not calculated for reasons of practical administration and economy. However, it would be erroneous to say that writers and publishers are not paid for these performances — it is simply that the revenue from cafés, etc., is distributed on the basis of radio and television performances (with an exception in the case of serious music).

An evening radio station performance is valued at one credit, *i.e.*, the writer and publisher each receive one credit; $3/4$ credit is given for each daytime performances (in conformity with the difference in advertising rates) and $1/2$ credit for each performance on a sustainer program. If the performance is carried by a network, then it is multiplied by the number of affiliated stations carrying it, *e.g.*, a performance on a 100 station network yields 100 credits to the writer and 100 credits to the publisher. If there is more than one writer, *e.g.*, composer and lyrist, they each receive 50% of the writer credits (in a later section we shall consider collaboration by ASCAP and BMI writers). The fact that the publisher is a member of ASCAP and receives credits in the publisher fund does not bear on the writer's credits and *vice versa*, as noted previously. The same credit is earned whether the performance is a live one or one on records. With regard to television, triple credit is given for each performance because despite the large amount of money ASCAP receives from television, there are considerably fewer television stations.

Program analysis.

Programs of national networks are completely analyzed and credit is given for each station affiliated with the network. Programs of stations with per program licenses are also fully analyzed and, in addition, programs of ten local stations in different sections of the country are completely analyzed, and the number of credits tabulated for the ten stations is multiplied by seven. These arbitrary figures may have changed by the time of publication since the number of stations checked and the multiplier are continually being increased because of the desire to give greater coverage to the local stations. To assist writers of serious music (at the expense of writers of light music) all programs of non-broadcaster licensees in the field of serious music (*e.g.*, concert halls) are analyzed and triple credit given.

Foreign societies.

Payment is spread over a considerable period of time, as shown in the Appendix, except in the case of the foreign societies. The foreign societies are paid solely on the basis of current performances, thus they receive the total value of a credit after the year of performance.[28b] The foreign societies affiliated with ASCAP pay the American society for the performance abroad of ASCAP music also according to a system of current performances. Therefore, ASCAP distributes this money to its members solely on the basis of the foreign societies' current performance records.

[28b] *E.g.*, If ASCAP writers receive seven dollar cents per credit from the Current Performance Fund then foreign writers would receive thirty-five dollar cents per performance.

40 PUBLIC PERFORMANCE OF MUSIC IN THE UNITED STATES

Performance values.

It should be noted that the credits per station performance, referred to earlier, are for original 3 minute light compositions. Background music receives as little as 1/1,000th of a credit and a symphonic work of one hour's duration as much as 124 credits. Copyrighted arrangements of works in the public domain receive 15% of the value given to original works.

Withdrawal from society.

As mentioned earlier, the member executes a long term assignment. Nevertheless, upon giving written notice within three months he may withdraw from membership in ASCAP at the end of any fiscal year. His resignation is subject to licenses then outstanding between ASCAP and users. Thus, until these licenses expire, performing rights in works in existence at the time of withdrawal are held by ASCAP. The member may deal with the performing rights in new compositions as he wishes. However, upon resignation the member takes a reduction in the royalties on performing rights remaining in ASCAP. [29]

Since common sense, and experience, tells us it is not likely that a writer or publisher will stay unaffiliated upon leaving ASCAP, *e.g.*, E.B. Marks Music Corp., discussed later, let us now examine ASCAP's major rival, BMI.

E. THE BMI STORY

I. Background

Radio broadcasting as a form of public entertainment is relatively young. In 1921 there were five such stations throughout the world. However, radio immediately began to grow by leaps and bounds and within a year there were over five hundred broadcasting stations in operation in the United States alone.

Radio opposes ASCAP.

The broadcasters thought that they should not be required to pay for performing music on the grounds that such performances, by popularizing songs, increased the sale of sheet music and,

---

[29] Articles of Association of the American Society of Composers A,uthors and Publishers, as in effect June 1, 1950, article III.

furthermore, that the broadcasts were not public performances for profit. When it became clear to the broadcasters that ASCAP *and the courts* took a dim view of this approach, they agreed to take out ASCAP licenses, which were on a "flat fee" basis, *i.e.*, a fixed, non-varying dollar amount.

This was the arrangement until 1932, when ASCAP presented the broadcasters with a new license fee system. Neville Miller, the president of the National Association of Broadcasters (NAB), had the following to say about ASCAP's new method of computing the license fee:

> "Having no source of music supply other than ASCAP and one or two individual publishers of classical music, broadcasters — on the eve of the final deadline, September 1, — were forced to submit to a principle which they then disapproved and have always regretted. That principle was the payment of a percentage of the broadcasters' gross receipts from the sale of broadcasting time, regardless of whether the time was consumed in playing ASCAP music, non-ASCAP music or no music at all. This principle never has been applied by ASCAP to any other industry using music, to the hotels, cafes, theatres, etc." [30, 31]

Thus in 1932 we have the beginning of the present percentage fee system of broadcast licensing used by ASCAP *and* BMI. The criticism of the broadcasters, quoted above, was directed not only at the percentage system but also against the blanket license, which was described earlier. As a result of the 1941 antitrust suit ASCAP was required to make available to broadcasters a per program license, also mentioned earlier, which is based on a percentage of the income from programs *using* ASCAP music. [32] With the conflict began NAB's attempt to provide radio stations with a large non-ASCAP repertory, *e.g.*, The Radio Program Foundation.

The purpose of this new organization was:

> "To create a music supply sufficiently large to allow all stations to forego their contracts with ASCAP (Society)." [33]

---

[30] Miller and Mills, *ASCAP-NAB Controversy, The Issues*, 11 AIR L. REV. 394, 399 (1940).

[31] The percentage-of-receipts license is now used in the ASCAP agreement with the National Ballroom Operators Association.

[32] Consent Decree, ASCAP, civil action No. 13-95 entered March 4, 1941, p. 3.

[33] Defendant's Answer, p. 26, U.S. v. ASCAP, E 78-388, S.D. N.Y. (1934).

The Foundation acquired the radio performance rights for the United States in the music catalog of G. Ricordi and Co. of Milan, Italy, as well as the broadcasting performance rights in several American catalogs of music.[34] However, with ASCAP's membership and catalog continuing to increase in size and importance, and with radio's increased need for music, the broadcasters had to continue to do business with the Society.

II. Birth of BMI

At the expiration of the ASCAP licenses in December, 1940, ASCAP again put forth a new license fee system. Whereas before, *each station*, whether independent or network owned or affiliated, paid a percentage of time sales to ASCAP, the new system provided that a levy should also be placed at *the source*, *i.e.*, the network should pay for programs carried, and which were also paid for, by their owned or affiliated stations. The theory was that although the network station originating the broadcast (and the other stations carrying it) paid a percentage of its advertising income to ASCAP, the network company was receiving large sums from which ASCAP received nothing. Whereupon we see the *Birth of BMI*:

> "Radio in the form of the NAB had taken as much as it thought it could or should and despite earlier losses and failures to defeat ASCAP [*e.g.*, competitive societies], refused to succumb to this latest directive.
> NAB's strategy was simple: it would not use ASCAP music. Since music was vital to radio's existence, it would: (1) compose its own, and (2) tap the always available source of music which is in the public domain and available for the asking. Pursuing this strategy, NAB formed its own music pool, BMI, which was stocked by independent non-ASCAP compositions and those publishers not ASCAP affiliated."[35]

ASCAP's reaction to radio's efforts is clearly shown in the following quotation from an article by Society official, E.C. Mills:

> "The National and Columbia networks have publicly announced a boycott of ASCAP music to commence January 1, 1941. It will, of course, never be put into effect. It is merely one more bluff, and it will be called."[36]

---

[34] Defendant's Answer, p. 26, U.S. v. ASCAP, E 78–388, S.D.N.Y. (1934).

[35] White, *Musical Copyrights v. the Anti-Trust Laws*, 30 NEBRASKA L. REV. 50, 54 (1950).

[36] Miller and Mills, *ASCAP-NAB Controversy, The Issues*, 11 AIR L. REV. 394, 397 (1940).

However, the networks *did* stop using ASCAP music upon the expiration of the licenses at midnight, December 31, 1940. The results were not as catastrophic to radio as ASCAP had predicted (and hoped). In fact, they were chiefly catastrophic to the sale of sheet music and phonograph records consisting of works in the ASCAP catalog, and the performing animal Sharkey, the trained seal (N.Y. Times, March 7, 1941, p. 11):

> "Sharkey, the trained seal, is going to have to broaden his repertoire to get back on the air unless the ASCAP-BMI controversy ends shortly. He knows how to play "Where the River Shannon Flows," and that is all. It's an ASCAP tune. He was due to broadcast here to-nite on the program of the Southern sportsman show, but the lawyers said no."

Radio and ASCAP settle dispute.

After the passage of a few months, with ASCAP being confronted on the one side by an indifferent public and on the other side by a government antitrust suit (which we referred to earlier), a new license was negotiated, with both ASCAP and BMI giving some ground. During the conflict NAB President Miller had said:

> "The battle has progressed so far that it seems certain that the broadcasters will never go back to the old percentage system."[37]

However, the percentage basis remained a major factor in the new license. Nevertheless, ASCAP's proposal was not the basis of the final agreement either, as can be ascertained from the following section in the Consent Decree, entered into with the Government on March 4, 1941:

> "In so far as network radio broadcasting is concerned, the issuance of a single license, authorizing and fixing a single license fee for such performance for network radio broadcasting, shall permit the simultaneous broadcasting of such performance by all stations on the network which shall broadcast such performance, without requiring separate licenses for such several stations for such performance." [38]

Thus, the contracts now provide that ASCAP receives from a network company a percentage of the gross amount paid by sponsors after deductions of sales commissions and the cost of

---
[37] *Id.* at 399.
[38] Consent Decree, ASCAP, civil action No. 13-95, entered March 4, 1941, section II, 4.

interconnecting facilities. The gross amount means the total amount paid for the use of broadcasting facilities by the sponsor of each program broadcast by the network, whether those payments are made to the network company or the affiliated stations.

With the signing of the new ASCAP agreement, radio did not disband BMI nor allow it to fall apart from lack of attention. BMI had made its mark:

> "Even ASCAP, a little begrudgingly to be sure, has admitted that BMI has coralled some excellent music both in the serious and in the popular fields. In many and varied quarters BMI has uncovered the minority heretofore unknown composers who had the ability to make the grade." [39]

Thus BMI was here to stay: (1) to be developed into a competitor to ASCAP, and (2) to remain as a buffer in future bargaining with ASCAP. [40]

III. Contracts *

Licenses.

The licensing arrangement between BMI and commercial users is similar to that of ASCAP except that BMI's licenses include dramatic performance rights and the rates are lower, in keeping with BMI's smaller catalog. [41]

Exclusive assignments.

A typical grant of music performing rights to BMI, from the writer of popular music, is for two years with options for five one year renewals. It is an *exclusive* assignment, which means that only BMI can give permission to perform the work. Although the

---

[39] N. Y. Times, March 9, 1941, p. 7.

[40] In fact, BMI was the object of a federal antitrust suit in 1941 and entered into a consent decree May 14, 1941. U.S. v. BMI (E.D. Wisc.), see Appendix.

The decree, however, does not appear to have had any major effect on BMI. At present there is a civil antitrust suit pending against BMI, brought by a number of ASCAP writer members. The plaintiffs seek the separation of BMI from the broadcasting companies, the dissolution of the national association of broadcasters, and treble damages. Variety, November 11, 1953, p. 1.

[41] Gross income of BMI and subsidiaries for the fiscal year ending July 31, 1952: $ 5,607,842. Broadcasting-Telecasting, October 27, 1952, p. 30.

Gross income of ASCAP for 1952: $ 17,672,000. Variety, April 8, 1953, p. 1.

* BMI informed us that their writer and publisher agreements were being revised, however, they were not yet prepared at the time of our printer's deadline.

grant is to all music performing rights, without distinguishing between dramatic and non-dramatic, it specifically reserves to the writer the rights in "performances of longer than thirty (30) minutes duration of operas, operettas and musical comedies." These rights are usually negotiated for separately by the broadcaster, or other user, with the publisher of the work. However, even in this area, BMI is pioneering to alter the somewhat cumbersome situation, as indicated in the following article from Variety:

> "Broadcast Music Inc., has opened a new frontier in its promotion of longhair music by wrapping up an agreement permitting BMI radio licensees to program complete performances of operas copyrighted by the G. Ricordi Music Company of Milan. Heretofore stations were permitted to perform operatic or dramatic musical work in portions not exceeding 30 minutes without special permission from the copyright owner. The BMI-Ricordi deal is the first such permission granted to a U.S. performing rights group."[41a]

As noted earlier, ASCAP only receives non-dramatic rights from its members, and considers operatic works as dramatic compositions.

The performing rights revert to the copyright proprietor at the end of the contract, unless a new contract is entered into, *i.e.*, the grants are not for the term of the copyright but rather for two to seven years depending upon the option renewals. However, BMI attorney Theodora Zavin pointed out (in our correspondence with BMI) that "as a practical matter most of the publishers who become affiliated with BMI continue to remain affiliated after the term of their agreement has expired." This factor is important because as an additional practical matter the publisher is usually the copyright proprietor, the writer receiving various royalty commitments from him in return. Nevertheless, BMI will lose some performance rights where the publisher is not a BMIer and the rights revert to him. Even this likelihood is minimized because some ASCAP publishers have affiliated companies which have contracts with BMI, and the BMI writers will be published through those firms, *e.g.*:

> "Publisher Ivan Mogull last week set up a Broadcast Music

[41a] Variety, July 29, 1953, p. 105.

Inc. affiliate, Harvard Music. Mogull also operates an ASCAP affiliate, Mogull Music." [42]

Secondly, the writer contract with BMI provides in section 7b that if he signs publishing agreements with regard to more than one work which has not yet been composed, then BMI has the option to exclude such works from the royalty provisions of the contract or to terminate the contract immediately. The purpose of section 7b, according to BMI, is to give all their affiliated publishers a chance to bid for the works of BMI writers.

Film music.

As noted earlier, the grant to BMI includes dramatic performances, but it specifically provides:

"In each instance that you are employed or commissioned by a motion picture producer to write during the period of the contract, all or part of the score of a motion picture, or by the producer of a revue for the legitimate stage to write during the period of the contract all or part of the musical compositions contained therein, we agree to confirm to the producers of the film that such part of the score as is written by you may be performed as part of the exhibition of said film without compensation to us, and to the producer of the revue that your compositions embodied therein may be exhibited on the stage with living artists without compensation to us."

If the music is sought for the stage or screen *after* composition, then BMI can license the performance rights without royalties to writer or publisher. However, they may decide not to do so upon consideration of other factors present in the particular commercial relationship. This may not be important, as a practical matter, since BMI does not acquire motion picture synchronization rights, without which film performing rights are valueless, and it does not acquire the performing rights to musical comedies. This point, however, should be kept in mind throughout any examination of BMI: it is a private corporation, able to meet the *varying* needs of the marketplace. Thus, unlike ASCAP, we find, (1) BMI enters into *varying* types of contracts with its writer and publisher affiliates, and what may apply to one need have no relation to another, and (2) BMI serves customers the way it thinks a business should: it tries to make the license more valua-

---

[42] Variety, February 4, 1953, p. 41.

ble, through promotional means, to the small stations that do not have the selection staffs of large networks.

Right to record.

A typical agreement between publishers and BMI contains a grant of exclusive performance rights for a period of five years with the rights reverting at the end of the period. [43] The agreement permits BMI (non-exclusively) to make arrangements of the work and allow others to do so, and also provides (in section 2c) that BMI shall have:

> "The non-exclusive right to record, or cause or permit to be recorded ... upon payment of the customary royalty rate then prevailing but in no event in excess of present statutory royalties."

Acting under this section which is also present in the writer's grant, BMI can make works fully available (*i.e.*, various artists and arrangements) to stations in instances when, because a work is not published and statutory copyright is not sought, mechanical rights could be vested exclusively in one recording company through the non-applicability of the compulsory license clause of section 1e of the Copyright Act. BMI can also act under this clause when the work is copyrighted but not yet recorded so as to subject the work to the compulsory licensing provision.

Writer and publisher royalties.

In theory, of course, if a writer has granted his performing rights to BMI, he has no performing rights which he can subsequently grant to a publisher and which the publisher can grant to BMI. However, for payment purposes, BMI, as do the other performing rights groups, treats the situation as one in which they have secured performing rights from both sources. An unusual aspect of the publisher and writer performance grants to BMI is that the writer gives his exclusive *and* non-exclusive rights, whereas the publisher conveys only exclusive rights. One can

---

[43] This is the interpretation given by BMI. The reader, however, should examine the contract (see appendix) because it does not seem clear. It appears that there may be an alternative interpretation: all performance rights acquired by the publisher during the term of the contract are granted without the grant being limited to the term. Since the publisher is the owner of the performing right, upon the expiration of the writer's grant, the performing right would remain in BMI for the duration of the original term of copyright.

imagine a situation in which an affiliated BMI publisher publishes a joint work of an ASCAP member and an unaffiliated writer. The ASCAP writer gives ASCAP a non-exclusive performing right and, presumably, the unaffiliated writer gives his non-exclusive right to the publisher. Thus, in this case, BMI is not acquiring from the publisher all of his available performing rights.

The type of warranty that appears in the typical performing right contract between BMI and its publishers and writers is too broad and subjects the publisher and writer to unlimited liability for which they may not be to blame. For example, the writer agrees (and the publisher contracts similarly) to indemnify BMI "against all loss and/or damage resulting from any and all claims of whatsoever name and nature arising from or in connection with the exercise of anyone or more of the rights granted ... in this agreement."

Additional catalogs.

The license from BMI to the commercial users includes, in addition to the performance rights resulting from the above mentioned contracts, the catalog of the privately owned American Performing Right Society, Inc. and the catalog of G. Ricordi, mentioned previously in connection with operatic performances and the BMI forerunner, the Radio Program Foundation. Also included in the BMI radio and television licenses is the repertory of the American Composers Alliance, whereby BMI assists composers of unpublished serious music by paying a blanket fee for the broadcasting rights. The American Composers Alliance is somewhat similar to the Dutch organization DONEMUS, which will be mentioned later.

IV. *Other Departments*

BMI has its own publishing department for popular music. The contract it uses includes a provision for royalties for broadcasting performances, however, the section is not applicable if the writer is an affiliated BMI writer. Nor would it serve BMI's purpose to publish the work of an ASCAP writer. Since the BMI affiliated writer is not assigning to the Publishing Department any performing rights, he receives performing royalties on the basis of the earlier, or underlying, affiliation agreement.

Section 3h of the Publishing Department contract provides:

"Except as is specifically provided for ... no other royalties of any kind shall be paid by Publisher to Writer."

The other specific items for which BMI pays royalties are sheet music, orchestrations, folios,[44] records, and films. Therefore the contract does not give the writer a share in additional income occasionally produced by novelty songs, such as "Rudoph the Red-Nosed Reindeer." The importance of this omission can best be shown by a passage from "Business Practices in the Copyright Field," by BMI's Robert J. Burton (vice-president and counsel):

"I have before me a list of 75 articles of commerce currently available, all of them based on a character suggested by the title of a song. Rudolph the Red-Nosed Reindeer ... was a previously unknown, imaginary character ... a two million dollar income has resulted because of the projection of a mere song title into visual objects of commerce ... This is an amazing list of products ranging all the way from lollipops to bubble bath to curtains, and including dozens of items of clothing and all sorts of toys and household utilities ... I have examined many of these objects and everyone bears a specific copyright notice referring back to the title of a musical composition."[45]

In the field of serious music BMI is represented by a subsidiary, Associated Music Publishers (AMP). A usual procedure in regard to performing rights is for the composer to receive from AMP a share of the concert hall royalties and a blanket fee for broadcasting rights.

Another important function of BMI, because of the number of young affiliated writers and publishers, is its counseling and guidance, *e.g.*, to go to Paris for further study, to buy a home in the country, etc. Furthermore, BMI, as does ASCAP, subsidizes concerts and festivals, works closely with music educators, etc. The theory is to make the music writers feel they are getting more than simply money, although, as BMI readily points out, without money no one will be attracted.

---

[44] Folio: ollection of popular songs bound in paper covers. Size mostly 9 × 12 (inches). SHAW, LINGO OF TIN PAN ALLEY (1950).
[45] Burton, *Business Practices in the Copyright Field*, 7 COPYRIGHT PROBLEMS ANALYZED 93 (1952).

V. Royalties

Fixed amount per broadcast performance.

Since BMI is not a nonprofit association it need not, and does not, divide its receipts among its affiliated publisher and writer members.[45a] BMI's contracts with publishers and writers generally provide for a fixed amount per broadcasting performance. For example, in 1953 the royalty usually paid to affiliated publishers was four dollar cents per local station performance and six dollar cents for network performances (or "plays" or "plugs" as they are sometimes called). In some publishing contracts, however, the six cents rate was limited: [45b]

> "BMI has evolved a system whereby network plays no longer have greater value than local plugs. In actuality, BMI would rather there were 40 local plugs, in widely scattered communities, than one chain plug originating from New York, Chicago or L.A., by a band or vocalist which might carry that play into 40 different cities.
> BMI wants to saturate its song catalog on a grass roots or local level, in line with the fact that the broadcasters, who underwrite Broadcast Music, Inc. likewise operate on a local level — not everything is a major network in radio.
> BMI was moved into this local vs. network wariness by the fact that *cut-ins, payolas* and other angles could put some tune up in fallacious high brackets via a series of blanket network performances and it would still not achieve the desired saturation that comes from multiplicity of local originations. As result, despite the normal 4 cents and 6 cents payoffs for local and network plugs, respectively, when computations are made, the payoff is not automatically made on network plugs. The local plug tallies at 4 cents, if less than network performances, automatically cut down the 6 cents per point payoffs to the sum total of the local plugs." (emphasis added).

Unethical practices.

The purpose of emphasizing *cut-in* and *payola* is to point out that underhanded methods are sometimes used in order to acquire high performance ratings. In the case of BMI it results in royalties being paid for performances which do not honestly reflect quest of popularity or popularity (*i.e.*, value). At the same time these performances prevent compositions deserving of performances

---

[45a] BMI cannot do so under the consent decree, see Appendix E; *Cf.* note 51.
[45b] Variety, March 11, 1953, p. 41.

from being broadcasted. Such methods have similar evil results in ASCAP, because the more money member X receives in royalties the less money member Y receives, and because of the same factor which affects BMI, there can only be a limited number of performances. The definitions of *cut-in* and *payola* cast some light on the subject of broadcasting performance royalties. The definitions are of authority because the author of the invaluable little dictionary, *Lingo of Tin Pan Alley* (1950), is a BMI publisher of popular music, Arnold Shaw:

> "*Cut-in* refers to the practice, adopted sometimes by publishers, sometimes by writers, sometimes by both, of a performer to share in the credits and/or royalties of a song. SPA [45c] has largely eliminated the credit cut-in; but publishers occasionally make "side" deals with vocalists and bandleaders to insure co-operation on performances."
>
> "*Payola*. Act of paying an artist to perform a song, practice outlawed by agreement between the Music Publishers' Contact Employees, representing the contact men, and most of the publishing houses. While direct payment is seldom resorted to these days, various subterfuges have been developed. Among these indirect forms of payola are: (1) standing the cost of a special arrangement; (2) signing bandleaders and intrumentalists to writer contracts; (3) sending gifts at Christmas and on special occasions."

Writers receive $1/2$ as much as publishers.

The BMI royalty paid to affiliated *writers* in 1953, which was only upon works in which BMI received exclusive performing rights, was 50% of the current rates generally being paid to the affiliated publishers. The royalty rate for performances on television was the same as for radio. Therefore, in 1953, the writers received two cents for each local station performance and three cents for each station carrying a network performance. Thus the total royalty per performance that BMI usually paid was six cents and nine cents per station. BMI, as does ASCAP, distinguishes between sustainer and commercial program performances:

> "Whereas one indie plug is worth one performance credit, BMI gives each plug on a sustaining network show 75 performance credits, regardless of the number of stations which carry the show. Plugs on commercial shows get a minimum of

---

[45c] SPA (Songwriters' Protective Association) is an association of professional songwriters. See Klein, *Protective Societies for Authors and Creators*, 1953 COPYRIGHT PROBLEMS ANALYZED 19 (1953).

75 credits with additional credits for every station over 75 carrying the show." [46]

(A network program may be carried by as many as 200 radio stations).

The contract between BMI and the publisher provides that if a higher royalty rate is paid later under "substantially identical agreements" then the publisher shall receive the more favorable rate or shall have the right to terminate the agreement. It is therefore likely that the higher rate would become the rate generally paid. This would thereby result in an increase of the writer's royalty, which is based upon the publisher's rate, *i.e.*, 50% of same.

BMI does not pay royalties to writers for performances on copyrighted arrangements of works in the public domain, and in regard to publishers BMI retains the right to exclude such works from the terms of the agreement. Thus, if an affiliated writer's copyrighted arrangement of a work in the public domain becomes valuable, he is not entitled to any performance royalties for it. However, if the affiliated publisher has the performing right, *i.e.*, the writers are neither with ASCAP nor with BMI, and BMI excludes the work from their agreement, the publisher's position would not be very strong because he has no other market (or means of enforcement), as a practical matter, for the performing right to a single arrangement of a public domain work.

Foreign rights.

As to foreign performing fees, BMI deducts 10% for administrative expenses and the balance goes to the writer and publisher. However, if a BMI affiliated publisher has a contract with a non-affiliated writer, the 90% balance will be paid entirely to the publisher; the writer will share in this money to the extent that it is provided for in his publishing contract. In this connection it is interesting to note that BMI receives from publishers, in addition to the right of public performance for profit throughout the world, world broadcasting rights. Therefore, if performances by foreign broadcasting stations are deemed to be nonprofit, BMI has the rights nevertheless. However, by the terms of this assignment BMI does not receive the right to non-broadcasted performances which are not for profit, although such performances are protected in most foreign countries.

---

[46] Variety, March 11, 1953, p. 41.

The same flaw arises in the writer contract, due to the conveyance of world rights in the terminology of the American Act. The writer grants to BMI, "the sole and exclusive right publicly to perform for profit, and to license others publicly to perform for profit throughout the world." It would seem, therefore, on the basis of this contract alone, that BMI cannot convey broadcasting rights to societies in countries where broadcasting is not for profit.

Guarantee.

An important feature of BMI's contract with affiliated writers is found in section 5:

"We agree to pay you as a minimum payment against the royalties to be earned during each year of the period of the contract not less than $ — for each year of the period of the contract."

The five one year options contain similar provisions: BMI is to make minimum annual payments to the writers.

Analysis of broadcasting performances.

In determining the number of performances, BMI, as does ASCAP, analyzes the network performances completely, and the sampling technique is used in connection with independent stations. In regard to the networks, by examining the programs originating with a few stations they obtain the programs of hundreds of additional stations which simply relay the broadcast. In addition, over 100 different local stations are analyzed each month, with each performance during the month accounted for. The number of performances reported by the analyzed stations is then multiplied by a figure (approximately twelve), calculated to cover the number of performances on all the licensed local stations.

Now let us go on to compare some additional features of ASCAP and BMI.

F. BMI AND ASCAP - DIFFERENCES AND SIMILARITIES

I. Contracts

Dramatic and non-dramatic rights.

The performing rights assigned to ASCAP by its membership are non-dramatic, a result, in part, of the historical development of performing right societies. The performing rights acquired by

BMI are both dramatic and non-dramatic, although it does not include the rights in "performances of longer than thirty (30) minutes duration of operas, operettas and musical comedies." The latter rights, with the exception of G. Ricordi operas, are negotiated for by the broadcasters (or other users) as needed.

Exclusive and non-exclusive assignments.

The ASCAP assignment is non-exclusive in so far as it permits the members to issue non-exclusive licenses to users. The definition of the term, user, includes one who:

> "(1) owns or operates an establishment or enterprise where copyrighted musical compositions are performed publicly for profit ,or (2) is otherwise directly engaged in giving public performance of copyrighted musical compositions for profit." [47] (*i.e.*, user does not include BMI).

The BMI agreements are exclusive assignments but, as indicated earlier, in practice the result of both assignments is, in this respect, the same.

Disputes due to two licensors.

The licenses issued by both organizations are similar, but for the limited dramatic rights given by BMI. However, whereas most television stations take out BMI blanket licenses, there are many that take out per program licenses from ASCAP. ASCAP claims that this results in many stations playing ASCAP music only when it is absolutely necessary because the BMI music under the blanket license has to be paid for whether used or not, whereas under per program licensing music is only paid for when used. Because of this alleged disadvantage, ASCAP wants the Federal Court for the Southern District of New York to change the Amended Consent Decree under which it is now operating, so that they can refuse to issue a per program license to any broadcaster which has a BMI blanket license.

The asserted situation is allegedly reversed in the field of dance halls. Here the operators have an ASCAP license based upon a percentage of total receipts, whereas BMI has not been able to come to terms with the National Ballroom Operators Association:

---

[47] Articles of Association of the American Society of Composers, Authors and Publishers, as in effect June 1, 1950, section 6.

"It has been charged that ballroom operators had given orders to visiting bands not to play BMI tunes in order to avoid the need to make a deal with BMI."[47a]

This is due in part perhaps to the feeling among many users that "they should not be obliged to deal with more than one licensing agency anymore than they deal with more than one telephone company."[48]

Government supervision of license fees.

As a consequence of the 1950 Amended Consent Decree, the Federal Court has the final say on the cost of an ASCAP license. (See p. 34 *supra*). In this connection it is interesting to note that which was ASCAP's position for many years (*The ASCAP Story* (1950), p. 22):

> "In many European countries, where mass communications are owned and operated by the government, performing right societies similar to ASCAP occupy a quasi-judicial role. These foreign governments require each user to report to the society all uses of music.
> Under our American free enterprise, such an arrangement is neither possible nor desirable. As Americans, ASCAP members believe that the free artist can best survive and flourish when, individually or as a member of a group, he deals with the commercial enterprises which earn millions of dollars from the product of his genius."

However, ASCAP's views on the subject of governmental supervision have changed in recent years. The Society's General Attorney, Herman Finkelstein, writes:

> "Federal regulation is now effected through the machinery of consent decrees. In some countries rates are determined by administrative agencies. The American Society of Composers, Authors and Publishers is willing to submit to regulation of rates by either judicial or administrative branch of the Government on the theory that determination of rates by an impartial outside agency avoids a situation in which the public is denied access to the best music because of disputes between the users and the creators."[49]

[47a] Variety, March 11, 1953, p. 42.
[48] Finkelstein, *Marketing of the Arts, Anti-Trust Laws and the Arts*, U. OF CHICAGO LAW SCHOOL CONFERENCE ON THE ARTS PUBLISHING AND THE LAW 12 (March 5, 1952).
[49] Finkelstein, *Public Performance Rights In Music and Performance Right Societies*, 7 COPYRIGHT PROBLEMS ANALYZED 85 (1952).

"It is appropriate to consider whether groups engaged in licensing performing rights should be removed from the operation of the anti-trust laws upon submitting to statutory rate regulation as in the case of the shipping companies." [50]

BMI does not find itself in such a position because (1) the largest users are the broadcasters (and 700 stations are stockholders) and all broadcasters share in the profits, if any, via rebates, and (2) the BMI repertory has not yet achieved the size and quality of the ASCAP catalog so that action, such as that of the ballrooms, is not unlikely if BMI were to abuse its position (apart from the question of Justice Department action and civil suits under the antitrust laws).

Composition of ASCAP and BMI.

The BMI stock is owned by members of the broadcasting industry, and the Board of Directors is representative of same; the ASCAP board is composed of publishers and writers representative of its membership.

The broadcasters are among ASCAP's customers; publishers and writers are among BMI's customers. This does not mean that *no* users have a voice in ASCAP; there has been much comment regarding undue influence of the motion picture interests through their ASCAP publishing subsidiaries. The consent decree took cognizance of the problem and the last paragraph in our section on the management of ASCAP shows how it was dealt with.

Motion picture performing rights.

It is often pointed out that the film industry pays to ASCAP less than $ 1,000,000 per year as compared to over $ 12,000,000 paid-in by the broadcasting interests. This overlooks a fundamental fact. With regard to motion pictures there are two rights which have to be acquired: synchronization rights and performance rights. ASCAP only licenses the latter and members of ASCAP deal individually for the synchronization right. This does not mean that some examination into the question of Hollywood fees may not be warranted, but it should point up the fact that more than superficial consideration is needed. [51]

---

[50] Finkelstein, *Marketing of the Arts, Anti-Trust Laws and the Arts*, U. OF CHICAGO LAW SCHOOL CONFERENCE ON THE ARTS PUBLISHING AND THE LAW 16 (March 5, 1952).

[51] For example, several motion picture companies own publishing firms which causes a conflict of interests when the publisher sells synchronization rights, in which the writer has an interest, to the parent company.

Furthermore, in dealing with motion pictures it should be remembered that members deal individually with their dramatic rights for which they may receive as much as several hundred thousand dollars for a musical comedy.

In the case of BMI, unless the writer was commissioned to write the music for the film, these performance rights (dramatic as well as non-dramatic), subject to the thirty minute opera and musical comedy limitation, are acquired by the licensing organization without the need for paying royalties based thereon. This is somewhat similar to the ASCAP method in that music is licensed to non-broadcasting users as well as to broadcasters, but with royalties to writers and publishers calculated solely on the basis of broadcast performances. The situation is different, however, because ASCAP distributes the money it collects from film producers, although on the basis of broadcasting performances, whereas BMI does not. Therefore, when one affiliates with BMI he is engaging in a gamble to a larger degree. However, since here also the assignment does not include synchronization rights the copyright owners may still realize the true value of the composition.

II. Royalties

Rates; distribution formulas.

Whereas in principle ASCAP pays the same royalties to writers and publishers, the BMI royalty rate is two parts for the publisher to one part for the writer, with distribution based solely on current performances. ASCAP, however, pays out only a portion on the basis of the most recent performance, with the balance on averages, length of time, etc. One might say, in theory, that ASCAP earnings are based on current performances but that the entire payment is not made currently. Because of this difference in method if X wrote a hit and it was the only song played night and day, he would be the only writer collecting royalties from BMI (apart from the minimum guarantees), whereas in ASCAP he would be limited to the current performance fund (and to only a small portion of the remaining 80%). If the work was not performed at all in the second year or thereafter, the BMI writer would receive nothing (save the minimum guarantees), but the

ASCAP writer would continue to share in the remaining 80% non-current funds for some time to come. Thus the ASCAP plan is a tax benefit by spreading the performance royalties on current hits over a period of years, and not bunching them together with the royalties from sheet music and phonograph records. Furthermore BMI operates on a "fixed per performance price" basis.

Television performances.

ASCAP gives triple credit for television performances, whereas BMI does not (at least not in 1953). If BMI gave triple credit it would pay out three times as much with regard to television performances. However, when ASCAP gives triple credit for television it simply means the various distribution funds must be divided by more credits, with each credit worth less. Thus the ASCAP method results in higher royalties than otherwise to the writer whose works are more suitable for television, and lower royalties to the writer of non-televised works. This gives proper consideration to the small number of stations (one-eighth as many television stations as radio stations) which produce an increasingly large segment of the ASCAP revenue. [52] Perhaps BMI should lower the value of the radio performance and increase the payment for the television performance.

Program analysis.

Since ASCAP considers fewer non-network programs (70 stations in 1953) in the royalty distribution, the writer or publisher whose works are not likely to be performed on network shows but which will be played by the local stations, may be better suited for affiliation with BMI because of the very extensive analysis of independent stations (half of the nation's 2300 radio stations are non-network). According to Variety:

"It is understood that ASCAP approached BMI recently with a request to use the BMI indie stations' logs. BMI, however, nixed the request. ASCAP has been steadily increasing its coverage of the indie station picture as against it previous policy of paying off almost exclusively on network plugs." [53]

This difference, number of stations logged (analyzed), should be borne in mind if one seeks to compare the monetary value of

---

[52] *E.g.*, see *supra* note 14. The estimated ASCAP revenue from local and network television for 1954 is $ 8,000,000. Variety, March 10, 1954, p. 52.

[53] Variety, March 11, 1953, p. 41.

BMI and ASCAP performance credits. In addition one must bear in mind that independent stations rely much more heavily on music programs (usually in the form of gramaphone records) which results in the BMI affiliate receiving many more performance credits.

Non-exclusive rights.

When a writer from ASCAP joins with one from BMI to create a song, each having already conveyed the performing rights to their respective organizations, each organization acquires performance rights in the work. These rights are known as "non-exclusive" or "split" copyrights. ASCAP says that stations with ASCAP per program licenses and BMI blanket licenses refuse to pay ASCAP for the performance of these works claiming that they come within the BMI blanket license. Thus ASCAP is not paying royalties for these performances until the Federal Court requires the per program licensee to pay for them. Billboard reports:

> "One bitter music man claimed writers on split copyrights were being discouraged because the Society was not anxious to have its performance pay-off compared with BMI's." [53a]

This seems fallacious because the writer grant to BMI provides for royalties only upon works in "which we [BMI] obtain and retain exclusive performing rights." (section 4). The publishers agreement with BMI provides that with regard to "all rights granted by publisher under the term of this agreement ... no foreign or domestic performing rights licensing society or other organization has any performing, broadcasting or television rights in the works." (section 8b). Thus, in this case, there is no question of comparison of performance payments.

Royalty appeal systems.

In lieu of the ASCAP appeal system for royalty disputes, controversies between BMI and grantors are settled according to the arbitration laws of New York with the arbitrators selected by the American Arbitration Association.

[53a] Billboard, December 20, 1952, p. 1.

III. Withdrawal

Withdrawal from membership.

The ASCAP assignment (until 1965) though for a much longer period of time than the BMI agreements (publisher, five years; writer, two years, renewable to seven years) can be partially abrogated at the end of each year. The performing rights in existing works remain in ASCAP until existing user-licenses expire, and the rights to new works belong to the ex-member. Thus it appears to be a simple matter to resign from ASCAP. However, the reduced royalty on the works remaining with ASCAP is a deterrent to such action by members with a considerable number of currently performed compositions in their catalog. In the case of writers it is about a 50% reduction in the royalty rate. Therefore he must receive a good offer in order to take such action, this is again assuming that he has a considerable number of currently performed works.

An additional factor which may serve to deter a writer's resignation from ASCAP is the possibility that upon the expiration of ASCAP's outstanding licenses the writer will receive no performing royalties on the existing works in question for the balance of the original term of copyright. For example, SPA's (Songwriters' Protective Association) Uniform Popular Songwriters' Contract provides for an assignment to the publisher of the composition *subject to ASCAP agreements* in return for various royalties. Thus, when there is no longer an ASCAP agreement, and the outstanding ASCAP licenses, which are part of such agreement, have expired, then the publisher has the complete copyright subject to his own ASCAP or BMI assignment. If this analysis is correct, then ASCAP is not even under an obligation to provide reduced royalties during the period of existing licenses once membership has been terminated, since the writer no longer has any performing rights. Such action, including the reduction, however, may be contrary to the spirit of the Amended Consent Judgment which prohibits ASCAP from:

> "Restricting the right of any member to withdraw from membership in ASCAP at the end of any fiscal year upon (1) giving three months advance written notice to ASCAP, and (2) agreeing that his resignation shall be subject to any rights or obligations existing between ASCAP and its licensees under

then existing licenses and to the rights of the withdrawing member accruing under such licenses." (sect. IV,G).

BMI v. Taylor.

Similarly the publisher did not acquire the performing rights, in most instances, because they were vested immediately in ASCAP by virtue of the writer grant. In *BMI and Edward B. Marks Music Corp. v. Deems Taylor, as President of ASCAP, et al.*, 55 N.Y.S. 2d 94,103 (Sup.Ct. 1945), the Court said:

> "The fact that the license to BMI was not to take effect until the last five year contract between Marks and ASCAP has expired is immaterial. The expiration of that contract and the termination of Marks' membership in ASCAP did not discharge or end the rights which spring from the underlying relationship. When that stage was reached, Marks could take with it only that which it owned in its absolute and unqualified right; but it could take no more. It could not destroy the equitable rights which are attached to the songs in favor of ASCAP and its other members, including the authors and composers of the songs in suit. It still held the copyrights in trust for them.
>
> "This joint venture relationship, by its very nature, created certain mutual and reciprocal rights, benefits and obligations upon and between the publisher members of ASCAP as a class, and its author and composer members as another class.
>
> "Because of these mutual rights, benefits and obligations no publisher member could withdraw from ASCAP without the consent of the writer member who created the work of which the publisher held the copyright in trust, and take with him upon such withdrawal the absolute copyright rights freed from the burdens of that trust."

This reasoning would seem to apply with even greater force when the writer leaves ASCAP, because he does not generally own the copyright, as pointed out before. However, we shall refer to this case again (p. 125 *infra*).

The BMI publisher does not have this problem because after the expiration of the writer's short term grant to BMI the publisher has the performing rights as part of the entire copyright, subject to his own short term grant to BMI. The "joint venture relationship" of the ASCAP association would seem to be lacking. Furthermore, unless the BMI writer provides for royalties from his publisher to commence upon the expiration of the writer's short term grant to BMI, the writer will find himself without performing royalties in the near future as to the compositions composed during the term of the BMI contract. This statement, however, is too broad because when a writer's or a publisher's BMI contract is renewed, all of the works previously covered by the old contract are carried over as a part of the new agreement.

Dual membership.

Neither writer nor publisher can terminate his affiliation with BMI prior to the agreed date because there is no "escape" clause in the contract. The performing rights in existing and in future compositions are already conveyed for the term of the agreement, thus there is nothing further that the writer or publisher can do, or not do, in connection with the contract. Conceivably a publisher could set up a new corporation for publishing future compositions and a writer could surreptitiously have his new works published under a different name. The writer is certainly committing a breach of contract, which, if discovered, could be prevented. The publisher's action would have no purpose if the new corporation either: (1) did not join ASCAP, or (2) published works by BMI writers, since in neither case would such a company receive performing royalties. Thus the question is whether the publisher can establish an ASCAP affiliate for publishing works of non-BMI members. It appears to be the same case when an ASCAP publisher wishes to create a BMI affiliate. Neither organization would seem to have a justiciable claim against a new company publishing works of the rival organization's writers, since they would not have received those performing rights anyway. Both organizations however, may have a just claim to the performing rights of non-affiliated writers. Therefore it would seem that the organization with which the publisher first affiliated may have a right of action. It is also arguable in the case where a publisher's capital is limited so that he could only publish a certain number of works per year, that by establishing another company for publishing works of the rival organization he destroys or diminishes the value of the first contract. These cases, however, have not arisen (to my knowledge) and we can only speculate as to the probable result.

IV. Operation

Criticism of BMI.

As noted earlier BMI is a business organization which can treat one publisher or writer differently from another. This has resulted in disputes between some affiliates and BMI. An example is a resolution which had been presented by an affiliated publishing company, Life Music (no longer a BMI affiliate) at a BMI stockholders meeting, through means of proxies from some radio station stockholders:

> "Inquire into excessive and discriminatory payments, guarantees and subsidies to certain publishers and the reasons thereof."
> "Inquire into any practices of favoritism, nepotism, 'angles', 'deals' and preferential action."
> "Recommended uniform, fair and standard contract for all BMI publishers and songwriters." [53b]

Furthermore, BMI sends circulars to the stations to help them improve their programming — with BMI music. The promotional sheets cannot publicize all the BMI compositions at the same time so it must favor some to the disadvantage of the unpublicized. ASCAP's General Attorney claims that due to the nature of the ASCAP organization it cannot do any of these things, that it must treat all of its members equally, whether it be in connection with contracts or publicity. The antitrust decree requires distribution of royalties with "primary consideration" given to performances. *Quaere*, however, whether "primary consideration" forbids necessary competitive action by ASCAP when the purpose of the suit against ASCAP was to induce competition into the field of music performing rights. As to making users "ASCAP conscious" by promotional means, why cannot ASCAP use a sampling system in choosing the compositions to be the object of its publicity, since it uses that technique in program analysis?

BMI, however, does not feel any such restraint and makes special arrangements, *e.g.*, with writers and publishers who are also performers. Such writers are valuable to BMI because they have an assured number of performances and they can

---

[53b] Billboard, October 31, 1953, p. 15.

64 PUBLIC PERFORMANCE OF MUSIC IN THE UNITED STATES

"push" other compositions in the organization's repertory. The following news item is an example of the possible types of performer-writer-publisher tie-ins:

> "Bandleader Sammy Kaye has turned songplugger for a new tune written by Carmen Lombardo, composer-sideman with his brother Guy's band. Song, "Blue Willows," is being published by Kaye's firm, World Music." [54]

Alleged favoritism.

Once we are in this area we read of other advantages which a BMI affiliate is said to possess:

> (1) "Key to sales is widespread promotion and the radio and disk jockey are most potent." [54a]

> (2) "The Society takes the position that deejays [disk jockeys] on the local level, whether by tacit rooting interest or directive from the locally owned broadcasters, seem to favor BMI-originated tunes, else how come the cornballs hit the top with greater frequency?" [54b]

> (3) "The Society ... looks warily upon the accord between interests known as Broadcast Music Inc. underwritten by broadcasters, and (in the case of the two major networks, CBS and NBC) with affiliated major phonograph companies. Columbia and RCA Victor, of course, deny any 'casting' of tunes whether from ASCAP or BMI sources." [54c]

> *Definitions: disk jockey or deejay — a radio station employee who has a program in which he plays records and says a few words about them.*
> *cornball — hillbilly song, and the like.*

The other side of the balance sheet, however, reveals that a major ASCAP publishing interest, Metro-Goldwyn-Mayer, owns M-G-M Records, which is one of the "big five" in the American recording field. And, the very lucrative source of income to music publishers and writers, Hollywood, contains several of the major ASCAP publishing interests: M-G-M., Twentieth Century-Fox Films and Warner Bros.

Conclusion.

In view of this, one can appreciate the statement of Sigmund Timberg:

---

[54] Variety, February 4, 1953, p. 41.
[54a] Variety, October 17, 1951, p. 63.
[54b] Variety, March 11, 1953, p. 41.
[54c] Ibid.

"Once organized on a broad commercial scale for profit, even the aesthetic pursuit of dreams, music, and other evidences of the free spirit may engender commercial repressions inconsistent with our basic antitrust philosophy of free trade and fair competition." [55]

Many countries do not have an antitrust policy in the performing right field nor do they always treat copyright in general in the same way as the United States. Therefore, let us proceed to Part II, an examination of copyright and performing right societies in Great Britain, the Netherlands and France.

---

[55] Timberg, *The Antitrust Aspects of Merchandising Modern Music: The ASCAP Consent Judgment of 1950*, 19 LAW AND CONTEMPORARY PROBLEMS 294 (1954).

Part II

GREAT BRITAIN, THE NETHERLANDS, FRANCE

CHAPTER III

EUROPEAN COPYRIGHT

A. BERNE UNION

International Copyright Union.

European countries, as well as many other countries, are members of the Berne Union. [1, 2] The Union is a result of the Convention drafted at an international conference at Berne, Switzerland in 1885 which sought to introduce uniformity into the area of international copyright. Prior to the Convention, which was signed in 1886, literary and artistic works were generally not protected in a foreign country unless there was a treaty between the author's country and the country in which he sought protection. [3]

National treatment.

The basic principle underlying the Convention is found in Articles 4, 5 and 6 (Articles refer to the Rome Convention unless indicated otherwise). [4] Article 4 (1) provides:

"Authors who are nationals of any of the countries of the Union shall enjoy in countries other than the country of origin of the

---

[1] Union Internationale Pour La Protection Des Oeuvres Littéraires et Artistiques.

[2] Members of the Union on January 1, 1954: Australia, Austria, Belgium, Brazil, Bulgaria, Canada, Czechoslavakia, Denmark, Finland, France, Great Britain and Northern Ireland, Germany, Greece, Hungary, Iceland, India, Israel, Eire, Italy, Japan, Lebanon, Liechtenstein, Luxembourg, Monaco, Morocco (French Zone), New Zealand, Netherlands, Norway, Pakistan, Philippine Islands, Poland, Portugal, Rumania, Spain, Switzerland, Union of South Africa, Siam, Sweden, Syria, Tunisia, Turkey, Vatican, Yugoslavia. Droit d'Auteur 1954, pp. 2–3.

[3] The Convention was most recently revised at the Brussels Conference in 1948. This latest revision, however, has not yet been ratified by all the member countries. Other revisions of the 1886 Convention (which was completed at Paris in 1896) took place at Berlin in 1908 (which was completed at Berne in 1914) and at Rome in 1928. The 1928 revision at Rome was ratified by all the members of the Union except Siam and South West Africa which adhere to the revision at Berlin in 1908.

[4] The Rome text has been chosen instead of the later Brussels Revision because the latter has not yet been ratified by half of the member countries. The text quoted is an "equivalent" English text appearing in COPINGER, THE LAW OF COPYRIGHT (8th ed., Skone James, 1948). The official text is in French.

work, for their works, whether unpublished or first published in a country of the Union, the rights which the respective laws do now or may hereafter grant to natives, as well as the rights specially granted by the present Convention." [5]

This Article does not protect an author in the "country of origin." The country of origin is defined, to some extent, in Article 4 (3). In the case of unpublished works it is the country to which the author belongs and in the case of published works it the country of first publication. The Brussels Revision attempts to make the definition more explicit in more complex situations, such as successive and simultaneous publications. When the Union author of a published work is not a national of the country of origin, *i.e.*, the place of first publication, he receives protection therein under Article 5:

"Authors who are nationals of one of the countries of the Union, and who first publish their works in another country of the Union, shall have in the latter country the same rights as native authors."

Thus it will be seen that Articles 4 and 5 do not protect a national of a non-Union country, *e.g.*, the United States of America. Protection for such authors is found in Article 6:

"Authors who are not nationals of one of the countries of the Union, and who first publish their works in one of those countries, shall enjoy in that country the same rights as native authors, and in the other countries of the Union the same rights granted by the present Convention."

Limitation on formalities.

The protection under Article 6 is limited, however, since it extends only to published works. [6] Unpublished works of non-Union authors do not receive protection in Union countries via the Convention. As stated earlier, the basic principle underlying the Convention is found in Articles 4-6. It is the concept of national treatment: each country shall protect foreign works according

---

[5] The Berlin Convention contains the phrase, "subjects or citizens," instead of the term, "nationals."

[6] Article 4 provides: "In the case of works published simultaneously in a country outside the Union and in a country of the Union, the latter country shall be considered exclusively as the country of origin."

Under the Brussels Revision "a work shall be considered as having been published simultaneously in several Countries which has been published in two or more Countries within thirty days of its first publication."

to its own laws. Nevertheless, the author is not required to observe formalities of the Union countries in which he seeks protection. However, this does not apply to the country of origin since each country may prescribe conditions for works published therein. Article 4 (2) states:

> "The enjoyment and the exercise of these rights [the rights which the laws of countries other than the country of origin do now or may hereafter grant to their nationals, as well as the rights specially granted by this Convention] shall not be subject to any formality; such enjoyment and such exercise shall be independent of the existence of protection in the Country of origin of the work. Consequently, apart from the provisions of this Convention, the extent of protection, as well as the means of redress afforded to the author to protect his rights, shall be governed exclusively by the laws of the Country where protection is claimed."

Restrictions on nonmembers.

The Convention, in addition to *not* providing protection for nationals of non-Union countries in respect to their unpublished works and works first published in a non-Union country, states:

> "Nevertheless, where any Country outside the Union fails to protect in an adequate manner the works of authors who are nationals of one of the Countries of the Union, the latter Country may restrict the protection given to the works of authors who are, at the date of the first publication thereof, nationals of the other Country and are not effectively domiciled in one of the Countries of the Union." (Article 6 (2)).

Since the United States, for example, has restrictions in the nature of copyright notices and domestic manufacture, affected Berne Union countries can hereby retaliate by placing restrictions on the protection given to works of American authors. The Brussels Revision, by permitting other Convention countries to join in the retaliation, emphasizes the possibility of the United States, or any other non-Union country, losing its "back door" entrée to Berne Union protection:

> "If the Country of first publication avails itself of this right [retaliation], the other Countries of the Union shall not be required to grant to works thus subjected to special treatment a wider protection than that granted to them in the Country of first publication." (Article 6 (2)).

First publication in nonmember country.

It should be noted that in the case of first publication in a non-Union country authors do not receive protection under the Convention. The requirement of first publication in a Union country applies to authors of Union (Articles 4 and 5) as well as non-Union countries (Article 6). Thus the author from a Union country *terminates* his Berne protection by authorizing first publication in a non-Union country and the non-Union author by such publication *loses the opportunity* of obtaining Berne protection.

Definition of publication.

Since procurement or termination of protection depends on whether or not there has been a publication, the definition is of considerable importance. Article (4) 4 provides:

> "By "published works" must be understood, for the purposes of the present Convention, works copies of which have been issued to the public. The presentation of a dramatic or dramatico-musical work, the performance of a musical work, the exhibition of a work of art, and the construction of a work of architecture shall not constitute a publication." [7]

Therefore, an American playwright would not secure Berne protection in an unpublished drama by first performing it in a Union country. The Union author, on the other hand, can give the first performance of such a work in a non-Union country without losing protection under the Convention. The definition of the term, publication, is inadequate, however, to serve as a guide in determining which of all the possible exploitative acts that an author may authorize, are, or are not, publications within the meaning of the Convention. For example, is the distribution of gramophone records a publication, or the distribution of motion picture films, or the mere placing on sale of copies of a book with the printing of it and the major commercial risk centered elsewhere? Since the Convention does not supply the answer, each country in which protection is sought must decide it for itself.

---

[7] The Brussels Revision elaborated on the definition of published works: copies of which have been issued *and made available in sufficient quantities* to the public, *whatever may be the means of manufacture of the copies*. It also added the following to the acts which shall not constitute publication: the presentation of a cinematographic work, the public recitation of a literary work and the transmission or the radiodiffusion of literary or artistic works.

In Belgium the Court of Cassation, in 1907, held that gramophone records do not come within the meaning of issuance of copies because they are not of utility to human knowledge without the use of gramophone machines. In France, on the other hand, the Paris Court of Appeals, in 1905, held that the issuance of gramophone records does constitute a publication. [8,9] This appears to be the same conflict that exists in the United States. *Quaere*, should the Belgian court reach the same result in answer to the question: Is distribution of motion picture films a publication? [10]

Netherlands: sale is not publication.

In 1935 the question arose whether a Union author retained protection, under Article 4 of the Convention, in the Netherlands by the simple process of placing copies of the work on sale in Canada simultaneously with its publication in the United States. The case involved a *Fu Manchu* story by A.H.S. Ward which appeared in the American magazine, Colliers. The District Court (*Arrondissements Rechtbank*) of Rotterdam held that the Canadian distribution was not sufficient to constitute a publication within the meaning of the Berne Convention. The decision was affirmed by the Supreme Court (*Hooge Raad*). [11] The basis for the holding was the Convention's definition of the term, publication: "Par oeuvres publiées il faut ... entendre les oeuvres éditées" (French is the official language of the Convention). If the unofficial English text had been intended ("By published works must be understood works which have been issued to the public"), the appropriate French version would have been: "Les oeuvres placées en circu-

---

[8] 1 LADAS, THE INTERNATIONAL PROTECTION OF LITERARY AND ARTISTIC PROPERTY 298 (1938).

[9] "Whether the word 'copies' as used in this article [4 (4) of the Berne Convention] is to be interpreted as including records and like contrivances appears to be a question on which opinions differ. We understand, however, that a proposal to revise the Article clearly to include the issue of records in the definition of publication was made at the Brussels Conference in 1948 and was not accepted, and that it was then made clear that all countries were not prepared to accept that the issue of records to the public constituted publication." REPORT OF THE COPYRIGHT COMMITTEE TO PARLIAMENT, Cmd 8662 (London, 1952), p. 109.

[10] See p. 84 for a British view on the question.

[11] A. H. S. Ward v. de Handelsvennootschap onder de firma Uitgeversmaatschappij "De Combinatie", Arrondissements Rechtbank, Rotterdam, April 29, 1935; Hooge Raad, June 26, 1936 (Nederlandsche Jurisprudentie 1936, no. 1059, annotated by Prof. E. M. Meijers).

lation." Therefore, it was concluded, the act of simply distributing copies of the work in a Union country is not sufficient to comply with the requirement of publication. Consequently, in order to comply with the Dutch interpretation of the Convention the distributor in the Union country must participate in the publishing venture by, perhaps, taking financial risks greater than those of a mere bookseller or wholesaler.

The Gone With The Wind case.

The *Ward* case serves to show what acts are not sufficient to meet the Dutch requirements of the Convention. A subsequent case, on the other hand, *Margaret Mitchell (Marsh) v. N.V. Zuid-Hollandsche Boek- en Handelsdrukkerij*, Hooge Raad, May 23, 1941 (Nederlandsche Jurisprudentie 1941, no. 931, annotated by Prof. E. M. Meijers), involving the American novel *Gone With The Wind*, indicates what constitutes publication within the Dutch meaning of the Convention. The American publisher sold the printed pages to a Canadian publisher and the latter did its own binding and promotional work for the sale of the book in Canada. The Canadian company even inserted a new title page which listed its name as publisher.

Once again the lower courts (District Court and Court of Appeal (*Gerechtshof*) for the Hague) held that the acts performed in Canada were insufficient to constitute a publication. The Supreme Court, however, reversed the lower courts and remanded the case for further consideration of the facts in view of the high court's contrary interpretation of publication. The Supreme Court stated that a publication was not necessarily fictitious because it was for the purpose of securing Berne protection nor did it have to be printed in a Union country or independent of publication in a non-Union country. The important consideration, according to the Court, was whether the Canadian publisher undertook in its own name at its own risk the acts usually undertaken by a publisher. Unfortunately, after this exposition of what acts are, and are not, necessary to constitute a publication the lower court did not get an opportunity to reconsider the case because it was settled out-of-court by the parties. Nonetheless, the Supreme Court's opinion is a source of encouragement to advocates of a less stringent interpretation of publication. The copyright advisor to the Dutch Book-Trade Association, E. D. Hirsch-Ballin, said:

> "The case is a great advance over the earlier one since it shows a tendency to brush aside technical objections... by contenting itself with a simultaneous publication in which the publisher in the Union country, authorized by the copyright owner has performed the usual functions of a publisher rather than those of a mere distributor." [12]

The late Arthur E. Farmer, Attorney for the American Book Publishers Council (which, incidentally, published Dr. Hirsch-Ballin's views), however, took a less optimistic view of the *Gone With The Wind* case:

> "The case was never retried, so we still don't know what "editée" means in The Netherlands, except that it means something more than a mere sale to the public and less than a requirement of "manufacture"." [13]

England re publication.

As pointed out earlier each country must decide for itself whether the acts performed constitute a publication. Therefore, it is no surprise to find — as we found in the Belgian-French approach to gramophone records — that another Union country has different views than the Netherlands on the question of publication. In *Francis, Day and Co. v. Feldman and Co.*, 2 Ch. 728 (1914), a New York company acquired the rights to the now-famous light musical composition, *You Made Me Love You (I Didn't Want To Do It)*, which was written by an American author. The company sent twelve copies to Francis, Day and Hunter, music publishers in London, of which the latter placed six copies on sale in their retail department. Subsequently the composition became very successful and the London publisher, the plaintiff, acquired the copyright for the United Kingdom. In the ensuing infringement suit the court had to decide whether plaintiff's acts in London were sufficient to satisfy the requirement of publication. The court held that such issuance of copies

---

[12] HIRSCH-BALLIN, COPYRIGHT PROTECTION OF AMERICAN BOOKS IN THE NETHERLANDS 9 (1950).
[13] Farmer, *The Perils of (Publisher) Pauline — Or the Peculiar Problems of Book Publishers Featuring Copyright, Defamation and Right of Privacy*, 7 COPYRIGHT PROBLEMS ANALYZED 127 (1952).

to the public was a publication since it was adequate to show an intention to satisfy the public demand. We thus find a more liberal approach to the concept of publication, although it must be borne in mind that since the question arose in England the court was not confronted with the language of the Convention. The Union countries can comply with the Convention by making it part of the law of the land (*e.g.*, the Netherlands) [14] or by enacting special legislation to carry out its provisions. Britain has adopted the latter method:

> "The scheme of the Act of 1911 is to give to British works rights as large as those required by the Convention and by Orders in Council to extend these rights to foreign works. The Berne Convention is therefore not now the subject of interpretation by the Courts of this country, except, in so far as reference is made in the Orders in Council to certain sections." [15]

Therefore, Mr. Farmer was not wholly correct when he wrote that merely placing copies on sale in Canada "will secure Berne Convention copyright in Great Britain and Canada, because in those countries 'editée' means issuance to the public," [16] since these countries have not enacted the Berne Convention but have extended their internal legislation to Berne countries.

Term of publication.

Article 7 (1) states that "the term of protection granted by the present Convention shall be the life of the author and fifty years after his death." However, due to the inability of the contracting countries to agree upon the adoption of this uniform term of protection, Article 7 (2) makes Article 7 (1) an objective rather than an achievement:

> "Nevertheless ... the term shall be regulated by the law of the country where protection is claimed, and must not exceed the term fixed in the country of origin of the work. Consequently the countries of the Union shall only be bound to apply the

---

[14] Art. 60, 65-67 Netherlands Constitution, 1953, cited in Panhuys, *The Netherlands Constitution and International Law*, 47 AMERICAN JOURNAL OF INTERNATIONAL LAW 537.

[15] COPINGER, LAW OF COPYRIGHT 289 (8th ed., Skone James, 1948).

[16] Farmer, *The Perils of (Publisher) Pauline — Or the Peculiar Problems of Book Publishers Featuring Copyright, Defamation and Right of Privacy*, 7 COPYRIGHT PROBLEMS ANALYZED 127 (1952).

provisions of the preceding paragraph in so far as such provisions are consistent with their domestic laws." [17]

In view of Article 7 (2), Union countries providing long terms of protection would appear to be likely candidates for the place of first publication so that they may serve as the country of origin.

Distinction between published and unpublished works.

With the emphasis placed on country of origin and not on the author's nationality it is possible for an author to receive protection abroad for longer periods of time than in his native country. Moreover, until Berne countries invoke the permissive retaliatory measures against the United States, American authors with Berne publication will generally retain protection (in Berne countries) until long after their American copyrights have expired. The Convention does not distinguish between published and unpublished works in the sense of the American law nor do the copyright laws of the member countries. However, as noted earlier, because the Berne Convention does not apply to the works of a non-Union author unless first published in a Union country, the American author's unpublished works are not protected in Union countries via the Convention. Since Union authors lose their Berne protection upon first publication in a non-Union country and seeing how a non-Union author may acquire Berne protection, one may ask: Is the Convention aimed chiefly at securing protection for Berne authors or Berne publishers?

Universal Copyright Convention.

Under the Universal Copyright Convention adopted by the Inter-governmental Copyright Conference in Geneva, Switzerland in 1952, although not yet in force, [18] this inequity is eliminated.

---

[17] COPINGER, *op. cit. supra* at 276, states that the correct interpretation of the phrase, "must not exceed the term fixed," is that the country in which protection is claimed *need not* give protection for a longer period than the country of origin but it *may* do so if it wishes.

[18] "Article IX: 1. This Convention shall come into force three months after the deposit of twelve instruments of ratification, acceptance, or accession, among which there shall be those of four States which are not members of the International Union for the Protection of Literary and Artistic Works. 2. Subsequently, this Convention shall come into force in respect of each State three months after that State has deposited its instruments of ratification, acceptance or accession."

A published work need not have its first publication in a member country:

> "Published works of nationals of any Contracting State and works first published in that State shall enjoy in each other Contracting State the same protection as that other State accords to works of its nationals first published in its own territory." (Article II (I)).

The principle of national treatment, *i.e.*, assimilation of foreigners and nationals, it will be observed, is retained. [19] For other differences between the Universal Copyright Convention and the Berne Convention, *e.g.*, formalities, term of protection, and translation rights, the reader should consult the text of the Universal Convention and the official reports thereon. [20] It should be noted, however, that this Convention is limited in its application to member countries of the Berne Convention:

> "(a) Works which, according to the Berne Convention, have as their country of origin a country which has withdrawn from the International Union created by said Convention, after January 1, 1951, shall not be protected by the Universal Copyright Convention in the countries of the Berne Union;
> "(b) The Universal Copyright Convention shall not be applicable to the relationships among countries of the Berne Union insofar as it relates to the protection of works having as their country of origin, within the meaning of the Berne Convention, a country of the International Union created by the said Convention." [21]

In view of the fact that the above mentioned Conventions require the author, for the most part, to look to the national legislation of each country to determine the extent of his protection, let us examine the copyright acts of some of the Berne countries.

B. GREAT BRITAIN

England abolishes common law copyright.

The first Copyright Act in England was the Statute of Anne (1710). The Act was limited to the protection of published works.

---

[19] In regard to unpublished works the Berne rule applies: "Article II (2). Unpublished works of nationals of each Contracting State shall enjoy in each other Contracting State the same protection as that other State accords to unpublished works of its own nationals."

[20] 5 UNESCO Copyright Bulletin nos. 3–4 (1952).

[21] Appendix Declaration relating to Article XVII.

In *Donaldson* v. *Beckett*, 4 Bur. 2408 (1774), the House of Lords held that the effect of the Act was to terminate protection for published works under the common law. Unpublished works, however, continued to receive common law protection. As soon as the work was published common law protection ceased and the work was subjected to the limitations of the Act as to nationality of the author, rights protected, etc. Thus the situation was similar to the dual system of protection which exists in the United States. In 1911, however, the new Copyright Act undertook to protect unpublished works, thereby eliminating the common law copyright. Section 1 (1) of the Act provides:

> "Subject to the provisions of this Act, copyright shall subsist throughout the parts of His Majesty's dominions to which this Act extends for the term hereinafter mentioned in every original literary, dramatic, musical and artistic work, if — (*a*) in the case of a published work, the work was first published within such parts of His Majesty's dominions as aforesaid; and (*b*) in the case of an unpublished work the author was at the date of the making of the work a British subject or resident within such parts of His Majesty's dominions as aforesaid; but in no other works, except in so far as the protection conferred by this Act is extended by Orders in Council thereunder relating to self-governing dominions to which this Act does not extend and to foreign countries."

First publication in U.S.

A nonresident alien does not, therefore, receive protection for his unpublished works unless the Act is extended by an Order in Council [22] to include his country. By Order in Council in 1915 the Act was extended to unpublished works of subjects, citizens, and residents of the United States [23] and the Rome Convention Order of 1933 states that "the Copyright Act, 1911, shall apply — (a) to works first published in a foreign country of the Copyright

---

[22] Orders in Council are issued by "His Majesty, by and with the advice of His Privy Council, and by virtue of the authority conferred upon Him by the Copyright Act, 1911."

[23] The Order provides that the term of copyright "shall not exceed that conferred by the law of the United States of America." Since an unpublished American work which is not registered under the American Copyright Act is protected in the United States under the common law until publication, the British term would thus apply. If the work, however, is registered under the American Act the American term of fifty-six years from the date of registration will usually apply. The British term of copyright is discussed on pages 81, 86.

Union, in like manner as if they were first published within the parts of His Majesty's dominions to which the said Act extends: (b) to literary, dramatic, musical and artistic works, or any class thereof, the authors whereof were at the time of the making of the work subjects or citizens of a foreign country of the Copyright Union, in like manner as if the authors were British subjects." Works first published in the United States, however, are not protected in Great Britain. This limitation applies, unfortunately, to the Briton as well as to the American or other foreigner. Thus, an unpublished American work can retain protection in Britain by first publication therein and the work of a British subject or resident (or non-Briton) loses British copyright by first publication in the United States. In this connection the English view as to the nature of publication should be remembered:

> "It would appear that it is the place where copies are received by the public, or at least capable of being so received, and not the place where copies are printed or produced." [24]

Simultaneous publication.

When the first publication is not in the United Kingdom or a Union country the Act's definition of simultaneous publication may be of significance:

> "A work shall be deemed to be first published within the parts of His Majesty's dominions to which this Act extends, notwithstanding that it has been published simultaneously in some other place... and a work shall be deemed to be published simultaneously in two places if the time between the publication in one such place and the publication in the other place does not exceed fourteen days." [25]

Thus if the work is placed on sale in Great Britain within fourteen days after its first publication elsewhere the work will be considered as simultaneously published and therefore as first published in Britain in compliance with the Act. If the second publication were to take place, however, in a Union country instead of, and other than, Great Britain, would the work receive Berne protection in Britain? In other words, since an Order in Council assimilates Union countries to the United Kingdom, does

---

[24] COPINGER, LAW OF COPYRIGHT 28 (8th ed., Skone James, 1948).
[25] Section 35 (3).

the liberal English definition of simultaneous publication apply to publications occurring *simultaneously* in a Union and non-Union country? The question has not yet been decided, however, working by analogy, if England determines the nature of publication by reference to its internal legislation it should do likewise with regard to the question of simultaneity. [26]

Definition of publication.

The Act is not much clearer than the Berne Convention or the United States Copyright Act as to which acts constitute a publication. Section 1 (3) states:

"For the purposes of this Act, publication, in relation to any work, means the issue of copies of the work to the public, and does not include the performance in public of a dramatic or musical work, the delivery in public of a lecture."

As noted before, a publication of printed matter occurs when copies are placed on sale. This is similar to the American view of publication. The question of publication is, however, more difficult in connection with the distribution of phonograph records, as was shown to be the case in the United States. If the first distribution of a work to the public is by means of phonograph records then it is essential to know whether this is, or is not, a publication. Loss or acquisition of copyright may depend on whether the distribution is a publication, as indicated by the discussion of first publication. This question also arises with regard to British participation in the Berne Convention. However, as shown in note 9, each country appears free to adopt its own interpretation.

Indefinite duration of protection.

The issue also presents itself when we seek to apply section 17:

"In the case of a literary, dramatic or musical work, or an engraving, in which copyright subsists at the date of the death of the author or, in the case of a work of joint authorship, at or immediately before the date of the death of the author

---

[26] Farmer, *The Perils of (Publisher) Pauline — Or the Peculiar Problems of Book Publishers Featuring Copyright Defamation and Right of Privacy*, 7 COPYRIGHT PROBLEMS ANALYZED 127 (1952), writes: And we aren't even sure in such instances, because there is no case of which I know that decides whether or not that particular provision [simultaneous publication] of the British copyright law shall apply as well to the interpretation of the Berne Convention as to the British copyright law."

who dies last, but which has not been published, nor, in the case of a dramatic or musical work, been performed in public, nor in the case of a lecture, been delivered in public, before that date, copyright shall subsist till publication, or performance or delivery in public, whichever may first happen, and for a term of fifty years thereafter."

By virtue of this section of the Act if the work has not been published or publicly performed it is the object of copyright protection, conceivably, forever. Thus the Act has incorporated one of the basic attributes of common law copyright and, therefore, the American enigma of the *Miracle* case is present here, too. Can the copyright owner distribute phonograph records, which is certainly a deliverance to the public, and still have his work treated as an unpublished work? In commenting on the affirmative view to the question, the Copyright Committee pointed out:

"If this should appear to be a strange conclusion, it is to be remembered that the word "publication" is given a narrow meaning by Section 1 (3) and must in any case involve something more than merely making a work known to the public, however widely this is done. For example, a work can be made widely known by public performance without the issue of copies or even of records, and therefore without being regarded as "published", whatever meaning is given to the word "copies"."[27]

This argument does not appear to be wholly sound because the Act (section 1) itself specifically states that publication does not include public performance, *i.e.*, making the work known to the public by means other than public performance may be a publication.

Another viewpoint, as was expressed by Skone James in an early edition of his treatise, is that it is an infringement of the copyright in a work to make a record of it and therefore the distribution of records is a publication of the work.[28] This analysis, however, is also not necessarily correct. Simply because the copyright proprietor has the sole right to make recordings of his work (section 1 (2d)) and it is an infringement for any person to do "anything the sole right to do which is by this Act conferred on the owner of the copyright" (section 2 (1)), it does not thereby follow that when such right is exercised by the owner it is a

---

[27] REPORT TO PARLIAMENT, Cmd 8662 (London, 1952), p. 108.
[28] COPINGER, LAW OF COPYRIGHT 27 (7th ed., Skone James, 1936).

publication. Once again the right of public performance serves as an example. In the later edition of his work, Mr. Skone James provides stronger support for his viewpoint:

> "In the case of a musical work, the issue to the public of records or mechanical contrivances by which the work may be performed in public does constitute a publication of the music therein embodied since such contrivances constitute just as much a fixed and permanent record of the music as publication of a musical score." [29]

Records and pre-1911 law.

Prior to the Act of 1911 the British copyright law made no mention of the right of mechanical reproduction. With the invention of various mechanical means of reproducing music the question arose whether or not such acts constituted an infringement of the copyright of the reproduced work. In England, as was likewise shown to be the case in the United States, the court held in *Boosey v. Whight*, 1 Ch. 122 (1900), that the right to make and issue mechanical contrivances could not be understood to be included within the right to make and sell *copies* of the work. The English courts, in fact, went one step further than the American courts and held that the records and the other forms of mechanical instruments did not infringe common law copyright, *i.e.*, the rights in an unpublished work. [30] The Act of 1911, however, corrected this inequitable situation. Unpublished works were given statutory protection (consequently many foreign authors ceased to be protected) and the statute was extended to include the manufacture and distribution of records, perforated rolls, cinematograph films, and other means of mechanical reproduction. [31] It is thus arguable that now when the Act defines publication as an issuance of copies it must include records because Parliament did not intend to ignore technological advances and, in fact, recognized the author's right to control such versions of his work. This is in essence the Skone James' position. However, if Parliament intended to change the *Boosey v. Whight* interpretation of the expression, copies, it could have done so instead of merely altering the situation by granting the author the right of

---

[29] COPINGER, LAW OF COPYRIGHT 27 (8th ed., Skone James, 1948).
[30] Monckton v. Gramophone Co., 106 L.T. 84 (1912).
[31] Section 1 (2d).

mechanical reproduction. It is submitted, therefore, that Parliamentary silence on the interpretation of the term, copies, is a retention of the Court's view that records are not copies and thus a distribution of gramophone records is not a publication. The consequence of this interpretation is that the acquisition or forfeiture of copyright protection will not depend on the issuance of gramophone records. Therefore the possibility exists for unpublished works to retain copyright protection indefinitely despite a distribution to the public of gramophone records embodying the work. Although such application of section 17 may appear to be contrary to the spirit of the Act, in actual practice abuse of the provision is an unlikely occurrence. In order to have a successful sale of gramophone records a campaign involving public performances is most likely necessary. Thereupon the term of protection would be limited to fifty years. It is conceivable that in the future there will be a large market for gramophone recordings of literary and dramatic works. Nevertheless, it is unlikely that the owners would foresake the possible profits of the publishing and theatrical fields for, in effect, perpetual recording rights.

Distribution of motion pictures.

In our chapter on American copyright the question of the distribution of motion pictures as a publication was considered, and shown to be unsettled. In view of the fact that many American films are produced from unpublished scripts it may be of considerable importance whether the wide commercial distribution of these films is considered to be a publication of the stories they are based upon. Skone James states:

> "It is thought that inasmuch as publication means the issue of "copies" of the work to the public, the exhibition of a film ... upon the cinematograph screen would not be a publication of the work." [32]

Mr. Skone James does not discuss the commercial distribution which precedes the exhibition of a film. However, since his discussion made mention "of the fact that many films originate in the United States of America" it can be assumed that he was not considering the exhibition of a film as something separate and

---

[32] COPINGER, LAW OF COPYRIGHT 222 (8th ed., Skone James, 1948).

apart from its distribution. Thus his view on the question would appear to be in conformity with that of Mr. Tannenbaum (p. 15).

Compulsory licensing.

While on the subject of mechanical contrivances it should be noted that the British Act, as does the United States Copyright Act, provides for compulsory licensing of musical works. The language is quite similar to that used in section 1 (e) of the American Act. [33] The important difference between the American and British Acts is that the former provides a fixed sum per instrument regardless of the sale price. The British royalty rate, however, is more sensibly calculated on a percentage of the ordinary retail selling price. [34] In addition, the American inequity of allowing authors of works copyrighted before the mechanical right came into existence to be deprived of the right is not present. In view of the percentage system of calculating mechanical royalties it is unlikely that a dispute would arise, such as did in the United States, as to whether the sound track of a film is subjet to the compulsory license clause. Furthermore, the language of the Act indicates that the compulsory license is intended to apply to contrivances sold to the public, thus it would have application to *home movies* and not to films for use in cinema theatres. Copyright in mechanical contrivances, apart from the musical work embodied therein, and the right of public performance will be considered in the next chapter dealing with performing right organizations.

Compulsory licensing, although of a much more limited nature, is also provided for in fields other than mechanical reproduction of music. [35] Such provisions are unknown to American copyright law.

---

[33] "(a) that such contrivances have previously been made by, or with the consent or acquiescence of, the owner of the copyright in the work; and (b) that he [user] has given the prescribed notice of his intention to make the contrivance, and has paid in the prescribed manner to, or for the benefit of, the owner of the copyright in the work royalties in respect of all such contrivances sold by him, calculated at the rate hereinafter mentioned." (Section 19 (2)).

[34] In case of contrivances sold within two years after the commencement of the Act the rate is 3 and 1/8 per cent, and it is 6 and $\frac{1}{2}$ per cent after the expiration of that period. Copyright Order Confirmation (Mechanical Instruments: Royalties) Act, 1928.

[35] Section 3: "The term for which copyright shall subsist shall, except as otherwise expressly provided by this Act, be the life of the author and a period of fifty years after his death:

Provided that at any time after the expiration of twenty-five years, or in the case

Term of protection.

As was noted in the discussion of copyrighted works which are unpublished at the time of the author's death the British copyright term is different than that found in the American Act. Under the latter legislation the term of protection for each work is calculated from the date of its publication (or registration) whereas all the protected works of an author under the British Act will be protected during his lifetime and fifty years thereafter except for a few special situations and where the author forfeits his protection by first publication in an undeclared country. The exceptions are the unpublished works (discussed earlier), joint works, Government publications, mechanical instruments and photographs. The term of copyright for joint works is simply a slight variation of the normal period. [36] In the other three cases, however, the method of calculating the term of protection is similar to that found in the United States Act. Government owned copyrights last "for a period of fifty years from the date of the first publication of the work." [37] Copyright in mechanical contrivances lasts for "fifty years from the making of the original plate from which the contrivance was directly or indirectly derived." [38] "The term for which copyright shall subsist in photographs shall be fifty years from the making of the original negative." [39]

Absence of formalities.

The Act of 1911 does not require the registration of unpublished

of a work in which copyright subsists at the passing of this Act thirty years, from the death of the author of a published work, copyright in the work shall not be deemed to be infringed by the reproduction of the work for sale if the person reproducing the work proves that he has given prescribed notice in writing of his intention to reproduce the work, and that he has paid in the prescribed manner to, or for the benefit of, the owner of the copyright royalties in respect of all copies of the work sold by him calculated at the rate of ten per cent on the price at which he published the work."

Section 4: "If at any time after the death of the author of a literary, dramatic, or musical work which has been published or performed in public a complaint is made to the Judicial Committee of the Privy Council that the owner of the copyright in the work has refused to republish or to allow the republication of the work or has refused to allow the performance in public of the work, and that by reason of such refusal the work is withheld from the public, the owner of the copyright may be ordered to grant a license to reproduce the work or perform the work in public, as the case may be, on such terms and subject to such conditions as the Judicial Committee may think fit."

[36] Section 16 (1) (2).
[37] Section 18.
[38] Section 19.
[39] Section 21.

works in order to confer protection nor does it require published works to bear a notice or be printed and bound in Britain when they are books in the English language. Thus the major formalities of the American Act are absent. Although section 15 does require a deposit of copies, it is limited to books and is not a condition for securing copyright nor does failure to comply with a written demand result in a loss of copyright. [40] It appears to be more like a tax on publishers than copyright legislation since it is the publisher that must fulfill the requirement and it is he that is liable to a fine for noncompliance. Furthermore, there is no indication that the work must be first published in the United Kingdom or a work in which copyright subsists for the deposit requirement to apply.

Limitation on right to assign.

In section 5 (2) [41] the Act contains a provision, similar to that found in the renewal section of the United States Act, which places a limitation on the author's right to assign. British copyright during the last twenty-five years of the fifty year period following death belongs to the author's heirs. However, contrary to the American rule, the author cannot assign this portion of the copyright. This section operates when (and only when) the author is the first copyright owner, therefore it includes American and Berne authors. They (or their employer) receive copyright in their works immediately upon creation thereof, *i.e.*, while it is in manuscript form, and it is simply a question of whether they have foresaken protection by a first publication in an undeclared country. When copyright is obtained by first publication in a Berne country the author is not necessarily the first copyright owner since the publisher may

---

[40] Section 15 (1), (2), (6).

[41] "Provided that, where the author of a work is the first owner of the copyright therein, no assignment of the copyright, and no grant of any interest therein, made by him (otherwise than by will) after the passing of this Act, shall be operative to vest in the assignee or grantee any rights with respect to the copyright in the work beyond the expiration of twenty-five years from the death of the author, and the reversionary interest in the copyright expectant on the termination of that period shall, on the death of the author, notwithstanding any agreement to the contrary, devolve on his legal personal representatives as part of his estate, and any agreement entered into by him as to the disposition of such reversionary interest shall be null and void, but nothing in this proviso shall be construed as applying to the assignment of the copyright in a collective work or a license to publish a work or part of a work as part of a collective work."

have received, by assignment prior to publication, the right to secure copyright.

Criminal provisions.

Whereas the United State Copyright Act provides criminal measures only for willful infringements which are for profit, [42] some of the criminal proceedings under the Act of 1911 apply irrespective of the profit element so long as the infringer acts knowingly. [43]

Originality is not novelty.

The Act does not list a variety of works in which copyright may be acquired — as is found in the United States Act — instead it simply provides for copyright "in every original literary, dramatic, musical and artistic work." [44] The English courts have interpreted the expression, original, in much the same way as their American counterparts:

> "The originality which is required relates to the expression of the thought. But the Act does not require that the expression must be in an original or novel form, but that the work must not be copied from another work — that it should originate from the author." [45]

Infringement must be substantial.

Since the copyright owner's right is to reproduce the work "or any substantial part thereof" it follows that in order to show an infringement he must prove that the defendant has reproduced

---

[42] "Any person who willfully and for profit shall infringe any copyright secured by this title, or who shall knowingly and willfully aid or abet such infringement, shall be deemed guilty of a misdemeanor, and upon conviction thereof shall be punished by imprisonment for not exceeding one year or by a fine of not less than $ 100 nor more than $ 1,000, or both, in the discretion of the court." (section 104).

[43] Section 11 (1): "If any person knowingly — (c) distributes infringing copies of any such work either for the purposes of trade or to such an extent as to affect prejudicially the owner of the copyright ... he shall be guilty of an offence under this Act and be liable on summary conviction to a fine not exceeding forty shillings for every copy dealt with in contravention of this section, but not exceeding fifty pounds in respect of the same transaction.

Section 11 (2): "If any person knowingly makes or has in his possession any plate for the purpose of making infringing copies of any work in which copyright subsists ... he shall be guilty of an offence under this Act, and be liable to summary conviction to a fine not exceeding fifty pounds."

[44] Section 1 (1).

[45] University of London Press, Ltd. v. University Tutorial Press, Ltd., 2 Ch. 601, 608–609 (1916).

a substantial part of the copyrighted work. As in the United States, the substantial nature of the part copied is determined by its importance to the entire work. [46] Thus again as in the United States, the doctrine of *fair use* is applicable to copyrighted works. In England, however, the principle has found enunciation in the Copyright Act. [47]

C. NETHERLANDS AND FRANCE

We shall now examine some of the differences found on the Continent.

The moral right.

"Philosophically speaking, two great conceptions of what it has been agreed to call "copyright" are in opposition and conflict: the Anglo-Saxon and the Latin conceptions.

"According to the former, a work of the mind is a saleable work, a personal property similar to any other commercial article, the ownership of which can pass, and in fact does pass, in its entirety from the head of the author to that of the publisher, the transfer having the effect of eliminating the author from the exploitation of his work, at least as owner of the publishing and reproduction rights.

"According to the latter conception, the work of the mind, which is inseparable from the author and which remains indissolubly attached to the person of the author, excludes all possibility of an absolute transfer, the personal, moral element retaining always a pre-eminence over the pecuniary, commercial element in the exploitation of the work." [48]

Netherlands: Act contains moral right.

The *droit moral*, or moral right, is expressed in the following manner in Article 25 of the Dutch Copyright Law (Auteurswet 1912):

"No alteration may be made in a work mentioned in article 10 (1–9) [all copyrighted works except works of applied art] without permission of the copyright owner. If the author has

---

[46] Warne & Co. v. Seebohm, 39 Ch. D. 73 (1888).

[47] Also: "Provided that the following acts shall not constitute an infringement of copyright: — (i) Any fair dealing with any work for the purpose of private study, research, criticism, review, or newspaper summary." (Section 2 (1)).

[48] Parès, *The French Conception of Copyright*, 2 REVUE INTERNATIONALE DU DROIT D'AUTEUR 4 (Jan., 1954).

assigned his copyright his permission is, nevertheless, also necessary during his life.

"The same applies with regard to the name of the work and designation of the author, so far as it appears in or upon the work.

"The first paragraph is not of application with regard to alterations of such character that the author or his assignees could not in good faith refuse permission thereto. The author also has the right, even if he has assigned his copyright, to make in good faith such alterations in the work as the rules of social intercourse permit." *

France: recognition by jurisprudence.

Oddly enough, France, the country which pays the greatest homage to the moral right has no legislation on the matter. The doctrine, however, has been recognized and accepted by the French courts. [49] Mr. Parès gives a rather strong definition of protection of the right of personality which is certain to be met with objection by users of literary property in the United States and Great Britain:

"Strongly impregnated with the personal aspect, this right is interpreted essentially by the obligation of third parties to respect the absolute will of the author, by penal sanctions against any violation of whatever kind of this will. [50]

U.S. and Britain: no moral right.

The *Report of the Copyright Committee* noted that under the common law the United Kingdom protects the author's honor and reputation [51] and that with respect to the moral right provision of the Berne Convention [52] "no other Berne Union country has complained that the United Kingdom has failed to discharge its obligations." Ladas points out that in the United States although all of an author's rights in his work end, apart from contract, when he assigns his copyright and the assignee may

---

* Translations from Dutch are by the author.

[49] 2 UNESCO Copyright Bulletin nos. 2–3, p. 58 (1949).

[50] Parès, *The French Conception of Copyright*, 2 REVUE INTERNATIONALE DU DROIT D'AUTEUR 14 (Jan., 1954).

[51] REPORT TO PARLIAMENT, Cmd 8662 (London, 1952), p. 80. See also The Fine Arts Copyright Act, 1862, which prohibits alterations in paintings, drawings and photographs.

[52] Article 6bis: "(1) Independently of the author's copyright and even after the transfer of the said copyright, the author shall have the right to claim authorship of the work as well as the right to object to any distortion, mutilation or other modification of the said work which would be prejudicial to his honour or reputation."

alter the work, nevertheless, the author has the right not to have his work altered so as to libel him, *i.e.*, to bring him into ridicule or contempt. [53] However, the author does not have a moral right. For example, in *Vargas v. Esquire*, 164 F. 2d 522 (7th Cir. 1947), the court held that an artist who sells his rights in a work has no right of paternity (which is part of the moral right), *i.e.*, the magazine may publish the work without listing the artist's name.

Nationals first published in U.S., etc.

In contradistinction to the British law, which does not protect British nationals if first published in undeclared countries, and the American law, which does not protect non-domiciled nationals of undeclared countries despite first publication in the United States, the French and Dutch laws, as do the laws of most of the Continental countries, provide protection for such publications. [54] For example, Article 47 of the Dutch Copyright Law states:

"This law is of application to all works of literature, science or art which either before or after the coming into operation of the law were published for the first time by or on account of the author in the Kingdom of the Netherlands in Europe or in the Dutch East Indies, as well as all works not so published, the authors of which are Dutch or other Dutch subjects.

"A work is published in the sense of this article, when it appears in print or, in general, when multiplications thereof are made public; the presentation of a stage work or dramatico-musical work, the performance of a musical work, the exhibition of a work of art and the construction of a building are not such publications in the sense considered."

In addition, the Berne Convention is part of the law of the Netherlands and France. [54a]

Films and records: performance of music.

By virtue of the above-quoted definition of the term, published, the distribution of a motion picture film or phonograph record is a publication and thus if the distribution is in conformity with the rules laid down in the *Gone With The Wind* case protection may be obtained in the Netherlands. Public performance of music, however, is not a publication. Therefore, if a

---

[53] 2 LADAS, THE INTERNATIONAL PROTECTION OF LITERARY AND ARTISTIC PROPERTY 803 (1938).
[54] 4 UNESCO Copyright Bulletin nos. 1–2, p. 101 *et seq.* (1951).
[54a] France, Constitution of 1946, Articles 26–28.

foreign work is first made public via performance in a non-Union country this does not forfeit copyright or prevent acquiring copyright. On the other hand, if it is first made public by means of a performance in the Netherlands (or other Berne country) it is not adequate to satisfy the condition of publication required by the Berne Convention or the Dutch internal law of 1912.

France protects all authors.

Whereas the Netherlands does not protect unpublished works of non-Berne authors or works of foreign authors first published in non-Berne countries, France does not make such distinctions and extends protection to all authors. However, it is not certain whether this protection can exceed that given in the country of first publication or in the author's country in the case of an unpublished work, nor whether the protection includes the right of public performance. [55]

Fair Use; compulsory licenses; formalities.

The compulsory licenses of the United States and British Copyright Acts are not found in the Dutch or French law nor the American theory of conditioning copyright upon the observance of formalities. The Anglo-Saxon doctrine of fair use, however, finds expression in French decisions [56] and is expressly provided for in the Dutch law. [57]

Posthumous works and phonograph records.

The gramophone problem noted in connection with the American common law and with posthumous works under the English Act is not present in France or the Netherlands. Although the French law protects posthumous works for fifty years after the death of the heir who publishes the work, [58] the distribution of gramophone records is considered to be a publication. In the Dutch law it is provided that the copyright in the posthumous work terminates fifty years from the date the work was first made public by the rightful claimant. [59] According to Article

---

[55] 2 Ladas, The International Protection of Literary and Artistic Property 1017 (1938); 1 World Copyright 211 (Pinner ed. 1953); *But cf.* Sté "Le Chant du Monde" v. Sté Fox Europa et al., Paris Court of Appeals (1st Chamber), Jan. 13, 1953, cited in Inter-Auteurs, no. 112, p. 124 (1953).

[56] 2 UNESCO Copyright Bulletin nos. 2–3, p. 93 (1949).

[57] Articles 16, 17, etc.

[58] 2 UNESCO Copyright Bulletin nos. 2–3, p. 74 (1949).

[59] Article 38.

12 (1), by the expression, making public (*openbaarmaking*), is to be understood:

"The making public of a multiplication of the whole or a part of the work."

Article 12 (1), taken in conjunction with Article 14 which provides that the manufacture of rolls, records and other instruments comes under the multiplication of a work, will cause the fifty year period of protection in the posthumous work to begin running with the distribution of records.

With the foregoing account of United States and European copyright to serve as background let us proceed to an examination of European practices in music performing rights and how they compare with the American situation.

Chapter IV

PUBLIC PERFORMANCE OF MUSIC IN EUROPE

A. THE STATUTORY LAW

Profit requirement absent.

In Great Britain, France and the Netherlands the right of public performance in music is not limited to performances which are for profit. [1] For example, the Dutch Copyright Law provides that the copyright includes "the exclusive right of the author of a work ... to make it public," [2] and states that the expression, "making public," is understood to include "the delivery or performance or presentation in public of the whole or part of the work or of a reproduction thereof." [3] Thus the American distinction between musical and dramatico-musical compositions is not made and an unauthorized musical performance invades a right of the copyright owner even if the performance is not for profit. [4]

No jukebox exception.

Furthermore, exceptions in favor of a special interest, such as the juke box industry, are conspicuously absent. For example, several articles of the Dutch Act make clear that the author of a musical work has not only the exclusive right to make rolls, discs and other articles intended to mechanically reproduce the work so as to make it audible [5] but also the exclusive right to perform the work in public by the use of such instruments. [6]

---

[1] Great Britain: section 1 (2); France: Law of 1791; the Netherlands: Article 1.
[2] Article 1.
[3] Article 12 (3).
[4] In France, as noted earlier, (Chapter III, note 55), it is not certain whether the copyright extended to the United States and other countries (apart from treaty or convention) includes the performing right. Nevertheless, the performing right societies do not allow such considerations to enter into their distribution of royalties for performances of foreign compositions.
[5] Article 1, 12 (1), 14.
[6] Article 50 (*b*)

Britain: copyright in records.

In the British Copyright Act of 1911 in addition to extending copyright to include the right to make mechanical contrivances [7] it was provided in section 19 (1) that:

> "Copyright shall subsist in records, perforated rolls, and other contrivances by means of which sounds may be mechanically reproduced, in like manner as if such contrivances were musical works, but the term of copyright shall be fifty years from the making of the plate from which the contrivance was directly or indirectly derived, and the person [or corporate body] who was the owner of such original plate at the time when such plate was made shall be deemed to be the author of the work."

B. CASE LAW

Gramophone Co. v. Carwardine.

According to Skone James' view of section 19 (1), "the intention probably was simply to prevent one record from being copied directly or indirectly from another record," [8] however, in *Gramophone Co. Ltd. v. Carwardine & Co.*, 1 Ch. 450 (1934) it was held that section 19 (1) went beyond simply conferring a right to prevent copying. The court said that the gramophone company was given, in addition, rights in the public performance of their records. Thus a performance license from the copyright owner of a musical work is not sufficient when the licensee seeks to publicly perform the work by means of a gramophone record. Similarly, where a work is in the public domain a license for public performance is nevertheless necessary if the intended performance is via records which are still protected.

France: performance of records.

In France we find another interesting deviation in the field of performing rights. The right of mechanical reproduction, which was held to be a part of the right of publication (*édition*), [9] is viewed by some as including the right to control public per-

---

[7] Section 1 (2).

[8] COPINGER, LAW OF COPYRIGHT 240 (8th ed., Skone James, 1948).

[9] Halevy v. Rouart-Lerolle, D. P. 1932,1.29 note by M. Nast, cited in MAK, RIGHTS AFFECTING THE MANUFACTURE AND USE OF GRAMOPHONE RECORDS 49 (1952); Laurens, *The Idea of Destination' in the Turning to Account of Intellectual Works*, 3 REVUE INTERNATIONALE DU DROIT D'AUTEUR 40 (April, 1954)

formances of copyrighted works embodied in mechanical instruments. [10] Writing in the *Revue International du Droit d'Auteur*, [11] in regard to a Belgian judgment to this effect, the Directeur General of B.I.E.M. (Bureau International de l'Edition Mechanique) pointed out:

> "The author ... may forbid by sovereign right all publication of his work. Likewise, and as justifiably, he may authorise a particular publication, i.e., within limits he has fixed. Thus he can authorise the gramophone publication of his work by limiting such publication to the sale of copies of records by retail for private use.
>
> "In this case, any exploitation or use of records outside retail sale for private use constitutes unauthorised publication: for instance, the use of the records for broadcasting.
>
> "The author's reproduction right is a right of a distinct nature, independent of that of public performance."

Britain and U.S.

Under the British copyright law, which, in regard to mechanical contrivances, gives the copyright owner the right of manufacture and not the right of publication, [12] it would be difficult to arrive at such a result. The United States Copyright Act, however provides:

> "To print, reprint, publish, copy, and vend the copyrighted work." [section 1 (*a*)].
>
> "And for the purposes set forth in subsection (*a*) hereof, to make any arrangement or setting of it [musical composition] or of the melody of it in any system of notation or any form of record in which the thought of an author may be recorded and from which it may be read or reproduced." [section 1 (*e*)]

Thus, it would seem, at first glance at least, that M. Tournier's statements could also apply to the American situation. However,

---

[10] Laurens, *supra* note 9, at 42–46. DESBOIS, LE DROIT D'AUTEUR (1950), cited in Laurens, *id.* at 42–44, does not agree that the broadcasting company would be violating the right of reproduction by use of records without paying a supplement. He says, "it would merely be infringing a contractual obligation created by free agreement."

[11] Tournier, *Judgment of Brussels of May 9, 1953 on the Broadcast Use of Gramophone Records*, 1 REVUE INTERNATIONALE DU DROIT D'AUTEUR 22 (Oct., 1953).

[12] Section 1 (2): "For the purposes of this Act, 'copyright' means the sole right to produce or reproduce the work or any substantial part thereof in any material form whatsoever ... and shall include the sole right —

(*d*) in the case of a ... musical work, to make any record, perforated roll, cinematograph film, or other contrivance by means of which the work may be mechanically performed or delivered,

and to authorise any such acts as aforesaid".

to apply them would result, in effect, in the elimination of the last paragraph of section 1 (e) which states that "the reproduction or rendition of a musical composition by or upon coin-operated machines shall not be deemed a public performance for profit." Since it was the intent of Congress to free jukeboxes from performance royalties, it is unlikely that Congress intended a right of publication in records in the sense of the Belgian jurisprudence.

Netherlands.

The Dutch Act, Article 50 (b), presents a different situation. The Dutch Law states that in addition to the mechanical right [13] the copyright owner has the exclusive right of public performance by means of such instruments. [14] The usual view is that the second clause is superfluous because the right to make a copyrighted work public already existed. The clause becomes meaningful, however, if we consider it as a right complementary to the right of manufacture. M. Tournier says that there should be a relationship between the destination (use) and price of a recording.[15] Dr. Mak answers this proposition by stating that since the author has the exclusive performing right he can ask for a higher fee for performances by means of recordings. [16] As a practical matter, however, when two different organizations collect fees for the exercise of two different rights it usually results in a greater amount being collected (and, of course, higher administrative costs). [17] Dr. Mak also asserts that the BIEM position is unsound "seeing that the author may only assert such right against anyone putting records on the market and once, however, the manufacturer has put, with the author's consent, the records into circulation, this right of the author is exhausted." [18] However, by assuming that the author can only have rights against third persons by contractual agreement, Dr. Mak begs the question as to the right against everyone possibly created by the Act.

---

[13] Article 1.
[14] Article 50 (*b*).
[15] Tournier, *supra* note 11, at 16–18.
[16] MAK, RIGHTS AFFECTING THE MANUFACTURE AND USE OF GRAMOPHONE RECORDS 170 (1952).
[17] Consider the separation of the film synchronization right from the right to publicly perform the film.
[18] MAK, *op. cit. supra* note 16.

Summary.

In Great Britain, therefore, the public performance of music requires a license from the copyright owner if it is protected by copyright and an additional license, from the manufacturer, if the music — copyrighted or not — is embodied in a record still protected. In France the public performance of a record containing copyrighted music also involves two licenses: one from the holder of the right of public performance and one from the owner of the right of mechanical reproduction. In the Netherlands, however, only a license from the holder of the performing right is necessary.

Right of broadcasting not specified.

In these countries, as in the United States, the copyright legislation does not expressly give authors the right of broadcasting. Therefore, the authors are protected in the relatively new media by virtue of their other rights.

Britain.

In Great Britain the broadcasting of music is viewed as the exercise of the author's right of public performance. Section 35 (1) provides: "performance" means any acoustic representation of a work ... including such a representation made by means of any mechanical instrument." Thus the courts held:

> "The defendants, by modulating the waves in the ether, were able to effect, as they intended to affect, a vast number of electrical instruments possessed by members of the public and thereby to render audible to that public the performance given within the walls of the defendant's studio. In my view, however, the defendants, in doing what they did, clearly gave a public performance. Instead of gathering the public into a vast assembly room, they set in motion certain ether waves knowing that millions of instruments in houses and flats were tuned to the waves sent forth, and knowing and intending also that acoustic representation of the opera would thereby be given to an enormous number of listeners." [19]

---

[19] Messager v. British Broadcasting Co., 2 K.B. 543 (1927); although Messager was overruled (on different grounds), the view on broadcasting was confirmed in Performing Right Society, Ltd. v. Hammond's Bradford Brewery Co., Ch. 121 (1934).

The *Report of the Copyright Committee*, however, expressed a desire to see the point clarified in the Act. [20]

France.

The *Hammond's* case (see footnote 19) involved the question of whether someone receiving such a broadcast of music was giving a public performance when he made it available to the public. It was answered in the affirmative despite the fact that the broadcaster was licensed. In France, too, broadcasting copyrighted music is viewed as an invasion of the author's right of public performance (Act of 1791) [21] and the receiver is also deemed to be giving a public performance if he places his receiving set in public, *e.g.*, in a restaurant. [22] However, in both countries, as noted, if the work is embodied in a record the additional rights of the manufacturer and mechanical right owner must be reckoned with.

Netherlands.

In the Netherlands, in *A.V.R.O. v. BUMA*, Hooge Raad, March 4, 1938 (Nederlandsche Jurisprudentie 1938, no. 948, annotated by Prof. P. Scholten), the Supreme Court did not decide whether the broadcasting of copyrighted music is an invasion of the author's exclusive right to make his work public, however, this would seem to be a necessary conclusion from its decision granting a prohibition against the use of musical works in the repertory of the Dutch performing right society (*BUMA*) by the radio station, *A.V.R.O.* In *Frans Lehar v. P. Verbeek*, Hooge Raad, May 6, 1938 (Nederlandsche Jurisprudentie 1938, no. 635, annotated by Prof. E. M. Meijers), the same court held that although the author gave consent to a radio broadcaster he did

---

[20] "There is no doubt that if a radio set is turned on in a public place while the music is being played, or poetry is being recited, a public performance is being given by the set. But it is not entirely clear from the Copyright Act whether the mere fact of playing copyright music or reciting poetry in a Broadcasting Studio constitutes a public performance, so as to require the authority of the copyright owner. We therefore recommend that it should be made abundantly clear that a copyright owner has the sole right to authorise any broadcasting organisation to make use of his work over their system and to communicate that work to the public, irrespective of whether or not some recipient of the programme emitted is giving a performance of the programme in public." REPORT TO PARLIAMENT, Cmd 8662 (London, 1952), p. 41.

[21] DESBOIS, LE DROIT D'AUTEUR 399 (1950).

[22] SACEM v. Kubler, D. 1946. J. 335, cited in DESBOIS, *id.* at 405.

not thereby authorize third persons to place a receiving set in public to make broadcasts of his work audible.

This decision appears to overrule the earlier case, *Vereeniging Het Genootschap van Nederlandsche Componisten v. Amersfoortsche Radiocentrale*, Hooge Raad, April 30, 1930 (Nederlandsche Jurisprudentie 1931, p. 53 annotated by Prof. E. M. Meijers), which involved a relay station that transmitted to its subscribers programs broadcast by regular broadcasting stations. In this case the Supreme Court held that that the relayer was not *performing* the work in the sense of Article 12 (3). Rather, the court said, the broadcaster performed the work and the relayer merely made it possible for its subscribers to receive it. Since this is all that (or rather more than) the defendant did in the later case it is safe to say that the earlier decision is no longer law. One reason for the earlier result was the unfortunate way in which the issue was framed. The question argued was whether the relayer was giving a performance (*uitvoering*) whereas the second suit was based on the broader issue of the right to make a work public.

Now that we have some idea of the nature of the rights in question let us examine the organizations [23] that exploit (or prevent exploitation of) such rights.

C. GREAT BRITAIN

1. Performing Right Society, Ltd.

a. Membership and Management

One sometimes hears the statement that publishers have no place in such organizations. Such commentators overlook the fact, quite often, that, as in the case of the Performing Right Society Limited (PRS) of Great Britain, "in order to establish the Society on a sound basis, the publishers vested in the Society for the common benefit of all members the performing rights in a very large and valuable repertory of copyrighted music" and "the

---

[23] In chapter II we noted the reasons for their formation and the reasons for the exclusion of dramatic performing rights from their scope of operation.

publishers undertook to provide the necessary funds for the formation and preliminary expenses." [24, 25]

PRS thus consists of composers, lyric writers, publishers, and, upon their death, their personal representatives. It is a nonprofit association, *i.e.*, all receipts after costs of administration are distributed to the members. It was organized in the same year as ASCAP, 1914, and at present has a membership of approximately 2,500.

The Society is managed by a General Council of twenty-four Directors, twelve of whom are writer members and twelve of whom are publisher members. Four of the writer Directors are authors and eight are composers. There is not a definite number of directorships designated for writers and publishers of standard *i.e.*, serious or classical music, although a balance is sought. Every two years the six Directors longest in office retire (three publishers, two composers, and one author) and the Society at the annual general meetings fills the vacancies. All full members are eligible for election upon nomination by a full member and directors are eligible for re-election.

The President and Vice President of the Society — one of whom shall be a writer and the other a publisher — are elected by the General Council from among the Directors for a term of three years. They are eligible for re-election as long as they are Directors and while they serve in office they are not subject to retirement by rotation. The Council also appoints the General Manager to whom it may delegate all of the General Council's administrative powers deemed necessary for the full and proper administration of the affairs of the Society.

A Director is disqualified to serve if he or his firm is interested in any contract with the Society unless he declares the nature of the interest. And, of course, he may not vote in respect of such contracts.

Questions arising at general meetings are decided by a majority of votes with each full member having one vote. It is within the discretion of the General Council to admit a member to full membership (without which he does not have voting rights). The

---

[24] JAMES, CHARLES F., THE STORY OF THE PERFORMING RIGHT SOCIETY 17 (1951).
[25] One publisher, speaking frankly, said: "The best gamekeeper is an old poacher." A writer, on the other hand, put it this way: "A publisher of serious music *needs* the performance royalties and a publisher of popular music *earns* the money."

other classification — Associate membership — carries with it the right to royalties without a voice in its determination. Additional material concerning the management of the Society can be found in the PRS Articles of Association (as amended 25th June 1953).

b. Assignments

Present and future rights.

Each member, writer and publisher alike, assigns to the Society the performing rights in all musical works, present and future, of which he is the writer or publisher (or proprietor, in the case of legal successors) or which will vest in him during membership. [26] Present assignments last until December 31, 1954, and if not terminated within three months of said date are extended automatically for seven years.

Definition of performing rights.

""Performing right" means and includes ... the right of performing in public in all parts of the world, by any means and in any manner whatsoever including wireless transmission and rediffusion, all musical works or parts thereof and such words or parts thereof (if any) as are associated therewith, including ... the vocal and instrumental music in cinematograph films ... and the right of authorising any such performance but ... shall not include the right of performing or authorising the performance of any of the following classes of work (except by means of cinematograph films), *viz.*: (i) dramatico-musical works in their entirety; (ii) excerpts from such parts of any dramatico-musical work as consist of words and music written expressly therefor, if accompanied by dramatic action, dumb show, costume, scenic accessories or other visual representation of the same work; (iii) the whole or any part of the music of a choreographic work if accompanied by a visual representation of the same work." [27]

""Dramatico-musical works" means operas, operettas, musical plays, revues or pantomines in so far as they consist of words

---

[26] "The copyright in a non-existing work cannot be assigned because the assignment cannot be signed by the owner of the copyright therein (*cf.* Copyright Act, 1911, s. 5 sub-s. 2), but an agreement to assign the copyright in a non-existent work may be enforceable as an equitable assignment (Macdonald v. Eyles, [1921], 1 Ch. 631; Sims v. Marryat 17 Q.B. 281), and the equitable assignee could sue for damages if the legal owner is joined as a party." 1 WORLD COPYRIGHT 385–386 (Pinner ed. 1953).

[27] PRS Articles of Association, section 1 (u).

and music written expressly therefor, but do not include cinematograph films." [28]

Thus, if merely the music from a dramatico-musical work is performed, *i.e.*, if a visual representation is absent, such as the radio broadcast of an opera, it comes within the performing right held by the Society. In the case of motion pictures, however, the Society has the dramatic performing rights despite a visual representation. Nevertheless, because the author retains the synchronization right, he is in no worse (in fact, better) position than if his work were being performed on the legitimate stage and he merely had a performing right since in this way he is collecting for the exercise of two rights. Furthermore, PRS gives twice as much credit for visual use of a composition than when it serves as background music.

In PRS pamphlet H there is a summary of the organization's performing right:

> "The operations of the Society extend only to *musical works*. It is not concerned with the performance of non-musical plays or sketches, nor with operas, musical plays, or other dramatico-musical works when performed in their entirety by living persons on the stage."

Warranties.

The assignment from a writer differs in only one respect from the assignment granted by a publisher. The former contract contains an additional clause providing that the writer "hereby warrants that the musical works, in respect of which the rights assigned are hereby assigned or purported to be assigned do not or will not as the case may be infringe the copyright in any other work." Obviously a publisher is in no position to give such a warranty. Both assignments, however, contain the following warranty which is too broad in coverage:

> "The assignor will at all times hereafter keep the Society harmless and indemnified against all loss damages costs charges and expenses which the Society may suffer or incur in respect of any claims which may be made upon or against the Society in respect of or as a result of any exercise by the Society of any of the rights assigned which are hereby assigned".

---

[28] *Id.*, section 1 (t).

C. Licenses

Users must deal with PRS.

PRS issues licenses to all types of users of non-dramatic performing rights: the British Broadcasting Corporation (BBC), cinema theatres, hotels, restaurants, factories, dance halls, passenger ships, and many others. Since the members' assignments are not non-exclusive the users cannot deal with the individual copyright proprietors. In fact, because members upon being admitted to membership in the Society agree to be bound by the Articles of Association, they relinquished their performing rights immediately upon acceptance to the Society. [29]

Broadcasting.

The license to the BBC provides for the broadcasting corporation to pay one shilling (approximately fourteen cents) per annum for each listener license it issues. [30] The BBC is a noncommercial monopoly which receives one pound (approximately $ 2.85) annually from each owner of a radio receiving set and two pounds per television set. Since Eire does not have its own Society the PRS grants the performing rights directly to the Irish radio — at a fee of nine pence (approximatley ten cents) per licensed listener. For the year 1952 PRS received £ 660,713 from the BBC and the Irish broadcasting authorities. Non-broadcasting fees from British licensees, on the other hand, totaled only £ 527,573. This was supplemented by £ 97,049 from British Overseas Territories and £ 353,948 from affiliated foreign societies. Due to the relative ease in analyzing broadcasting performances and collecting such fees, and the heavy costs, on the other hand, of supervising tens of thousands of places of entertainment, the administration expenses attributable to the broadcasting fees is 3% as opposed to 13.41% in the case of the general fees (which include £ 42,683 derived chiefly from interest on monies

---

[29] Articles of Association, 4 (b): "Pending ... assignment, and in so far as it may not extend, every Member by virtue of his election grants to the Society ... the sole power and authority: — (i) to authorise or permit or forbid the exercise of the performing right ... (ii) to grant licenses on his behalf ... (iv) to delegate authority to do any acts as aforesaid to any affiliated society."

[30] Due to the high costs of television broadcasting the BBC receives a larger license fee from television-set owners than it receives from radio-set owners. Thus the question arises whether PRS is entitled to a higher fee in respect to such listeners. The argument against a higher fee is that the performing right is not a visual right whereas the viewer receives both sight and sound.

invested). Thus with a gross income in 1952 of £ 1,681,966, the expenses amounted to £ 156,787, or 9.32% of the gross income.

General licenses.

The method of calculating license fees for general licensees varies with the nature of the establishment. For example, cinema theatres pay a percentage ($1^1/_2$ to 3% depending on income) of fifty-two times the monetary value of the full seating capacity at maximum evening prices excluding Saturdays (after deducting the entertainment tax). Therefore, if the monetary value is £ 100 the fee is 2% of 5200 or £ 104 per annum. On the other hand, fees for large hotels which engage orchestras are based on a percentage of the salaries paid to the musicians.

It is interesting to note that contrary to the practice of licensing the proprietor of the establishment where the performance takes place (*e.g.*, the cinema theatre as opposed to the film producer), in the case of juke boxes PRS licenses the operators, *i.e.*, distributors, rather than the individual innkeepers. In addition, the annual fee of ten guineas (approximately $ 30) per machine is reduced to seven guineas if the operator "comes forward on his own". The Kefauver hearings before the United States Senate indicated that in the United States, too, the distribution and operation of juke boxes has fallen into unreliable hands. The fee is considerably higher than in the case of ordinary gramophones or radio-receiving sets because the customer is paying directly to hear a particular composition.

d. Programs

One of the conditions of securing a license is:

"The Licensee shall, for the duration of this License, supply to the Society or its authorised agent weekly by post, on the forms obtainable from the Society, a list, signed by or on behalf of the Licensee, of ALL MUSICAL WORKS, WHETHER PUBLISHED OR IN MANUSCRIPT, PERFORMED EITHER VOCALLY, INSTRUMENTALLY OR MECHANICALLY at the premises, with the names of the Composer, Author, Arranger and Publisher (if any) of each such work, and the number of times each had been performed during the week, for the purpose of enabling the Society to distribute the fees attributable thereto in accordance with its system of distribution."

The expression, mechanically, means by the use of a gramophone. Thus a licensee who has a radio-receiving set need not submit a program. Despite the requirement PRS does not receive programs from all of its licensees. It receives from the BBC, of course ,all the programs, and of the cinema theatres 95% co-operate fully. In regard to music in films, they need merely note the title of the film shown and the number of performances. The film producers issue *cue sheets* containing the titles of compositions used in each film, their duration, and the names of the writers and publishers. However, from the other licensees it does not receive all the programs performed. Nevertheless, the Society receives 400,000 programs from licensees in the general distribution group (*i.e.*, non-broadcasting). Since PRS receives about 50% of its revenue (excluding sums from affiliated foreign societies) from licensees other than broadcasters as opposed to over 75% received by ASCAP from radio and television, the Society cannot place such complete stress on broadcasting performances as does ASCAP. Of course, if British broadcasting accurately reflected the country-wide popularity of compositions it would be possible to base royalty distributions solely thereon, however, such is not the case. This is due, in large part, to the greater amount of foreign music performed by the BBC than in the country cafés and the like. However, since the broadcasting fees are kept separate from the other fees, the distribution of royalties based on the former performances is not prejudiced by the much higher administrative costs attached to the collection and distribution of the general license fees. One criticism may, nevertheless, be made with regard to the system of placing fees which are collected from licensees with radio-receiving sets into the general distribution fund. If the broadcasting performances do not reflect general popularity then the general distribution fund is not entitled to fees from establishments with radio receiving sets.

Accuracy of programs.

Apart from the high costs attached to the analysis of programs from general licenses located throughout the country there is the question of their accuracy. Several writers, with experience as musicians, have stated that there is a tendency for the proprietor, or his orchestra leader, to hurriedly fill out the form at the end of the week. In this way, the writers claim, many people will fill in such short titles as *Secret Love* and *Amor*, rather than more elaborate ones (which were actually performed) such as *I Don't See Me In Your Eyes Anymore* or *In A Golden Coach There's A Heart Of Gold*. If radio, television and films reflected general popularity the solution is easy. It is not an easy one when such is not the case. Thus PRS puts aside a percentage of the receipts for members whose works, it is thought, were performed and yet did not appear on programs.

Film performances in U.S.

In the discussion of ASCAP it was stated that ASCAP is prohibited from collecting performing fees for films from cinema theatres and must collect such fees from the film producers. Therefore, when a British (or other foreign) film is exhibited in the United States, ASCAP does not collect performing fees for the music therein from the theatres. On the other hand, neither ASCAP nor the foreign societies can collect fees from the British (or foreign) producers since the latter are not performing the music. Thus the American consent decree has, in effect, deprived writers and publishers (American and foreign) of their performing rights to music appearing in foreign films. The solution is for the writers and publishers to take this into account when negotiating the sale of their mechanical rights. If PRS sought to enforce the performing right it might very well subject itself to an antitrust suit. At present PRS puts aside a small percentage of its ASCAP revenue for the benefit of writers and publishers whose music appeared in such films shown in the United States.

e. Distribution

The royalties for each composition are distributed on the basis of $1/3$ to the composer, $1/3$ to the author, and $1/3$ to the publisher, *unless* the parties contract otherwise. It is provided, however, that the publisher's share cannot exceed $1/2$. Thus, as might be expected, $1/2$ to the writers and $1/2$ to the publishers is more often the case than not. It should be borne in mind, however, that with the increased costs of exploitation and the very marked diminution in the sale of sheet music and gramophone records the publishers have been forced to rely more and more upon performing fees in order to stay solvent.[30a] Nevertheless, on the other side of the coin, we find that the writers are confronted with the same economic dilemma.[30b] However, with regard to fees from foreign performances writers get $1/2$ irrespective of portions that may have to go to sub-publishers, publishers agents, or the like.

Assignments by nonmembers.

In the event that the writer or writers of a composition are not members of PRS and the publisher member has the performing rights the publisher receives 100% of the royalties earned by the composition. On the other hand, if a work is not published the writers will receive 100% of the royalties. In addition a nonmember may assign his performing rights to a member and the latter can collect the royalties in his behalf. This practice is followed, for example, when a member collaborates with a nonmember in creating a work.

Popularity of American works.

Theoretically, since each full member has one vote, the writers, of which there are many more than there are publishers, could alter the Articles of Association at a General Meeting to provide for higher writer royalties. However, such action is unlikely because the publishers would probably resort to publishing more American works. Although they must share such performing fees with the American publisher there is considerably less expense and risk in undertaking a work which has already achieved success in the United States and has been recorded by many famous vocalists and orchestras. On the other hand, if the American works were not in demand there would undoubtedly be a corresponding increase in the popularity of British works which would enable the publishers to return to the $1/3$ - $1/3$ - $1/3$ division of performing fees.[31]

[30a] See, for example, Variety, April 21, 1954, p. 53.

[30b] Finkelstein, *The Composer and the Public Interest-Regulation of Performing Right Socicties*, 19 LAW AND CONTEMPORARY PROBLEMS 279 (1954).

[31] In order to obtain the rights to sub-publish an American work the English publisher usually gives the American publisher an 'advance' (a sum of money paid before royalties are earned). Therefore, instead of the usual division of 6/12 to the American writers, 3/12 to the American publisher and 3/12 to the English publisher, the latter generally receives 6/12 until the 'advance' is recouped.

GREAT BRITAIN

Broadcasting fees.

Due to a less complex broadcasting system than is found in the United States it is relatively easy to distribute the income due to broadcast performances. There are three national BBC "networks" — the Light Programme, Third Programme, and the Home Service. They service transmitters in the seven regions into which the country is divided, *e.g.*, London, Scottish, Midland, etc. In addition, the regional transmitters often carry local programs in place of the network productions. In theory, a four minute composition [32] can earn £ 10.2.3, however, this could only occur if the work were performed simultaneously on all three Programmes (or if only one Programme was broadcasting) and were carried by all the regions. In practice, two, or all three, of the Programmes are *on the air* (with different programs) except for the $2^{1}/_{2}$ hour period from 6:30 a.m. to 9 a.m. From 9 a.m. to 6 p.m., for example, the Home Service and the Light Programme are broadcasting, which would result in each four minute composition performed earning £ 5.1.2, *if* the Programme is carried by all the regional transmitters. The monetary value attached to each region depends on the number of licensed receiving sets in the area, thus the London region accounts for $^{2}/_{7}$ th of the above-mentioned £ 5.1.2. Since the Third Programme broadcasts programs of a more serious nature it usually has a smaller audience and thus a performance thereon does not receive as much money as a performance on one of the other two Programmes. For example from 6 p.m. to 11 p.m., when all three Programmes are broadcasting, a performance of a four minute composition on the Home Service or Light Programme is given £ 3.18.0. whereas such a performance on the Third Programme receives £ 2.6.3 (once again assuming all seven regions are transmitting the broadcast). Compositions which are longer, or shorter, than four minutes receive proportionately more, or less, than the afore-mentioned amounts. The nature of the composition, *e.g.*, whether it is serious or light, is not material in determining the broadcasting royalty, except in a few cases such as *signature tunes* and copyrighted arrangements of works in the public domain. [33]

---

[32] Standard British ballad.
[33] Copyrighted arrangements of works in the public domain: royalty varies from 1/1 to 1/24 depending on the amount of original work superimposed upon the original

Thus, it is the duration of the composition on the air and the audience potential that determines the amount of the royalty. In the general performance fund, however, distributions are not based solely on the duration of the work. A committee, chosen by the Executive Committee of the Board of Directors, classifies the various types of works so that a *dance tune* may receive 1 point compared to a 120 points for a symphony.

f. Mechanical societies

In addition to collecting performing fees for its members, PRS collects performance fees for the Mechanical Copyright Protection Society (MCPS). Although the latter organization is essentially interested in collecting royalties for the exercise of recording rights, it also serves as a "junior" performing right group for people not eligible for PRS membership. MCPS is not a member of BIEM, an international organization of mechanical right collection societies. Thus BIEM has a British agent, the British Copyright Protection Co., Ltd. (Britico), which collects recording royalties from British recording companies and the BBC for works in the Biem catalogue.

II. *Phonographic Performance, Ltd.*

a. Recording companies and Musicians' Union

It was noted earlier, in the *Carwardine* case, that the recording companies have a copyright in their records and therefore a right of public performance therein. Following this decision the companies formed Phonographic Performance, Ltd. (which we shall refer to as PPL), to enforce this right. The PPL does not, however, have the same policy as PRS (*i.e.*, to secure as many licensees and performances as possible). This is due to an agreement between PPL and the Musicians' Union. [34] The latter group does not want

---

composition. Signature tunes (compositions used at the opening and or closing of a program) receive 1/5 of the regular royalty. In regard to television, since there is only one Programme (broadcasting only several hours per day), which has relatively few licensed listeners, the royalty is only £ 2.18.71 for the performance of a 4 minute composition.

[34] REPORT TO PARLIAMENT, Cmd 8662 (London 1952), p. 55, rejected a second reason given for restrictions on performances, *viz.*, that unlimited performances of records caused a decrease in sales.

its members to create their own unemployment via recordings for public performances. Therefore, PPL sometimes refuses to issue licenses and all the licenses which are issued include the following provisions:

"This license is issued subject to the following conditions inserted at the request of the Musicians' Union, namely: —
(a) No record shall be played, used or performed or permitted to be played, used or performed by the Licensee ... at any theatre, music hall, dance hall or other place of entertainment if a trade dispute directly affecting the rights or interests of musicians as such shall be in existence or threatened or contemplated to the knowledge of the Licensee ... between the Musicians' Union and/or its members or any of them on the one hand and any Company, firm or person on the other, unless such trade dispute shall be unaffected by the enjoyment of this License.
(b) No record shall be played, used or performed or permitted to be played, used or performed by the Licensee ... at any theatre, music hall, dance hall or other place of entertainment
(1) in complete or partial substitution for musicians employed or
(2) where musicians would have been employed but for the exigencies of war or national emergency or
(3) where musicians could, having regard to the size and nature of the theatre, music hall, dance hall, or other place of entertainment, be employed."

Although performers do not have a "performers' right" which would enable them to control, or receive compensation for, public performances of their recordings, [35] PPL gives $32^1/_2$ % of its net distributable revenue to the Musicians' Union and the recording artists. Furthermore, although the theory of treating a public performance of a record as an exercise of the mechanical right is not recognized, PPL gives 10% of the fees due to copyrighted music (which is about 70%) to the agents or holders of the mechanical rights, *i.e.*, Britico, MCPS, and Chappells Music (not all publishers turn their mechanical rights over to Britico).

---

[35] The Dramatic and Musical Performers' Protection Act (1925) does not create a "performers' right." It merely prohibits making, distributing or performing a record which is made without the consent of the performers. The Act does not create a right of civil action and, presumably, the lack of a developed doctrine of Unfair Competition would prevent the performer from securing a judgment for damages or a portion of the offender's profits.

b. Monopoly

As in the case of the PRS, PPL has almost a monopoly. Both, however, may be circumvented. A PRS license is not necessary if the work is in the public domain, and a PPL license can perhaps be avoided by using live music or records pressed (directly or indirectly) from an original plate made in the United States (see p. 95).

Despite the fact that one *can* find a way to perform music without securing a license (or two licenses), a regular user of music, such as a café, theatre, BBC, and the like, must deal with the PRS and perhaps with the PPL, too. Therefore, the monopoly positions, which are not subject to Government control, enable the two organizations to set their own unappealable license fees, [36] and in the case of the PPL, to issue licenses subject to severe restrictions or to refuse licenses altogether. [37]

III. Recommended Tribunal

Thus the Copyright Committee in its *Report to Parliament* recommended a standing Tribunal to review disputes between the licensing groups and music users. [38] The Tribunal's power would not extend to the internal operation of the societies, which we find in the Federal Court supervision of the American Consent Decrees, nor would the Tribunal consider all the license fees whether in dispute or not as is the practice of the Canadian Copyright Appeal Board. [39]. The Report recommends that "the Tribunals should be empowered on application made to them:

(*a*) to review and revise tariffs actually in operation, both as to the class of entertainment covered by a tariff and the fees chargeable thereunder;

(*b*) to make new tariffs where none exist or where the scope of any existing tariff seems to them not to be appropriate; and

(*c*) to determine whether or not refusals to grant licenses (or

---

[36] PRS and the BBC settled a dispute by submitting to arbitration, but this was accomplished voluntarily by the parties.

[37] The Musicians' Union, however, has stated: "Should control over the public use of records become less effective from the view of performers than it is to-day, whatever the attitude of the manufacturers might be, performers would almost certainly cease to record." REPORT TO PARLIAMENT, Cmd 8662 (London 1952), p. 56.

[38] The Committee considered arbitration, as resorted to in the PRS-BBC dispute, to be too expensive for many users and that "continuity is most desirable." *Id.* at 76.

[39] Section 10, The Copyright Amendment Act, 1931.

whether any conditions attached to licenses issued) are detrimental to the public interest, and if so to grant licenses of right, subject to such conditions as the Tribunal may decide." [40]

The Performing Right Society does not appear to be opposed to such a system of rate-supervision. Phonographic Performance, Ltd., on the other hand, which frequently refuses to issue licenses and severly restricts those licenses it does issue, is opposed to such outside review.

D. FRANCE

One society; no government supervision.

In France, as in England, there is neither government supervision of the performing right society's license fees nor is permission from the State necessary in order to form a society for the exercise of the performing right (*petit droit*). However, again as in England, there is only the one society, which is, as a practical matter, a monopoly.

SACEM; programs.

The Société des Auteurs, Compositeurs et Éditeurs de Musique (SACEM), the French society, follows the same system of requiring each licensee to submit a program listing the works performed. Due to the difficulty — which might be overcome in the future by the use of some mechanical recorder — of obtaining an accurate program of works performed by means of juke boxes, SACEM, as does PRS, obtains lists of the records contained in the machines. Although this practice is better than obtaining no programs at all, it is not an accurate reflection of the works actually performed.

ASCAP royalties.

Since ASCAP distributes its royalties almost solely on the basis of radio and television performances, SACEM does not distribute the money it receives from the American Society on the basis of the latter organization's programs alone. Instead, it also considers its own programs, operating on the theory that a successful French composition which does not appear on the

---

[40] REPORT TO PARLIAMENT, Cmd 866 (London 1952), p. 77.

ASCAP radio-television programs may nevertheless have been performed in the United States.

Operas.

With regard to a radio broadcast of a French opera, permission must be secured from the publisher and/or the society for dramatic performing rights, Société des Auteurs et Compositeurs Dramatiques (S.A.C.D.). However, it comes within the SACEM license if only a fragment of the opera is broadcasted.

Broadcasting.

The radio authority pays a bulk sum to four societies for use of various rights they represent: SACEM; the dramatic right society, (S.A.C.D.); the literary society (Société des Gens de Lettres de France); and the international mechanical right collection organization, BIEM. SACEM receives 48% of this sum which is based on a fixed amount for each licensed receiving set. In France, as in England and the Netherlands, broadcasting is supported by a receiving set license-fee.

The "right" to broadcast a musical composition embodied in a phonograph record, it was mentioned earlier, is additional to the right to broadcast the work. This aspect of the right of mechanical reproduction is exercised by the Société pour l'Administration du Droit de Reproduction Mécanique des Auteurs, Compositeurs et Éditeurs (S.D.R.M.), which also issues recording licenses to gramophone record manufacturers. [41] The broadcasting authority gives S.D.R.M. programs containing the recorded (and copyrighted) music performed and the society distributes the fees on a 50-50 basis between writers and publishers. The fees collected for the manufacture of records, however, are distributed according to the contracts between the writers and publishers. These contracts usually provide for the writers to receive from $1/3$ to $1/2$ of the mechanical royalties. SACEM, on the

---

[41] In actual practice because S.D.R.M. is a member of the international society of mechanical right societies, BIEM, it does not grant mechanical rights to the record manufacturers. The manufacturers contract, through the international society of records manufacturers, with BIEM, which receives the rights from the various national societies. Each company thereby has access to the entire BIEM repertory. Thus, as a practical matter, there is no need for the compulsory licensing provision of the United States and British copyright laws.

other hand, distributes its fees on the basis of $^2/_3$ to the writers and $^1/_3$ to the publisher.

E. THE NETHERLANDS

a. Government control

BUMA

In the Netherlands, we noted previously, neither copyright in a record, distinct from the composition embodied therein, nor a mechanical right in the public performance of a record, is recognized. Therefore only one license is necessary for the public performance of music, whether live or mechanical. The enforcement of this right, however, is subject to restrictions not found in either England or France.

Article 30a, Copyright Law.

Prior to 1932 two nonprofit societies were operating in the Netherlands. One was Het Bureau Voor Muziek-Auteursrecht (BUMA) and the other was the French society, SACEM. The former society was founded by the trade union of Dutch composers of serious music, Genootschap van Nederlandsche Componisten, and the association of Dutch music dealers and publishers, Vereniging van Muziekhandelaren en -Uitgevers in Nederland. It represented serious Dutch music and some foreign repertories. The French society, which maintained a branch office in the Netherlands, controlled most of the Dutch light music, in addition to its own large national repertory and most of the foreign music. The presence of two competing societies resulted in innumerable difficulties, especially for the users. Then, Mr. Wiessing, the Directeur of BUMA, writes: "The situation got to such an untenable point that the Dutch government decided to intervene."[42] In 1932, the Copyright Law was amended by the addition of Article 30 (a). The Article provides that permission from the Minister of Justice is necessary in order to engage in the business of acting as an intermediary in the field of music performing rights, [43] and performing right licenses issued by such intermediaries without ministerial consent are void. In addition, the

---
[42] Wiessing, *La Buma*, INTER-AUTEURS, no. 109, p. 173 (1952).

[43] Performances of dramatico-musical works, choreographic works and pantomines are not included if accompanied by visual representations. Thus there is more than one organization operating in this area.

Article provides that further rules can be made by Royal Decree, including control over the intermediary (*i.e.*, the performing right group) and that the interested parties, which presumably means the users of the music although this is not clearly stated, can be consulted in the exercise of this control.

In 1933 the Minister of Justice issued a decree giving the necessary authorization to BUMA. This meant that SACEM, having not obtained consent to continue its operation, was forced to cease acting as a performing right organization in the Netherlands. The French society thereupon transferred its repertory for the Netherlands to BUMA which is, as a practical matter, through the absence of other authorizations, a monopoly.

b. Membership and management

Since BUMA consisted of the associations of serious composers and publishers, the writers of serious lyrics (*e.g.*, the words for operas) and the composers and authors of light music were not represented. Therefore, two new societies subsequently became members of BUMA: the association of men of letters, Nederlandse Vereniging van Letterkundigen, and the trade union of composers and authors of light music, Vereniging Woord- en Toondichters der Lichte Muziek. The four organizations are the members of BUMA, not the individual writers and publishers. The latter are referred to as *adherents* and by virtue of membership in one of the four member associations are automatically eligible for affiliation with BUMA. Writers and publishers that are not members of one of the four member associations are, nevertheless, eligible as adherents. A publisher, for example, that has not been admitted to the music publishers and dealers association, will be accepted for adherence to BUMA if he is listed in the Commercial Register. A writer, on the other hand, need merely have three works published or performed. Such adherents, however, would not have a voice in choosing the Board of Directors of BUMA. The Board consists of seventeen directors of which thirteen are elected by the four member associations and four appointed by the Minister of Justice.[44] The thirteen directorships for the member

---

[44] The directors selected by the Minister of Justice include men such as the Director of the Academy of Plastic Arts and the Chancellor of the University of Amsterdam.

associations are apportioned as follows: serious music composers, four; light music composers and lyric writers, four; publishers, three; men of letters, two. Each association, at a general meeting, elects its quota of BUMA directors. The term of office is two years with one-half of the Board members retiring each year.

In addition, there is an Executive Committee consisting of seven members. Six of the Committee members are chosen by the Board of Directors from among the adherents, and one member, who need not be an adherent, is designated by the Minister of Justice. The Minister also designates the President, who, according to the Statutes of BUMA, shall preferably be a composer of serious music. The President, (in addition), holds the same office in the General Council. Of the Committee members chosen by the Board, there must be two composers of serious music, two writers of light music, one man of letters, and one publisher. They serve a term of three years.

Division of power.

The administrative responsibilities are divided between the two bodies and they cannot interfere in each others duties. For example, the Board fixes the rules by which the revenue is distributed and the Executive Committee decides whether or not to accept applications from prospective adherents. The Board, however, has the power to remove the Executive Committee from office.

The day-to-day management and administration of the Society is in the hands of a Directeur (or General Manager), who is appointed by the Board and whose acts are supervised by the Executive Committee.

Government Commissioner.

The Government control over the Society, referred to in Article 30(a), is exercised by a Government Commissioner (*Regerings-Commissaris*). [45] He does not have the power to decide disputes

---

[45] The present Commissioner, appointed by the Minister of Justice, is G.H.C. Bodenhausen: Profesor of Law, Utrecht University; Member of the Permanent Committee of the Berne Convention and of its Executive Subcommittee; Vice President of the Association Littéraire et Artistic Internationale (Paris); Chairman of the Advisory Committee on Copyright to the Netherlands Ministry of Justice; Chairman of the Netherlands delegation at the Brussels Conference (1948) on Revision of the Berne Convention and at the Geneva Conference (1952) on the Universal Copyright Convention.

between the Society and users. He serves, rather, as an impartial observer to whom complainants can bring their grievances after they have reached an impasse with the management or Executive Committee. If he finds that the Society is not abusing its position, because of the prestige he carries as an impartial expert, the complainant is usually placated. On the other hand, if he thinks that the grievance is justified, BUMA will correct the situation — at least it has until now. Thus the effectiveness of such a system of government supervision depends, for the most part, on the qualifications, reputation and personality of the particular Commissioner. In addition, the Commissioner has the power of the Minister of Justice behind him. He can ask the Minister to issue an order in respect to matters in dispute because, it will be recalled, under Article 30 (a) of the Copyright Law the Minister can decide the conditions under which Ministerial Consent will be given to a performing right intermediary. [46]

c. Assignments

The publishers' and writers' contracts with BUMA for the exploitation of performing rights are similar. They are for a period of three years and include the performing rights in all existing works and in all works to be made during the term of the contract. In order to permit the exploitation the adherent agrees to assign the performing rights in the works already in existence and to assign the performing rights in future works upon their completion. In addition, the contract invests BUMA with an irrevocable power of attorney to exercise these rights. This latter clause is important because although the Dutch law does not recognize an assignment of works not yet in existence, the power of attorney is recognized. [47] The contract and power of attorney provide for BUMA to have the rights exclusively, *i.e.*, as stated in Articles I and II, BUMA has the world performing rights "as the trustee of the composer [or publisher] and to the exclusion of all others even of the composer [or publisher] himself" and

---

[46] In addition, under Article 17bis the use of copyrighted material by means of broadcasting is subject to regulation. However, the power given under this Article has not yet been exercised.

[47] GEMA v. Tuschinski's Exploitatie Maatschappij, Hooge Raad, February 13, 1936 (Nederlandsche Jurisprudentie 1936, no. 443, annotated by Prof. E. M. Meijers).

"irrevocable authority ... to the exclusion of all others, even of the composer himself." In order for foreign societies to validly delegate to BUMA rights in future works they must have such a power of attorney or assignments from their members upon the completion of each new work.

d. Licenses

In the Netherlands there are several broadcasting corporations representing different political and religious organizations. The broadcasters are members of the Radio Union which maintains two broadcasting stations — Hilversum I and Hilversum II. The Radio Union handles the technical side of Dutch broadcasting and the programs are under the supervision of the independent broadcasting organizations. The owners of each radio-receiving set must pay twelve guilders (approximately $ 3.36) per year and the Radio Union pays BUMA slightly more than one-third of a guilder annually per licensed set. Thus the 2,200,000 radio licenses yield approximately 750,000 guilders annually to BUMA.

In addition BUMA licenses all other users of copyrighted music. In this respect BUMA is assisted by the local authorities. In order for anyone to perform music publicly he must receive authorization which helps the police maintain public order. The police usually inform BUMA of each establishment or organization which has secured authorization or they withhold authorization until the proprietor obtains a BUMA license.

The method of determining the license fee depends on the type of user. For example, cinema theatres are licensed on the basis of a percentage of net receipts, and in the case of cabarets with live music the fee depends on the price of beer, gin and soft drinks during the performance of music and the size of the establishment.

e. Programs

All licensees submit programs listing the works performed except establishments with *mechanical* contracts (*i.e.*, users of radio receiving sets, television sets or gramophone). License fees from the Radio Union, cinema theatres, [48] concerts, and establish-

---

[48] The cinema theatres submit a list of the films exhibited and the number of times they are shown and BUMA distributes the fees according to the 'cue "sheets" issued by the film producers listing the music (and its duration) in each film.

ments with live music are distributed on the basis of the programs such licensees submit. In the case of mechanical music, however, BUMA distributes the fees on the basis of the programs for light and serious live music. The justification given for this action is the alleged difficulty in obtaining accurate programs for such performances. To the extent that the programs for light and serious live music do not accurately reflect the recorded and broadcasted music actually performed in cafés this is unfair. [49] This arrangement does not always affect only foreign writers and publishers — who are more heavily represented on records and the radio than in the live music category — but it can also deprive a Dutch composer of his rightful royalties. For example, take the case of a composition which extolls the virtues of Heineken's beer. It will not be broadcasted because of its commercial nature, yet recordings of the work will be played thousands of times throughout the year in the many cafés operated by the Brewery or serving their beer. Thus only to the extent that the work receives live performances will the writer receive royalties despite the fact that it receives countless performances throughout the country. [50]

f. Distribution

Separate funds.

There are five separate distribution funds: (a) serious music; (b) light music; (c) radio; (d) television; and (e) films. In (a) the royalties are distributed on the basis of the score of the work, *i.e.*, the number of different vocal and instrumental parts, its duration, and the proceeds of the program on which the work appears. In (b) and (e) only duration and receipts are considered. The radio and television funds are distributed on the basis of the nature of the work and manner of performance as well as on the basis of the score and duration. Serious music is given five times as much credit as light music and operettas receive three times as much as credit as light music. Serious music receives this favored

---

[49] In 1951, for example, the percentage of Dutch music in the light, serious, and radio categories, was 55%, 50% and 35%, respectively. Actually the figures are somewhat inflated because they include foreign works which are sub-published by a Dutch publisher. BUMA Report for 1953.

[50] The result would, of course, be the same in the United States where only broadcast performances are considered.

treatment in addition to increased credit in consideration of the score. When the performance is by means of live performers, as opposed to commercial records, [51] the work receives twice as much credit. We therefore find a reversal of the method that Dr. Mak suggested could be used in substitution for a separate fee for the broadcast of records. He said that the copyright owners could ask for a higher performing right fee when their works are performed by means of recordings. Instead we find that BUMA gives less credit to these performances than to live performances. The rationalization given is that since live performances cost the broadcaster more money the copyright owner should receive more money for such performances. On the other hand, however, since the right to perform by records saves the broadcaster a considerable amount of money it would seem that this right is equally, if not more, valuable to the broadcaster than the right to perform the work by means of live performers, and thus should yield the copyright owners more, or certainly not less, money.

Writers $^2/_3$, publishers $^1/_3$.

To arrive at the sum of money each work has earned, the amount of fees credited to each fund is divided by the total number of credits attributed to music in such fund. This yields the monetary value of a credit in the particular fund which is multiplied by the number of credits the work has earned. Then the money attributed to each work is divided on the basis of $^2/_3$ to the writers and $^1/_3$ to the publishers. [52] In the event the work is not published — which is not uncommon in the Netherlands — the writers receive the entire amount earned by the work. In this way, BUMA and PRS differ substantially from ASCAP, where the absence of a publisher does not benefit the writers. When the publisher member publishes a work by nonmember writers the $^2/_3$ writer portion serves to increase the value of credits generally, whereas in PRS the publisher would have received the entire

---

[51] Records and tapes made especially for broadcasting are treated as live broadcasts.

[52] When a foreign composition is sub-published (not merely distributed) in the Netherlands the division is $\frac{1}{2}$ to the writers, $\frac{1}{4}$ to the foreign publisher, and $\frac{1}{4}$ to the Dutch publisher. A 50–50 division, between writers and publishers, with respect to foreign works, is also made in distributing royalties for film music because, it is said, it would require too much work to check whether each composition was sub-published or merely distributed by the Dutch publisher.

royalty and in ASCAP it would have benefited only the member writers.

Serious music subsidy.

It should be noted that when the amount of fees in each fund is divided by the total number of credits attributed thereto, it is the gross amount less a portion of the Society's expenses except in the case of serious music. The live performance category of serious music is not charged with the expenses of administration. This is another of the ways in which BUMA subsidizes serious music at the expense of light music.

Extensive analysis.

Since BUMA analyzes the programs of all of its licensees, except those with mechanical contracts, as opposed to the more selective analyses undertaken by PRS and ASCAP, it has a much higher cost of administration percentage-wise. Whereas the latter two societies have operation expenses of slightly under 10% and 20% respectively, BUMA's administrative costs are 30%. BUMA, however, appears quite justified in extensive analysis of non-radio programs. The amount of Dutch music, for example, performed on the radio is much less than appears on the programs from live music licensees. [53] Furthermore, radio accounts for only about 27% of BUMA's income [54] as compared with over 50% and 75% in the case of PRS and ASCAP.

Accuracy.

BUMA faces the same problem, however, which was mentioned in connection with PRS, that of falsified programs. [55] Despite the need for analysis of café programs, if they do not honestly reflect the works actually performed the system should be changed.

---

[53] See note 49 *supra*.

[54] In 1952, of the 2,609,000 guilders received by BUMA from licensees, 713,000 guilders came from radio. Television is still in its infant stage in the Netherlands. In 1952 it yielded 993 guilders to BUMA.

[55] In April, 1954, the District Attorney of Amsterdam brought criminal proceedings against several writers who obtained the program sheets from orchestra leaders and filled in their own works. The judge, however, dismissed the suit because he found that the writers were not made aware of the importance of the program sheets, *i.e.*, that they did not realize they were stealing. Therefore, the fact that owners of intangible property have the same rights against theft as owners of tangible property must be made clear to the very people that benefit from such a rule. Nevertheless, a year earlier a conviction was obtained in Rotterdam on similar facts.

g. Other activities

To assist its adherents, and to contribute to the cultural welfare of the Netherlands, BUMA uses a portion of its income (maximum of 10%) to support, for example, such institutions as Donemus (Documentation in the Netherlands for Music) and Onze Lichte Muziek (Our Light Music). The former organization "has as its object the furtherance of the development of Dutch musical life, particularly by giving every support to Dutch creative musical art." The methods used to achieve this object are:

> "The establishment and upkeep of a library and a documentation office devoted to the sphere of music;
> "The encouragement of the performance of Dutch musical works, both in Holland itself and abroad, and, with this end in view, the reproduction of scores and provision of materials, with the aim of placing same, with or without payment, at the disposal of any interested persons." [56]

Whereas Donemus is active in the area of serious music, Onze Lichte Muziek, as its names implies, is interested in the light music field. The association is active in publicizing Dutch light music at home and abroad by means of interesting and "eye-catching" publications (*e.g.*, *Dutch Popular Music*), in addition to such tangible methods as arranging with foreign organizations having similar aims for the exchange of recorded programs on the radio stations of each other's country.

F. CISAC

Furthermore, BUMA is responsible for the formation of several other Dutch societies, which are administered by the BUMA management and which are also members of CISAC [57] (Confédér-

---

[56] Interestingly enough, a survey among American composers indicated that there is also a need in the United States for such a "national organization with a national office." Mr. Thor Johnson, conductor of the Cincinnati Symphony suggested that "its functions would include such things as managing the circulation of compositions, [and] providing copying and publication facilities." N. Y. Times, February 22, 1953, sect. 2, p. 7.

[57] Bureau Theaterrechten van de Stichting tot Exploitatie en Bescherming van Auteursrechten (SEBA), member of Ist Federation of CISAC.

Stichting tot Exploitatie van Mechanische Reproductie Rechten der Auteurs (STEMRA), IIIrd Federation.

Bureau Letterkunde van de Stichting tot Exploitatie en Bescherming van Auteursrechten (SEBA), IVth Federation.

See text (*infra*) for explanation of CISAC and the Federations.

ation Internationale des Sociétés d'Auteurs et Compositeurs).

BUMA, like SACEM and PRS, is a member of the Fédération des Sociétés de Droits d'Exécution (Federation of Performing Right Societies), which is one of the four federations [58] of CISAC. Unlike BIEM, which receives the mechanical rights from each of its society-members and then gives the total repertory to each society, each performing right society enters into reciprocal contracts with each other in the same manner as do member societies with a nonmember such as ASCAP. [59] The Confederation occasionally serves as an arbiter and also as the promulgator of uniform rules (or suggested rules) of operation.

An objection that may be raised against the reciprocal contracts entered into by the Societies is evident from an examination of Article 9 (I) in the BUMA-PRS agreement:

"Each Society undertakes not to accept any application, either individual or collective, for admission to membership of persons who may belong to the countries of the Society without the consent of the latter."

The Societies have not only a monopoly in their own country but, as far as their own nationals are concerned, their monopoly includes a great part of the world and thus restricts the individual in the exercise of his performing rights.

G. WITHDRAWAL FROM SOCIETIES

In the discussion of ASCAP it was pointed out that the publish-

---

[58] The other three federations are: (I) Fédération des Sociétés de Droits de Représentation (dramatic rights); (III) Fédération des Sociétés de Droits de Reproduction Méchanique (mechanical rights); (IV) Fédération des Sociétés de Gens de Lettres (literary rights). The feredation of performing right societies is designated as the IInd federation. The numbering system simply indicates the chronological order of the formation of the four federations.

[59] Section V of the 1950 Foreign Consent Judgment (Civil Action No. 42–245) prohibited ASCAP from maintaining membership in any international organization which:

"(A) Restricts the right of member societies to offer or to license musical performing rights to non-member societies, or

(B) Imposes numerical limitations on the number of societies which may be admitted to membership for any designated territory, or

(C) In any manner prevents any United States musical performing rights society from securing, accepting, transferring or licensing musical performing rights, without restriction, to or from any foreign society, or

(D) Has the purpose or effect of allocating or restricting territories or eliminating competition among societies in the licensing of musical performing rights."

Shortly thereafter ASCAP terminated its membership in CISAC.

er could not leave the Society and take performing rights with him if the writer was a member of the Society at the time the work was created. It was suggested that this reasoning applies equally to a writer who leaves the Society. Such a case has not arisen with regard to the European societies under study. However, it would seem that the same result should be reached. An objection that might be raised against the New York case is the decision reached with respect to the counterclaim by the writers against the publisher, Marks. The writers asked for a rescission of their copyright contracts with a return of the copyrights in the musical compositions, and the court held:

> "I think they have abundantly established their right to such relief. One who undertakes to work property, such as a copyright on a royalty arrangement, becomes obligated to work it in good faith and for the benefit of the recipient of the royalties, as well as for his own avail. If he fails so to do, and thereby destroys the essential object of the royalty contract, rescission thereof may be decreed." [60]

Without an interest in the performing rights the publisher would have had considerably less interest in promoting the work and therefore the writers were justified in asking for a rescission of the contract. Since ASCAP and BMI pay royalties on exclusive rights only, if the court had decided that *both* parties held the performing rights non-exclusively, it would, in effect, have stripped both parties of the performing rights.

This is another indication of the importance of the performing right fees in the area of music, since, as the court points out, "the principal income derived by song writers from their creations comes from the license fees paid for their performance rights." [61]

---

[60] BMI and Edward B. Marks Music Corp. v. Deems Taylor, as President of ASCAP, et al, 55 N.Y.S. 2d 94, 103 (Sup. Ct. 1945).
[61] *Ibid.*

CONCLUSION

The examination of several copyright acts and performing right societies indicates that there are marked differences (as well as similarities) between the law and practice in the United States and Europe as well as among the European countries.

In the United States there is the common law in addition to the statutory copyright. In the United States, the performing right does not extend to nonprofit performances nor to coin-operated machines, whereas in England and France, on the other hand, additional rights are recognized in regard to the performance of records. In the United States the usual treatment of the public performance of film music has been altered by the concept of "source licensing" and in the Netherlands the system of "radio distribution" has not yet been held to be a public performance.

Whereas the performing right societies in England and France are *de facto* monopolies, and in the Netherlands a monopoly by virtue of being the only authorized society, the United States antitrust laws have been applied to prevent a single society from having a monopoly. In the United States there are two performing right organizations — one on the order of the European societies and one operated by the broadcasters.

Whereas the activities of PRS and SACEM are not supervised by the Government, ASCAP, BMI, and BUMA are subject to controls.

The distribution of royalties varies with the organization: ASCAP, $1/2-1/2$; PRS, $1/3-1/3-1/3$ or $1/2-1/2$; SACEM and BUMA, $1/3-1/3-1/3$; and BMI, a fixed sum per broadcast performance. The analysis of performances varies with the major distinction being that the American organizations rely chiefly on radio and television programs and ASCAP uses an averaging system in its distribution which takes into account performances over a number of years. Furthermore, ASCAP does not receive an exclusive assignment from its members.

In the United States we also find a different system of internal control by the members. Each member of ASCAP has voting power in proportion to his share of the royalties and in BMI, due to the purely commercial relationship, management is vested entirely in the stockholders, *i.e.*, the broadcasters.

That there is room for improvement in this area, which is a mingling of law, commerce and the arts, should be clear. It is hoped that this book may be of assistance in this direction.

Appendix A

ASCAP DOMESTIC CONSENT DECREE

IN THE UNITED STATES DISTRICT COURT FOR THE SOUTHERN DISTRICT OF NEW YORK

UNITED STATES OF AMERICA,
                  Plaintiff,
v.

AMERICAN SOCIETY OF COMPOSERS, AUTHORS AND PUBLISHERS, et al.,
                  Defendants.

Civil Action No. 13–95

AMENDED FINAL JUDGMENT

Plaintiff having filed its complaint herein on February 26, 1941, the defendants having appeared and filed their answer to the complaint denying the substantive allegations thereof, all parties having consented, without trial or adjudication of any issue of fact or law therein, to the entry of a Civil Decree and Judgment, filed March 4, 1941, and jurisdiction having been retained in this Court pursuant to Section VI of said Civil Decree and Judgment for the purpose of granting such modifications of the Civil Decree and Judgment as may be necessary and appropriate; and

Plaintiff having moved the Court that said Civil Decree and Judgment should be modified in certain respects, and all parties hereto consenting to such modifications and the entry of this Amended Final Judgment,

Now, THEREFORE, no testimony having been taken and without trial or adjudication of any issue of fact or law herein and without admission by any defendant in respect of any such issue and upon consent of all parties hereto, it is hereby

ORDERED, ADJUDGED AND DECREED that the Civil Decree and Judgment of March 4, 1941 be amended to read as follows:

I. This Court had jurisdiction of the subject matter hereof and of all parties hereto with full power to enter this Judgment. The complaint states a cause of action against the defendants under Section 1 of the Act of Congress of July 2, 1890, entitled "An Act to Protect Trade and Commerce Against Unlawful Restraints and Monopolies," commonly known as the Sherman Act, as amended.

II. As used in this Judgment:

(A) "ASCAP" means the defendant American Society of Composers, Authors and Publishers;

(B) "Right of public performance" means the right to perform a copyrighted musical composition publicly for profit in a non-dramatic manner, sometimes referred to as "small performing right";

(C) "Motion picture performance right" means the right of public performance of music which is recorded in order to be performed in synchronism or timed relation to the exhibition of motion pictures;

(D) "ASCAP repertory" means those compositions the right of public performance of which ASCAP has or hereafter shall have the right to license or sublicense;

(E) "User" means any person, firm or corporation who or which (1) owns or operates an establishment or enterprise where copyrighted musical compositions are performed publicly for profit, or (2) is otherwise directly engaged in giving public performance of copyrighted musical compositions for profit, or (3) is entitled to obtain a license from ASCAP under Section V of this Judgment.

III. The provisions of this Judgment applicable to the defendant ASCAP shall apply to such defendant, its successors and assigns, and to each of their officers, directors, agents, employees, and to all other persons, including members, acting or claiming to act under, through or for such defendant. None of the injunctions or requirements herein imposed upon the defendants shall apply to the acquisition of or licensing of the right to perform musical compositions publicly for profit outside the United States of America, its territories or possessions, such acquisition or licensing being subject to the provisions of the Final Judgment entered this day in Civil Action No. 42–245.

IV. Defendant ASCAP is hereby enjoined and restrained from:

(A) Holding, acquiring, licensing, enforcing, or negotiating concerning any rights in copyrighted musical compositions other than rights of public performance on a non-exclusive basis;

(B) Limiting, restricting, or interfering with the right of any member to issue to a user non-exclusive licenses for rights of public performance;

(C) Entering into, recognizing, enforcing or claiming any rights under any license for rights of public performance which discriminates in license fees or other terms and conditions between licensees similarly situated;

(D) Hereafter granting any license for rights of public performance in excess of five years' duration, except for motion picture performance rights which are licensed pursuant to Section V (C) of this Judgment;

(E) Granting to, enforcing against, collecting any monies from, or negotiating with any motion picture theatre exhibitor concerning any motion picture performance rights;

(F) Instituting or threatening to institute, or maintaining or continuing any suit or proceeding (1) against any motion picture theatre exhibitor for copyright infringement relating to motion picture performance rights or (2) against any user for copyright infringement of any musical composition not contained in the ASCAP repertory. After the preparation of the list required to be maintained by Section XIV herein, the repertory shall be deemed to consist of only those compositions appearing on such list;

(G) Restricting the right of any member to withdraw from membership in ASCAP at the end of any fiscal year upon (1) giving three months' advance written notice to ASCAP, and (2) agreeing that his resignation shall be subject to any rights or obligations existing between ASCAP and its licensees under then existing licenses and to the rights of the withdrawing member accruing under such licenses;

(H) Asserting or exercising any right or power to restrict from public performance for profit by any licensee of ASCAP any composition in order to exact additional consideration for the performance thereof, or for the purpose of permitting the fixing or regulating of fees for the recording or transcribing of such composition. Nothing in this Subsection shall be construed to prevent ASCAP, when so directed by the member in interest in respect of a musical composition, from restricting performances of a composition in order reasonably to protect the composition against indiscriminate performances, or the value of the public performance for profit rights therein, or the dramatic performing rights therein, or to prevent ASCAP from restricting performances of a composition so far as may be reasonably necessary in connection with any claim or litigation involving the performing rights in any such composition.

V. Defendant ASCAP is hereby ordered and directed to issue, upon request, licenses for rights of public performance of compositions in the ASCAP repertory as follows:

(A) To a radio broadcasting network, telecasting network or wired music service (as illustrated by the organization known as "Muzak"), on terms which authorize the simultaneous and so-called "delayed" performance by broadcasting or telecasting, or simultaneous performance by wired music service, as the case may be, of the ASCAP repertory by any, some or all of the stations in the United States affiliated with such radio network or television network or by all subscriber outlets in the United States affiliated with any wired music service and do not require a separate license for each station or subscriber for such performances;

(B) To a manufacturer, producer or distributor of a transcription or recordation of a composition in ASCAP's repertory which is or shall be recorded for performance on specified commercially sponsored radio programs or television programs, as the case may be, on an electrical transcription or on other specially prepared recordation intended for radio broadcasting or for television broadcasting purposes (or to any advertiser or advertising agency on whose behalf such transcription or recordation shall have been made) of the right to authorize the broadcasting, by radio or by television, as the case may be, of the recorded composition by means of such transcription or recordation by all radio stations or television stations in the United States enumerated by the licensee, without requiring separate licenses for such enumerated stations for such performance;

(C) To any person engaged in producing motion pictures (herein referred to as a "motion picture producer"), so long as ASCAP shall not have divested itself of such rights, a single license of motion picture performance rights covering the United States, its territories and possessions, without requiring further licenses. Such single license shall be issued in accordance with the following requirements and in accordance with all other provisions of this Judgment not inconsistent therewith:

(1) Such license shall be limited to pictures produced or in production not later than one year after the effective date of the license, and shall not make any charge for any performance occurring prior to the date of this Judgment;

(2) Upon written request of any motion picture producer such licenses shall be issued on a "per film" basis for the compositions in such film which are in the ASCAP repertory;

(3) All licenses of motion picture performance rights under this Subsection (C) shall be negotiated with and issued to individual motion picture producers, and not on an "industry-wide" basis;

(4) Where within a period of nineteen (19) months prior to the entry of this Judgment a motion picture producer has obtained a license for motion picture performance rights directly from members of ASCAP and has paid a separately stated amount therefor, such licenses issued by ASCAP covering motion picture performance rights shall, at the request of such producer, include the rights conveyed by the previous license, in which event ASCAP shall allow the motion picture producer a credit against the amount otherwise payable, equal to the amount paid under the previous license;

(5) No writer or publisher member of the Board of Directors of ASCAP shall participate in or vote on any question relating to the negotiation, execution, performance or enforcement of any such license where such member at the time, directly or indirectly, has any pecuniary interest in any motion picture producer, in any subsidiary or affiliate of any motion picture producer, or in any contractual relationship with any such producer.

VI. Defendant ASCAP is hereby ordered and directed to grant to any user making written application therefor a non-exclusive license to perform all of the compositions in the ASCAP repertory. Defendant ASCAP shall not grant to any user a license to perform one or more specified compositions in the ASCAP repertory, unless both the user and member or members in interest shall have requested ASCAP in writing so to do, or unless ASCAP, at the written request of the prospective user shall have sent a written notice of the prospective user's request for a license to each such member at his last known address, and such member shall have failed to reply within thirty (30) days thereafter.

VII. Defendant ASCAP, in licensing rights for public performance for radio broadcasting and telecasting, is hereby:

(A) Enjoined and restrained from issuing any license, the fee for which

(1) in the case of commercial programs, is based upon a percentage of the income received by the licensee from programs which include no compositions in the ASCAP repertory, or

(2) in the case of sustaining programs, does not vary in proportion either (a) to the performance of compositions in the ASCAP repertory during the term of the license, or (b) to the number of programs on which such compositions or any of them are performed,

unless the radio broadcaster or telecaster to whom such license shall be issued shall desire a license on either or both of such bases;

(B) Ordered and directed to issue to any unlicensed radio or television broadcaster, upon written request, per program licenses, the fee for which

(1) in the case of commercial programs, is, at the option of ASCAP, either (a) expressed in terms of dollars, requiring the payment of a specified amount for each program in which compositions in the ASCAP repertory shall be performed, or (b) based upon the payment of a percentage of the sum paid by the sponsor of such program for the use of the broadcasting or telecasting facilities of such radio or television broadcaster,

(2) in the case of sustaining programs, is at the option of ASCAP, either (a) expressed in terms of dollars, requiring the payment of a specified amount for each program in which compositions in the ASCAP repertory shall be performed, or (b) based upon the payment of a percentage of the card rate which would have been applicable for the use of its broadcasting facilities in connection with such program if it had been commercial, and

(3) subject to the other provisions of Section VIII, takes into consideration the economic requirements and situation of those stations having relatively few commercial announcements and a relatively greater percentage of sustaining programs, with the objective that such stations shall have a genuine economic choice between per program and blanket licenses;

(C) Enjoined and restrained from requiring or influencing the prospective licensee to negotiate for a blanket license prior to negotiating for a per program license.

VIII. Defendant ASCAP, in fixing its fees for the licensing of compositions in the ASCAP repertory, is hereby ordered and directed to use its best efforts to avoid any discrimination among the respective fees fixed for the various types of licenses which would deprive the licensees or prospective licensees of a genuine choice from among such various types of licenses.

IX. (A) Defendant ASCAP shall, upon receipt of a written application for a license for the right of public performance of any, some or all of the compositions in the ASCAP repertory, advise the applicant in writing of the fee which it deems reasonable for the license requested. If the parties are unable to agree upon a reasonable fee within sixty (60) days from the date when such application is received by ASCAP, the applicant therefor may forthwith apply to this Court for the determination of a reasonable fee and ASCAP shall, upon receipt of notice of the filing of such application, promptly give notice thereof to the Attorney General. In any such proceeding the burden of proof shall be on ASCAP to establish the reasonableness of the fee requested by it. Pending the completion of any such negotiations or proceedings, the applicant shall have the right to use any, some or all of the compositions in the ASCAP repertory to which its application pertains, without payment of any fee or other compensation, but subject to the provisions of Subsection (B) hereof, and to the final order or judgment entered by this Court in such proceeding;

(B) When an applicant has the right to perform any compositions in the ASCAP repertory pending the completion of any negotiations or proceedings provided for in Subsection (A) hereof, either the applicant or ASCAP may apply to this Court to fix an interim fee pending final determination of what constitutes a reasonable fee. If the Court fixes such interim fee, ASCAP shall then issue and the applicant shall accept a license providing for the payment of a fee at such interim rate from the date of the filing of such application for an interim fee. If the applicant fails to accept such license or fails to pay the interim fee in accordance therewith, such failure shall be ground for the dismissal of his application. Where an interim license has been issued pursuant to this Subsection (B), the reasonable fee finally determined by this Court shall be retroactive to the date the applicant acquired the right to use any, some or all of the compositions in the ASCAP repertory pursuant to the provisions of this Section IX;

(C) When a reasonable fee has been finally determined by this Court, defendant ASCAP shall be required to offer a license at a comparable fee to all other applicants similarly situated who shall thereafter request a license of ASCAP, but any license agreement which has been executed without any Court intervention between ASCAP and another user similarly situated prior to such determination by the Court shall not be deemed to be in any way affected or altered by such determination for the term of such license agreement;

(D) Nothing in this Section IX shall prevent any applicant or licensee from attacking in the aforesaid proceedings or in any other controversy the validity of the copyright of any of the compositions in the ASCAP repertory nor shall this Judgment be construed as importing any validity or value to any of said copyrights.

X. No officer or director of ASCAP, or any person acting on its behalf, shall participate in or vote on any question relating to any transaction or negotiation involving ASCAP and a licensee, or prospective licensee, where such officer, director, or other person has any pecuniary interest in such licensee or prospective licensee, or in any subsidiary or affiliate thereof, or in any contractual relationship with any such licensee or prospective licensee.

XI. Defendant ASCAP is hereby ordered and directed to distribute to its members the monies received by licensing rights of public performance on a basis which gives primary consideration to the performance of the compositions of the members as indicated by objective surveys of performances (excluding those licensed by the member directly) periodically made by or for ASCAP.

XII. Defendant ASCAP is hereby ordered and directed, within three months after the entry of this Judgment, to provide in its Articles of Association, effective as of the date of this Judgment, that ASCAP's members be prohibited from:

(A) At any time, while a member of ASCAP or thereafter, instituting, or threatening to institute, or maintaining or continuing any suit or proceeding for acts of copyright infringement relating to motion picture performance rights (1) alleged to have occurred prior to the date of this Judgment, or (2) where corresponding synchronization rights have been granted prior to the date of this Judgment;

(B) While a member of ASCAP, granting a synchronization or recording right for any musical composition to any motion picture producer unless the member or members in interest or ASCAP grants corresponding motion picture performance rights in conformity with the provisions of this Judgment.

XIII. In order to insure a democratic administration of the affairs of defendant ASCAP, and to assure its members an opportunity to protect their rights through fair and impartial hearings based on adequate information, defendant ASCAP is hereby ordered and directed to provide in its Articles of Association:

(A) That the members of the Board of Directors shall be elected by a membership vote in which all author, composer and publisher members shall have the right to vote for their respective representatives to serve on the Board of Directors. Due weight may be given to the classification of the member within ASCAP in determining the number of votes each member may cast for the election of directors. Elections for the entire membership of the Board of Directors shall take place annually or every two years. The Board of Directors shall, as far as practicable, give representation to writer members and publisher members with different participations in ASCAP's revenue distributions;

(B) That the general basis of member classification for voting and revenue distribution purposes shall be set forth in writing and shall be made available to any member upon request;

(C) That any member may appeal from the final determination of his classification by any ASCAP committee or board to an impartial arbiter or panel;

(D) That records be maintained by the officers, committees, or boards of ASCAP, and the impartial arbiters or panels referred to in Subsection (C) of this Section dealing with the classification of members and distribution of revenues, which will adequately apprise the respective members of the determinations made and actions taken by such officers, committees and boards of ASCAP, and arbiters or panels as to such members and the basis therefor.

XIV. Immediately following entry of this Judgment, defendant ASCAP shall upon written request from any prospective user inform such user whether any compositions specified in such request are in the ASCAP repertory, and make available for public inspection such information as to the ASCAP repertory as it has. Defendant ASCAP is furthermore ordered and directed to prepare within two years, and to maintain and keep current and make available for inspection during regular office hours, a list of all musical compositions in the ASCAP repertory, which list will show the title, date of copyright and the author, composer and current publisher of each composition.

XV. Defendant ASCAP is hereby ordered and directed to admit to membership, non-participating or otherwise,

(A) Any composer or author of a copyrighted musical composition who shall have had at least one work of his composition or writing regularly published;

(B) Any person, firm, corporation or partnership actively engaged in the music publishing business, whose musical publications have been used or distributed on a commercial scale for at least one year, and who assumes the financial risk involved in the normal publication of musical works.

XVI. For the purpose of securing compliance with this Amended

Final Judgment, duly authorized representatives of the Department of Justice shall upon the written request of the Attorney General or an Assistant Attorney General, and on reasonable notice to defendant, be permitted (a) reasonable access, during the office hours of said defendant, to all books, ledgers, accounts, correspondence, memoranda, and other records and documents in the possession or under the control of said defendant, relating to any of the matters contained in this Amended Final Judgment; (b) subject to the reasonable convenience of said defendant and without restraint or interference from it, to interview officers or employees of said defendant, who may have counsel present, regarding any such matters; and said defendant, on such request, shall submit such reports in respect of any such matters as may from time to time be reasonably necessary for the proper enforcement of this Judgment, provided, however, that information received by the means permitted in this Section XVI shall not be divulged by any representative of the Department of Justice to any person other than a duly authorized representative of the Department of Justice, except in the course of legal proceedings in which the United States is a party or as otherwise required by law.

XVII. Jurisdiction of this cause is retained for the purpose of enabling any of the parties to this Amended Final Judgment to make application to the Court for such further orders and directions as may be necessary or appropriate in relation to the construction of or carrying out of this Judgment, for the modification thereof, for the enforcement of compliance therewith and for the punishment of violations thereof.

It is expressly understood, in addition to the foregoing, that the plaintiff may, upon reasonable notice, at any time after five (5) years from the date of entry of this Amended Final Judgment apply to this Court for the vacation of said Judgment, or its modification in any respect, including the dissolution of ASCAP (and any time within two (2) years from said date apply to this Court for the vacation or modification of Section V (C) hereof). During the applicable periods specified above, defendant ASCAP is hereby ordered and directed to conduct its affairs, including the making of agreements to acquire or license the rights of public performance, so as not unreasonably to complicate or delay the enforcement of any such further relief requested by plaintiff and granted by this Court pursuant to the terms of this Section.

XVIII. This Amended Final Judgment shall become effective from the date of entry hereof, except that the provisions of Sections IV (G), XIII and XV shall become effective three months after the date of entry hereof, and the provisions of Section XI shall become effective eight months after the date of entry hereof. This Amended Final Judgment supersedes the Civil Decree and Judgment entered herein on March 4, 1941, but shall not be construed to make proper or lawful or sanction any acts which occurred prior to the date hereof which were enjoined, restrained or prohibited by said Civil Decree and Judgment of March 4, 1941.

Approved:

March 14, 1950

HENRY W. GODDARD
United States District Judge

We hereby consent to the entry of the foregoing Judgment.
For the plaintiff

SIGMUND TIMBERG
   Special Assistant to the Attorney General
WILLIAM D. KILGORE, JR.
HAROLD LASSER
   Special Attorneys

HERBERT A. BERGSON
   Assistant Attorney General
MELVILLE C. WILLIAMS
   Special Assistant to the Attorney General
IRVING H. SAYPOL
   United States Attorney

For the defendants
   ROBERT P. PATTERSON
   HERMAN FINKELSTEIN
   OSCAR COX
   Schwartz & Frohlich
   By LOUIS D. FROHLICH

Judgment entered:
   WILLIAM V. CONNELL
      Clerk
   March 14, 1950

Appendix B

ASCAP FOREIGN CONSENT DECREE

IN THE UNITED STATES DISTRICT COURT FOR THE SOUTHERN DISTRICT OF NEW YORK

UNITED STATES OF AMERICA,
                              Plaintiff,
v.
THE AMERICAN SOCIETY OF COMPOSERS, AUTHORS AND PUBLISHERS,
                              Defendant.

Civil Action No. 42–245

FINAL JUDGMENT

Plaintiff having filed its complaint herein on June 23, 1947, the defendant having appeared and filed its answer to the complaint denying the substantive allegations thereof, and the plaintiff and defendant by their attorneys having each consented to the entry of this Final Judgment, without trial or adjudication of any issue of fact or law herein, and without admission by said defendant in respect to any such issue;

Now, THEREFORE, no testimony having been taken and without trial or adjudication of any issue of fact or law herein and without admission of the defendant in respect of any such issue and upon consent of all parties hereto,

IT IS HEREBY ORDERED, ADJUDGED AND DECREED, as follows:

I. This Court has jurisdiction of the subject matter hereof and of all parties hereto with full power to enter this Final Judgment. The complaint states a cause of action against the defendant under Sections 1 and 2 of the Act of Congress of July 2, 1890, entitled "An Act to Protect Trade and Commerce Against Unlawful Restraints and Monopolies," commonly known as the Sherman Act, as amended.

II. As used in this Final Judgment:

(A) "ASCAP" means the defendant American Society of Composers, Authors and Publishers;

(B) "Right of public performance" or "musical performing right" means the right to perform or the right to license the performance of a copyrighted musical composition publicly in a non-dramatic manner;

(C) "ASCAP repertory" means those compositions the right of public performance of which ASCAP has or hereafter shall have the right to license or sublicense;

(D) "Musical performing rights society" means any society, association, partnership, corporation, person or any other legal entity engaged in licensing or transferring musical performing rights;

(E) "Foreign society" means a musical performing rights society organized pursuant to the laws of any country other than the United States or having its principal place of business in any country other than the United States;

(F) "United States" means the United States of America, its territories, and possessions.

III. The provisions of this Final Judgment applicable to the defendant ASCAP shall apply to such defendant, its successors and assigns, and to each of their officers, directors, agents, employees, and to all other persons, including members, acting or claiming to act under, through or for such defendant.

IV. Defendant ASCAP is hereby enjoined and restrained from:

(A) Holding, acquiring, licensing, enforcing or negotiating concerning any rights in copyrighted musical compositions other than musical performing rights on a non-exclusive basis;

(B) Limiting, restricting, or interfering with the right of any member to issue non-exclusive licenses for musical performing rights in any area outside the United States;

(C) Hereafter accepting from any foreign society any licenses for or assignments of musical performing rights in excess of twelve months' duration;

(D) (1) Refusing to grant licenses for performing rights to any foreign society except where the foreign society has breached a substantial term of an existing license, or would not capably represent the ASCAP repertory in such foreign country,

(2) Granting any license for musical performing rights to any foreign society the expiration date of which does not occur at least six months following the expiration date of any license which the foreign society has granted to defendant ASCAP,

(3) Negotiating for or carrying on discussions concerning the issuance of any license to any foreign society during the period when negotiations or discussions are taking place as to the issuance to defendant ASCAP of a license from such foreign society;

(E) Entering into, claiming any rights under, adhering to or enforcing any contract, agreement or understanding with any muscial performing rights society, or unilaterally or otherwise taking any action for the purpose or with the effect of:

(1) Preventing any foreign society from making musical performing rights available on a non-exclusive, non-discriminatory basis to any musical performing rights society other than defendant AS-CAP, or

(2) Discriminating or retaliating against any foreign society which grants or negotiates to grant musical performing rights in the United States to any musical performing rights society other than ASCAP. This provision shall not be necessarily construed to mean that a contract between ASCAP and a foreign society may not contain mutually agreeable provisions, based on fair objective standards, governing the payment of compensation in respect of performances subject to coverage under a license, existing at the time of such performances, issued through or to another society or other person.

(F) Offering to grant or granting musical performing rights to any foreign society on condition, expressed or implied, that such foreign society shall grant or offer to grant the musical performing rights of such society in the United States to defendant ASCAP.

V. Defendant ASCAP is hereby enjoined and restrained from directly or indirectly (1) holding membership in, (2) entering into, claiming any rights under, adhering to or enforcing any contract, agreement or understanding with, or (3) otherwise participating in or dealing with any international organization, association, or group of performing rights societies which:

(A) Restricts the right of member societies to offer or to license musical performing rights to non-member societies, or

(B) Imposes numerical limitations on the number of societies which may be admitted to membership for any designated territory, or

(C) In any manner prevents any United States musical performing rights society from securing, accepting, transferring or licensing musical performing rights, without restriction, to or from any foreign society, or

(D) Has the purpose or effect of allocating or restricting territories or eliminating competition among societies in the licensing of musical performing rights.

VI. (A) Defendant ASCAP is hereby ordered and directed to initiate forthwith and to carry on in good faith and with diligence negotiations to terminate and cancel each and every one of the following agreements, and any agreements or arrangements amendatory thereof or supplemental thereto:

Parties to agreement	Date
ASCAP and SADAIC (Argentina)	Oct. 15, 1945
ASCAP and APRA (Australia)	March 1, 1947
ASCAP and AKM (Austria)	Jan. 18, 1946
ASCAP and SABAM (Belgium)	July 4, 1947
ASCAP and UBC (Brazil)	June 7, 1945
ASCAP and AVTOR (Bulgaria)	Jan. 1, 1936
ASCAP and OSA (Czechoslovakia)	Oct. 9, 1946
ASCAP and KODA (Denmark)	Jan. 1, 1946

ASCAP and PRS (England)	May	30, 1945
ASCAP and TEOSTO (Finland)	Jan.	1, 1932
ASCAP and SACEM (France)	June	19, 1933
ASCAP and GEMA (Germany)	Jan.	1, 1946
ASCAP and BUMA (Holland)	Dec.	27, 1946
ASCAP and MARS (Hungary)	July	8, 1947
ASCAP and STEF (Iceland)	July	1, 1949
ASCAP and SIAE (Italy	March	1948
ASCAP and TONO (Norway)	Apr.	11, 1946
ASCAP and AUTORES (Portugal)	Aug.	1, 1933
ASCAP and SOCORO (Rumania)	March	12, 1946
ASCAP and SGAE (Spain)	Jan.	1, 1936
ASCAP and STIM (Sweden)	May	28, 1946
ASCAP and SUISA (Switzerland)	Jan.	1, 1942
ASCAP and AGADU (Uruguay)	Nov.	7, 1945
ASCAP and UYMA (Yugoslavia)	July	1937

(B) Upon the termination of each such agreement, defendant ASCAP is hereby enjoined and restrained from entering into, adhering to, maintaining or furthering, directly or indirectly, or claiming any rights under any contract, understanding, plan or program which has as its purpose or effect the continuing or renewing of such agreement, without limiting in any way ASCAP's right to obtain payment under any such agreement for performances occurring before the date of termination thereof.

VII. Defendant ASCAP is hereby ordered and directed to send, within thirty days after the entry of this Final Judgment, to each society designated as a co-conspirator in the complaint in this action, a copy of this Final Judgment.

VIII. For the purpose of securing compliance with this Final Judgment, duly authorized representatives of the Department of Justice shall, upon the written request of the Attorney General or an Assistant Attorney General, and on reasonable notice to defendant, be permitted (a) reasonable access, during the office hours of said defendant, to all books, ledgers, accounts, correspondence, memoranda, and other records and documents in the possession or under the control of said defendant, relating to any of the matters contained in this Final Judgment; (b) subject to the reasonable convenience of said defendant and without restraint or interference from it, to interview officers or employees of said defendant, who may have counsel present, regarding any such matters; and said defendant, on such request, shall submit such reports in respect of any such matters as may from time to time be reasonably necessary for the proper enforcement of this Judgment; provided, however, that information received by the means permitted in this Section VIII shall not be divulged by any representative of the Department of Justice to any person other than a duly authorized representative of the Department of Justice, except in the course of legal proceedings in which the United States is a party or as otherwise required by law.

IX. Jurisdiction of this cause is retained for the purpose of enabling any of the parties to this Final Judgment to make application to the Court for such further orders and directions as may be necessary or appropriate in relation to the construction of or carrying out of this Judgment, for the modification thereof, for the enforcement of compliance therewith and for the punishment of violations thereof.

It is expressly understood, in addition to the foregoing, that the plaintiff may, upon reasonable notice, at any time after five (5) years from the date of entry of this Final Judgment apply to this Court for the vacation of said Judgment, or its modification in any respect, including the dissolution of ASCAP. During the applicable period specified above, defendant ASCAP is hereby ordered and directed to conduct its affairs, including the making of agreements to acquire or license the rights of public performance, so as not unreasonably to complicate or delay the enforcement of any such further relief requested by plaintiff and granted by this court pursuant to the terms of this paragraph.

Approved:
March 14, 1950

HENRY W. GODDARD
United States District Judge

We hereby consent to the entry of the foregoing Judgment.
For the plaintiff

SIGMUND TIMBERG
  Special Assistant to the
    Attorney General
BERT C. DEDMAN
  Special Attorney
WILLIAM D. KILGORE, JR.
  Special Attorney

HERBERT A. BERGSON
  Assistant Attorney General
MARCUS A. HOLLABAUGH
  Special Assistant to the
    Attorney General
MELVILLE C. WILLIAMS
  Special Assistant to the
    Attorney General
IRVING H. SAYPOL
  United States Attorney

For the defendants
  ROBERT P. PATTERSON
  HERMAN FINKELSTEIN
  OSCAR COX
  Schwartz and Frohlich
  By LOUIS D. FROHLICH

Judgment entered:
    WILLIAM V. CONNELL
      Clerk
    March 14, 1950

Appendix C

ASCAP MEMBERSHIP CONTRACT

AGREEMENT made between the Undersigned (for brevity called *"Owner"*) and the AMERICAN SOCIETY OF COMPOSERS, AUTHORS AND PUBLISHERS (for brevity called *"Society"*), in consideration of the premises and of the mutual covenants hereinafter contained, as follows:

The *Owner* sells, assigns, transfers and sets over unto the *Society* for the term hereof, the right of public performance (as hereinafter defined), in each musical work:

Of which the *Owner* is a copyright proprietor; or

Which the *Owner*, alone, or jointly, or in collaboration with others, wrote, composed, published, acquired or owned; or

In which the *Owner* now has any right, title, interest or control whatsoever, in whole or in part; or

Which hereafter, during the term hereof, may be written, composed, acquired, owned, published or copyrighted by the *Owner*, alone, jointly or in collaboration with others; or

In which the *Owner* may hereafter, during the term hereof, have any right, title, interest or control, whatsoever, in whole or in part.

The right of public performance in every such musical work shall be deemed assigned to the *Society* by this instrument and shall vest in and be the absolute property of the Society for the term hereof, immediately upon the work being written, composed, acquired, owned, published or copyrighted.

The rights hereby assigned shall include:

(a) All the rights and remedies for enforcing the copyright or copyrights of such musical works, whether such copyrights are in the name of the *Owner* and/or others, as well as the right to sue under such copyrights in the name of the *Society* and/or in the name of the *Owner* and/or others, to the end that the *Society* may effectively protect and be assured of all the rights hereby assigned.

(b) The exclusive right of public performance of the separate numbers, songs, fragments or arrangements, melodies or selections forming part or parts of musical plays and dramatico-musical compositions, the *Owner* reserving and excepting from this assignment the right of performance of musical plays and dramatico-musical compositions in their entirety, or any part of such plays or dramatico-musical compositions on the legitimate stage.

(c) The right of public performance by means of radio broadcasting, telephony, "wired wireless," all forms of synchronism with motion pictures and/or any method of transmitting sound; Provided, however, that the *Owner* shall have the right, in good faith, by written notice to the *Society*, to restrict, limit or prohibit the public performance by radio broadcasting of works the copyright of which is vested in the *Owner*, and the *Society* agrees that all licenses by it issued shall contain a provision reserving its right to restrict or limit, or to prohibit entirely, the performance by broadcasting of any works in its repertory; and Provided further, that if the *Owner* notify the *Society* in writing to restrict, limit or prohibit the public performance of such copyrighted work, the *Owner* shall not, by the service of such notice, become repossessed of any of the rights transferred to the *Society* by this assignment.

2. The term of this agreement shall be for a period of twenty-five (25) years from the first day of January, 1941, and expiring on the 31st day of December, 1965.

3. The *Society* agrees, during the term hereof, in good faith to use its best endeavors to promote and carry out the objects for which it was organized, and to hold and apply all royalties, profits, benefits and advantages arising from the exploitation of the rights assigned to it by its several members, including the *Owner*, to the uses and purposes as provided in its Articles of Association (to which reference is hereby made), as now in force or as hereafter amended.

4. The *Owner* hereby irrevocably, during the term hereof, authorizes, empowers and vests in the *Society* exclusively the right to enforce and protect such rights of public performance under any and all copyrights, whether standing in the name of the *Owner* and/or others, in any and all works copyrighted by the *Owner*, and/or by others; to prevent the infringement thereof, to litigate, collect and receipt for damages arising from infringement, and in its sole judgment to join the *Owner* and/or others in whose names the copyright may stand, as parties plaintiff or defendants in suits or proceedings; to bring suit in the name of the *Owner* and/or in the name of the *Society*, or others in whose name the copyright may stand, or otherwise, and to release, compromise, or refer to arbitration any actions in the same manner and to the same extent and to all intents and purposes as the *Owner* might or could do, had this instrument not been made.

5. The *Owner* hereby makes, constitutes and appoints the *Society*, or its successor, the *Owner's* true and lawful attorney, irrevocably during the term hereof, and in the name of the *Society* or its successor, or in the name of the *Owner*, or otherwise, to do all acts, take all proceedings, execute, acknowledge and deliver any and all instruments, papers, documents, process and pleadings that may be necessary, proper or expedient to

restrain infringements and recover damages in respect to or for the infringement or other violation of the rights of public performance in such works, and to discontinue, compromise or refer to arbitration any such proceedings or actions, or to make any other disposition of the differences in relation to the premises.

6. The *Owner* agrees from time to time, to execute, acknowledge and deliver to the *Society*, such assurances, powers of attorney or other authorizations or instruments as the *Society* may deem necessary or expedient to enable it to exercise, enjoy and enforce, in its own name or otherwise, all rights and remedies aforesaid.

7. It is mutually agreed that during the term hereof the Board of Directors of the *Society* shall be composed of an equal number of writers and publishers respectively, and that the royalties distributed by the Board of Directors shall be divided into two (2) equal sums, and one (1) each of such sums credited respectively to and for division amongst (a) the writer members, and (b) the publisher members, in accordance with the system of distribution and classification as determined by the Classification Committee of each group, in accordance with the Articles of Association as they may be amended from time to time, except that the classification of the *Owner* within his class may be changed.

8. The *Owner* agrees that his classification in the *Society* as determined from time to time by the Classification Committee of his group and/or The Board of Directors of the *Society*, in case of appeal by him, shall be final, conclusive and binding upon him.

The *Society* shall have the right to transfer the right of review of any classification from the Board of Directors to any other agency or instrumentality that in its discretion and good judgment it deems best adapted to assuring to the *Society's* membership a just, fair, equitable and accurate classification.

The *Society* shall have the right to adopt from time to time such systems, means, methods and formulae for the establishment of a member's status in respect of classification as will assure a fair, just and equitable distribution of royalties among the membership.

9. **"Public Performance" Defined.** The term *"public performance"* shall be construed to mean vocal, instrumental and/or mechanical renditions and representations in any manner or by any method whatsoever, including transmissions by radio broadcasting stations, transmission by telephony and/or "wired wireless"; and/or reproductions of performances and renditions by means of devices for reproducing sound recorded in synchronism or timed relation with the taking of motion pictures.

10. **"Musical Works" Defined.** The phrase *"musical works"* shall be construed to mean musical compositions and dramatico-musical compositions, the words and music thereof, and the respective arrangements there of, and the selections therefrom.

11. The powers, rights, authorities and privileges by this instrument vested in the *Society*, are deemed to include the World, provided, however, that such grant of rights for foreign countries shall be subject to any agreements now in effect, a list of which are noted on the reverse side hereof.

SIGNED, SEALED AND DELIVERED, on this....day of,....19..

Owner { ....

.... }

Society { AMERICAN SOCIETY OF COMPOSERS, AUTHORS AND PUBLISHERS,

By.. }

Secretary

The grant made herein by the owner is modified by and subject to the provisions of the Amended Final Judgment (Civil Action No. 13–95) and Final Judgment (Civil Action No. 42–245) in *U.S.A. v. ASCAP*, dated March 14, 1950, and the provisions of the Articles of Association and resolutions of the Board of Directors adopted pursuant thereto.

Appendix D

ASCAP ROYALTY DISTRIBUTION *

The writer fund: 20% is distributed according to current performances. 60% is paid out on the basis of a five year average; theoretically, if the member creates one song and it is played in only one year, he receives royalties (from this fund) 1/5 of his each year for five years. However, this is an oversimplification because in an effort to prevent sharp fluctuations in income, a member's average is permited to drop only a certain amount each year. Thus our hypothetical writer actually receives less than three times his current performance royalty during the five year period, but he will receive royalties from the 60% fund for longer than five years. The remaining 20% of the writers' fund is distributed on the basis of how long the compositions have been in the ASCAP catalog, *i.e.*, number of years of membership, in relation to the average number of performances, the writer ultimately receiving his 100% (theoretically), although more slowly than from the 60% five year plan.

The writers' five year fund is, however, not distributed by simply dividing the sum by the five year average of credits, rather, the sum is divided according to *points*, with 60,000 credits equal to 1,000 points, with a ceiling imposed upon the points of those members having a five year average of over 60,000 credits, *e.g.*, Irving Berlin averages 600,000 credits and is given only 1,500 points. Due to the ceiling, an Irving Berlin or a Cole Porter receives considerably less than they would on a straight mathematical basis, and the less frequently performed writers thereby receive larger royalties.

The publisher fund: 55% is distributed solely on the basis of current performances. 15% is distributed on the basis of length of membership and average of performances. The remaining 30% is distributed in the same manner as the current performance fund except that recent popular (or light) compositions are not included, the compositions must be in the ASCAP repertory at least 2 years.

Under the Amended Consent Judgment ASCAP is "directed to admit to membership, non-participating or otherwise" many composers and publishers (see section XV). The Articles of Association therefore provide for participating and non-participating classes. The latter class of members are not eligible to vote, hold office, or share in any of the rights of the participating class except as to royalties in the current performance fund. The additional requirement for the more favorable membership is professionalism on the part of the writer and performances regularly in the case of the music publisher (Article III).

---

* This is a simplified summary prepared by the author.

Appendix E

BMI CONSENT DECREE

IN THE DISTRICT COURT OF THE UNITED STATES FOR THE EASTERN DISTRICT OF WISCONSIN

Civil Action No. 459

United States of America, plaintiff

v,

Broadcast Music, Inc., defendant

MODIFIED CONSENT DECREE

A final decree having been filed herein on February 3, 1941, upon the consent of defendant, and the defendant having, pursuant to Paragraph VI of said decree, moved this Court upon the petition of the defendant verified May 9, 1941, for a decree modifying the said decree of February 3, 1941, so that it shall read as hereinafter provided, and the defendant having appeared by counsel, and the plaintiff having consented hereto and the Court being fully advised in the premises, now therefore it is

Ordered, adjudged, and decreed that the final decree made and filed herein on February 3, 1941, be and the same is hereby modified so as to read as follows:

Civil Action No. 459—Civil Decree
United States of America, plaintiff

against

Broadcast Music, Inc., defendant

This cause came on to be heard on this third day of February, 1941, the plaintiff being represented by Thurman Arnold, Assistant Attorney General, B. J. Husting, United States Attorney for the Eastern District of Wisconsin, Victor O. Waters, Special Assistant to the Attorney General, and Warren Cunningham, Jr., Special Attorney, and the defendant being represented by its counsel, and having appeared and filed its answer to the complaint herein.

It appears to the Court that defendant, Broadcast Music, Inc., has consented in writing to the making and entering of this decree, without any findings of fact, upon condition that neither such consent nor this decree shall be construed as an admission or adjudication that said defendant has violated any law.

It further appears to the Court that this decree will provide suitable relief concerning the matters alleged in the complaint filed herein and that by reason of the aforesaid consent of defendant, Broadcast Music, Inc., and its acceptance by plaintiff it is unnecessary to proceed with the trial of the action, or to take testimony therein, or that any adjudication be made of the facts.

Now, therefore, upon motion of plaintiff, and in accordance with said consent, it is hereby

ORDERED, ADJUDGED, AND DECREED

I. The Court has jurisdiction of the subject-matter set forth in the complaint and of the parties hereto with full power and authority to enter this decree and the complaint states a cause of action against defendant, Broadcast Music, Inc., under the Act of Congress of July 2, 1890, entitled "An Act to Protect Trade and Commerce Against Unlawful Restraints and Monopolies" and the acts amendatory thereof and supplemental thereto.

II. Defendant, Broadcast Music, Inc., its officers, directors, agents, servants, employees and all persons acting or claiming to act on its behalf are hereby perpetually enjoined and restrained from entering into or carrying out, directly or indirectly, any combination or conspiracy to restrain interstate trade and commerce, as alleged in the complaint, by doing, performing, agreeing upon, entering upon, or carrying out any of the acts or things hereinafter in this paragraph II prohibited:

(1) Defendant, Broadcast Music, Inc., shall not, with respect to any musical composition, acquire or assert any exclusive performing right as agent, trustee or otherwise on behalf of any copyright owner or other owner of the performing right, or pursuant to any understanding or agreement with such owner to pay for such right a share of, or an amount measured by, the receipts or revenues of said defendant. Nothing contained in this sub-paragraph (1) shall be construed as preventing defendant Broadcast Music, Inc., from acquiring or asserting exclusive performing rights (a) in any musical composition of which said defendant shall also own or acquire the copyright; (b) in any musical composition concurrently with the exclusive right to publish such composition in the United States of America; (c) in any musical composition as a purchaser, assignee or licensee (but not as agent, trustee or otherwise on behalf of another) in consideration of the payment or agreement to pay, as the sole compensation for such performing rights, a fixed sum stated in the contract of purchase, assignment or license; or (d) in any musical composition, as a purchaser, assignee, or licensee (but not as agent, trustee or otherwise on behalf of another) in consideration of the payment or agreement to pay as the sole compensation for such performing rights, an amount determinable by reference to the number of licensed performances of such composition at a fixed per performance price and basis stipulated in such contract.

(2) Defendant, Broadcast Music, Inc., shall not enter into, recognize

as valid or perform any performing license agreement which shall result in discriminating in price or terms between licensees similarly situated; provided, however, that differentials based upon applicable business factors which jusitfy different prices or terms shall not be considered discrimination within the meaning of this sub-paragraph; and provided further that nothing contained in this sub-paragraph shall prevent price changes from time to time by reason of changing conditions affecting the market for or marketability of performing rights.

(3) Defendant, Broadcast Music, Inc., shall not require, as a condition to any offer to license the public performance for profit of a musical composition or compositions for radio broadcasting, a license fee of which any part shall be (a) in respect of commercial programs based upon a percentage of the income received by the broadcaster from programs in which no musical composition or compositions licensed by said defendant for performance shall be performed, or (b) in respect of sustaining programs an amount which does not vary in proportion either to actual performances, during the term of the license, of the musical compositions licensed by said defendant for performance, or to the number of programs on which such compositions or any of them shall be performed; provided, however, that nothing herein contained shall prevent said defendant from licensing a radio broadcaster, on either or both of the foregoing bases, if desired by such broadcaster, or upon any other basis desired by such broadcaster.

With respect to any existing or future performing license agreement with a radio broadcaster, defendant, Broadcast Music, Inc., shall not, if required by such broadcaster, refuse to offer a per program basis of compensation on either or both of the following bases which may be specified by the broadcaster:

(i) in respect of sustaining programs a per program license fee, expressed in terms of dollars, requiring the payment of a stipulated amount for each program in which musical compositions licensed by said defendant shall be performed;

(ii) in respect of commercial programs, a per program license fee, either expressed in terms of dollars, requiring the payment of a stipulated amount for each program in which the musical compositions licensed by said defendant for performance shall be performed, or at the option of defendant, the payment of a percentage of the revenue derived by the licensee for the use of its broadcasting facilities in connection with such program.

In the event that defendant shall offer to license the public performance for profit of a musical composition or compositions for radio broadcasting upon either or both of the foregoing per program basis, and shall also offer to license such performance on a basis of compensation which shall not vary in direct proportion either to actual performances during the term of the licenses of the musical compositions licensed by said defendant for performance or to the number of programs on which musical compositions licensed by defendant shall be performed, defendant shall act in good faith so that there shall be a relationship between such per program basis and such other basis, justifiable by applicable business factors, including availability, so that there will be no frustration of the purpose of this sub-paragraph to afford radio broadcasters alternative basis of license compensation.

(4) Defendant, Broadcast Music, Inc., shall not license the public performance for profit of any musical composition or compositions except on a basis whereby, insofar as network radio broadcasting is concerned, the issuance of a single license, authorizing and fixing a single license fee for such performance by network radio broadcasting, shall permit the simultaneous broadcasting of such performance by all stations on the network which shall broadcast such performance, without requiring separate licenses for such several stations for such performance.

(5) With respect to any musical composition in defendant's catalogue of musical compositions licensed for radio broadcasting and which is or shall be lawfully recorded for performance on specified commercially sponsored programs on an electrical transcription or on other specially prepared recordation intended for broadcasting purposes, said defendant shall not refuse to offer to license the public performance for profit by designated radio broadcasting stations of such compositions by a single license to any manufacturer, producer or distributor of such transcription or recordation or to any advertiser or advertising agency on whose behalf such transcription or recordation shall have been made who may request such license, which single license shall authorize the broadcasting of the recorded composition by means of such transcription or recordation by all radio stations enumerated by the license, on terms and conditions fixed by said defendant, without requiring separate licenses for such enumerated stations.

(6) Defendant, Broadcast Music, Inc., shall not, in connection with any offer to license by it the public performance for profit of musical compositions by users other than broadcasters, refuse to offer a license at a price or prices to be fixed by said defendant for the performance of such specific (i.e., per piece) musical compositions, the use of which shall be requested by the prospective licensee.

(7) Defendant, Broadcast Music, Inc., shall not, in connection with any offer to license by it the public performance for profit of musical compositions by radio broadcasters, refuse to offer a license on a per performance or per program basis as provided for in paragraph II (3) hereof at a price or prices to be fixed by said defendant for the performance of such programs, the use of which shall be requested by the prospective licensee.

(8) Defendant, Broadcast Music, Inc., shall not assert or exercise any right or power to restrict from public performance for profit by any licensee of said defendant any copyrighted musical composition in order to exact additional consideration for the performance thereof, or for the purpose of permitting the fixing or regulating of fees for the recording or transcribing of such composition; provided, however, that nothing in this sub-paragraph shall prevent said defendant from restricting performances of a musical composition in order reasonably to protect the work against indiscriminate performances or the value of the public performance for

profit rights therein or to protect the dramatic performing rights therein, or, as may be reasonably necessary in connection with any claim or litigation involving the performing rights in any such composition.

III. The terms of this decree shall be binding upon, and shall extend to each and every one of the successors in interest of the defendant, Broadcast Music, Inc., and to any and all corporations, partnerships, associations and individuals who or which may acquire the ownership or control, directly or indirectly, of all or substantially all of the property, business and assets of defendant, Broadcast Music, Inc., whether by purchase, merger, consolidation, reorganization or otherwise. None of the restraints or requirements herein imposed upon the defendant shall apply to the acquisition of or licensing of the right to perform musical compositions publicly for profit outside the United States of America, its territories and possessions.

IV. For the purpose of securing compliance with paragraph II of this decree, and for no other purpose, duly authorized representatives of the Department of Justice shall, on the written request of the Attorney General or an Assistant Attorney General and on reasonable notice to defendant, Broadcast Music, Inc., made to the principal office of said defendant, be permitted (a) reasonable access, during the office hours of said defendant, to all books, ledgers, accounts, correspondence, memoranda, and other records and documents in the possession or under the control of said defendant, relating to any of the matters contained in this decree, (b) subject to the reasonable convenience of said defendant and without restraint or interference from it, and subject to any legally recognized privilege, to interview officers or employees of said defendant, who may have counsel present, regarding any such matters; and said defendant, on such request, shall submit such reports in respect of any such matters as may from time to time be reasonably necessary for the proper enforcement of this decree; provided, however, that information obtained by the means permitted in this paragraph shall not be divulged by any representative of the Deparment of Justice to any person other than a duly authorized representative of the Department of Justice except in the course of legal proceedings in which the United States is a party or as otherwise required by law.

V. The provisions of sub-paragraph (4) of Paragraph II of this decree shall not become effective until nine (9) months after June 11, 1941. None of the other provisions of Paragraph II of this decree shall become effective until June 11, 1941.

VI. Jurisdiction of this cause is retained for the purpose of enabling any of the parties to this decree to make application to the Court at any time for such further orders and directions as may be necessary or appropriate in relation to the construction of or carrying out of this decree, for the modification hereof upon any ground, for the enforcement of compliance herewith and the punishment of violations hereof. Jurisdiction of this cause is retained for the purpose of granting or denying such applications so made as justice may require and the right of the defendant to make such application and to obtain such relief is expressly granted.

Dated May 14, 1941.

F. RYAN DUFFY,
United States District Judge.

We hereby consent to the entry of the foregoing decree.
For the complainant:

THURMAN ARNOLD,
Assistant Attorney General
VICTOR O. WATERS,
Special Assistant to the Attorney General
WARREN CUNNINGHAM, JR.,
Special Attorney

Counsel for the defendant, Broacast Music, Inc.:

GODFREY GOLDMARK.

Appendix F

BMI CONTRACT FOR PUBLISHERS

AGREEMENT made this   day of   19 , between BROADCAST MUSIC, INC., a New York corporation, whose address is 580 Fifth Avenue, New York 36, N.Y.
(hereinafter called "BMI") and ....
a   corporation .... doing business under the firm name and style of .... whose address is

....

(Street or Avenue)   (City)   (State)

(hereinafter called "PUBLISHER").

WITNESSETH:

FIRST:

(a) The word "term," as used in this agreement shall mean and be restricted to a period of five (5) years from the date hereof and continuing thereafter unless cancelled by either party at the end of the said five-year period, or at the end of any subsequent five-year period, upon three (3) months' advance written notice;

(b) The word "works," as used in this agreement, shall mean and be restricted to all musical compositions, including individual compositions embraced within a dramatico-musical composition, whether published or unpublished, now owned or copyrighted, or hereafter during the term, acquired or copyrighted by Publisher, and all such musical compositions, whether published or unpublished, in which Publisher now, or hereafter during the term, owns or controls the right publicly to perform for profit or the right to broadcast or televise

SECOND: Publisher hereby sells, assigns and transfers to BMI, its successors and assigns, the following rights in all works, including but not limited to the work itemized in Schedule A annexed hereto and made a part hereof:

(a) The sole and exclusive right publicly to perform for profit, broadcast and televise, including the right to grant licenses publicly to perform for profit, broadcast and televise;

---

* BMI informed us that their writer and publisher agreements were being revised however, they were not yet prepared at the time of our printer's deadline.

(b) The non-exclusive right to adapt, arrange, translate, change and dramatize for performing, broadcasting and televising purposes, including the right to grant non-exclusive licenses to adapt, arrange, translate and dramatize for performing, broadcasting and televising purposes;

(c) The non-exclusive right to record, or to cause or permit to be recorded, for mechanical, electrical or other reproduction, performance of said works in any form or in any adaptation, arrangement ,translation or dramatization thereof, but not for motion picture synchronization, upon payment of the customary royalty rate then prevailing, but in no event in excess of present statutory royalties;

(d) The rights hereby conveyed under subdivisions (a), (b) and (c) hereof shall be exercised by BMI and/or its licensees only within the Western Hemisphere.

THIRD: In consideration of this agreement, BMI agrees to pay Publisher the following:

(a) Two cents (2c) * per performance by a commercial amplitude modulation United States broadcasting station licensed by BMI of each original work printed in the United States either in customary saleable form or in professional copies provided that said printings are in such quantities as make copies of said work generally available to broadcasts either without charge or at the customary price for such material;

(b) One cent (1c) * per performance by a commercial amplitude modulation United States broadcasting station licensed by BMI of each unpublished work (or published work which is not printed in accordance with subdivision (a) of this paragraph "THIRD") which has been recorded on phonograph records, distributed throughout the United States and available to broadcasters at customary phonograph record prices;

(c) One cent (1c) * per performance by a commercial amplitude modulation United States broadcasting station licensed by BMI of any copyrighted arrangement of a work in the public domain embraced within this agreement and printed in the United States in accordance with subdivision (a) of this paragraph "THIRD."

(d) The aforesaid payments shall be made irrespective of whether the performances referred to in subdivisions (a), (b) and (c) of this paragraph "THIRD" are by means of recordings or by living talent.

In the event that BMI shall hereafter pay, or agree to pay, royalties in excess of those set forth herein for works of the same type as are embraced within this agreement and acquired by BMI under substantially identical agreements, and in the event that BMI shall not tender to Publisher a modification of this agreement making available to said Publisher said more favorable rates, Publisher shall have the right to terminate this

---

* There rates have been raised, see p. 50.

agreement by giving BMI notice in writing, which notice shall be effective to so terminate this agreement sixty (60) days after its receipt by BMI, provided, however, that BMI may, within the said sixty day period, tender to Publisher an agreement containing said more favorable rates and upon such tender, any notice of termination theretofore given by Publisher shall be deemed to have been withdrawn.

FOURTH:

(a) The performances by commercial amplitude modulation United States broadcasting stations licensed by BMI, referred to in paragraph "THIRD" hereof, for which payment shall be made, shall consist of not less than a full chorus of a work. The number of such performances shall be estimated by BMI as accurately as shall be practicable from an actual check of performance records furnished to BMI by broadcasting stations constituting a representative cross-section of the industry;

(b) A statement showing the number of performances as computed by BMI pursuant to the provisions of subdivision (a) of this paragraph "FOURTH" and remittances of payments by BMI to Publisher with respect to the same, shall be furnished by BMI to Publisher at least twice during each calendar year during the term.

FIFTH:

(a) BMI shall have the right, upon written notice to Publisher, to exclude from the terms of this agreement, at any time, any work which, in its opinion (1) is similar to a previously existing work and might constitute an infringement thereof, (2) is similar to the title or music or lyrics of a previously existing work and which might constitute unfair competition with respect to such work, (3) is offensive, in bad taste, or against public morals, or (4) is not reasonably suitable for performance;

(b) In the case of arrangements of works in the public domain, BMI shall have the unrestricted right to exclude such arrangements from the terms of this agreement;

(c) In the event that any claim is made by a third party with respect to any work covered by this agreement, BMI shall have the right to exclude such work from the terms of this agreement until such time as the claim shall have been withdrawn or otherwise disposed of;

(d) In the event that any work is excluded pursuant to the provisions (a) or (b) of this paragraph "FIFTH," all rights in such work shall automatically revert to Publisher.

SIXTH: Publisher further covenants and agrees as follows:

(a) To submit to BMI supplements to Schedule A setting forth, with respect to additional works acquired by Publisher, (1) the titles of such works as are printed in accordance with subdivision (a) of paragraph "THIRD" hereof, (2) the titles of such works as are not so printed in accordance with subdivision (a) of paragraph "THIRD" hereof, (3) the name or names of the authors or composers of each individual work, (4) the United States copyright registration number of each work and the publication date, if any, and (5) the titles of works which have been recorded on phonograph records, including the manufacturer's name, catalog number and the name of the recording artist;

(b) To furnish promptly to BMI, from time to time during the term hereof, manuscript copies of all unpublished works;

(c) To furnish promptly to BMI, from time to time during the term hereof, not less than three (3) copies of each printed version of all works embraced within this agreement and with respect to works recorded on phonograph records, to furnish promptly to BMI a copy of each of said records;

(d) To obtain and deliver to BMI any written agreements, assignments, instruments or documents of any kind with respect to any works embraced within this agreement which BMI may require, and to procure and maintain at least United States copyright protection with respect to all published works embraced within this agreement.

SEVENTH: BMI agrees, after ascertaining the suitability of a work pursuant to subdivision (a) of paragraph "FIFTH" hereof, to inform all of its broadcasting station licensees of the availability of said works for broadcasting.

EIGHTH: Publisher represents and warrants that:

(a) Schedule A hereto annexed is a complete list of all titles of all works which are owned or controlled by Publisher as of the date of this agreement and shows thereon the information required under subdivision (a) of paragraph "SIXTH" hereof;

(b) All rights granted by Publisher, under the terms of this agreement, are Publisher's sole and exclusive property; that said rights are free from all encumbrances and claims; and that Publisher has full right and power to make the within agreement; and that there exists no adverse claim to or in the said rights and that no foreign or domestic performing rights licensing society or other organization has any performing, broadcasting or television rights in the works; Publisher agrees to defend, indemnify, save and hold BMI, its licensees, the advertisers of its licensees, and their respective agents, servants and employees, free and harmless from any and all claims, demands, suits, judgments and recoveries, including lawyers' fees, which may be made or brought against them or any of them arising out of the grant of rights herein or arising out of the performance of any work or works embraced by this agreement, provided, however, that the obligations of Publisher to indemnify, all as provided in this paragraph, shall not apply to any matter added to, or changes made in, any work by BMI or its licensees;

(c) Publisher has obtained, with respect to all works owned or controlled by it as of the date of this agreement, and will obtain, with respect to works acquired during the term, written agreements signed by all of the authors and composers of the works granting to Publisher the rights transferred by this agreement.

NINTH: Upon the service on any of the parties herein indemnified of any notice, demand, process, papers, writ or pleading upon which any such claim, demand, suit or proceeding is made or begun against them or any of them which Publisher shall be obliged to defend hereunder, BMI shall, as soon as may be practicable, give Publisher notice thereof and shall deliver to Publisher such papers or true copies thereof, and BMI shall have the right to participate in such suits by counsel of its own selection, at its own expense. Publisher agrees to cooperate with BMI in all such matters.

TENTH: BMI represents that it now has in excess of six hundred (600) broadcasting station licensees, and agrees that in the event the number of its licensees should be reduced to less than three hundred (300) at any time during the term, Publisher shall have the right to terminate this agreement at any time thereafter during the existence of such condition by giving BMI ninety (90) days' notice in writing.

ELEVENTH: In the event that Governmental Rules and Regulations, affecting a substantial number of BMI's commercial broadcasting station licensees or a substantial volume of the business of BMI's commercial broadcasting station licensees, are changed so as to forbid or restrict substantially the broadcasting of commercial programs, BMI shall have the right to terminate this agreement at any time thereafter, during the existence of either of such conditions, by giving Publisher thirty (30) days' notice in writing, provided that BMI shall, prior to the end of said thirty-day period, also terminate all agreements of a similar nature with other publishers containing a similar right of termination. In the event of such termination BMI shall be under no further liability to Publisher for payments hereunder, except that payments shall be made for all periods up to the effective date of such termination, and Publisher shall remain liable under the indemnity provisions of this agreement with respect to all performances made prior to the termination date.

TWELFTH: Publisher hereby makes, constitutes and appoints BMI, or its nominee, Publisher's true and lawful attorney, irrevocably during the term hereof, and in the name of BMI or its nominee, or in the name of Publisher, or otherwise, to do all acts, take all proceedings, execute, acknowledge and deliver any and all instruments, papers, documents, process or pleadings that may be necessary, proper or expedient to restrain infringements and to enforce and protect the rights conveyed by this agreement, and to recover damages in respect to or for the infringement or other violation of the said performing, broadcasting and television rights in the works, and in its sole judgment, to join Publisher and/or others in whose names the copyrights to any works may stand, to discontinue, compromise or refer to arbitration, any such actions or proceedings, or to make any other disposition of the differences in relation to the premises, provided, however, that any moneys received by BMI by way of damages or otherwise from any infringement or violation of the aforesaid right shall be the sole and exclusive property of BMI.

Any actions or proceedings commenced by BMI pursuant to the provisions of this paragraph "TWELFTH" shall be at BMI's sole expense.

THIRTEENTH: In the event that Publisher shall at any time during the term hereof engage in the business of soliciting lyrics or musical compositions for a fee or shall accept manuscripts from composers in consideration of any payments to be made by such composers either for arranging, promotion or any other services, then BMI shall have the right in its sole discretion to terminate this agreement upon thirty (30) days' written notice to Publisher.

FOURTEENTH: In the event of any dispute of any kind, nature or description whatsoever arising between BMI and Publisher in connection with the terms and conditions of this agreement, or arising out of the performance hereof, or based upon an alleged breach hereof, the same shall be submitted to arbitration in New York City by a board consisting of three arbitrators under the then prevailing rules of the American Arbitration Association pursuant to the New York arbitration law. Each of the parties hereto shall have the right to select one of the said three arbitrators and the two arbitrators so selected shall thereupon select the third arbitrator, provided, however, that in the event the said two arbitrators shall be unable to agree upon the selection of a third arbitrator, such third arbitrator shall be appointed by the American Arbitration Association, and the parties further agree to abide by and perform any award with respect to any such controversy rendered by the Arbitration in conformity with this agreement, and that the expenses of such arbitration shall be divided equally between the parties.

FIFTEENTH: This agreement and each of the provisions thereof shall bind and inure to the benefit of each of the parties hereto and their respective successors. This agreement shall be construed in accordance with the laws of the State of New York. This agreement shall not be assignable by either party without the consent of the other.

IN WITNESS WHEREOF, the parties hereto have caused this agreement to be duly executed as of the day and year first above written.

BROADCAST MUSIC, INC.
By ....
 ....
By ....

[See p. 160 for a modification of the contract].

APPENDIX F

BROADCAST MUSIC, INC.
580 Fifth Avenue
New York 36, New York

Gentlemen:

Our contract dated .... is hereby modified so that the territory for which the grant of rights is given shall be the entire world.

It is understood that you will notify us promptly when you consummate contracts conveying our said rights for any country or countries not included in our present contract prior to this modification, and that all revenue you receive therefrom which is allocable to publishers will be divided either in accordance with the accountings that you receive from abroad, or, in the absence of such accountings, in the proportion which our logged performances in the United States shall bear to the logged performances in the United States of the other publishers who shall have conveyed these foreign rights to you. It is further understood that you shall have the right to deduct ten percent (10%) of all monies received by you for performances outside the Western Hemisphere and to retain the sums so deducted to cover your handling and administrative expenses.

We shall be free to convey performance rights for the country of foreign publication to any publisher who may publish any one or more of our works abroad in any of the countries added to our contract by this modification until such date as contracts are actually made by you for the licensing of such works in such country, but we shall not be free, of course, to make such grant for any country with respect to which you shall have made any such contract and notified us thereof.

Your signature beneath the word "ACCEPTED" will constitute this a binding modification of the aforesaid contract between us, such contract being in all other respects specifically ratified and affirmed.

Very truly yours,

BY ....

ACCEPTED:
BROADCAST MUSIC, INC.

BY ....

Appendix G

BMI CONTRACT FOR WRITERS*

BROADCAST MUSIC, INC.

Date ...., 19......

Dear

The following shall constitute the agreement between you and us:
1. You warrant and represent:
(a) That Schedule "A" annexed hereto is an accurate and complete list setting forth the titles and all other information called for by the Schedule as to all musical and dramatico-musical compositions heretofore composed by you alone and/or as a collaborator, all of the performing rights in which have been alienated to others;

(b) That Schedule "B" annexed hereto is an accurate and complete list setting forth the titles and all other information called for by the Schedule as to all other musical and dramatico-musical compositions heretofore composed by you alone and/or as a collaborator; and

(c) That no rights in the musical and dramatico-musical compositions referred to in Schedule "B" have been alienated by you except as so indicated on said Schedule.

2. You hereby grant to us for a period of two years commencing .... 19 ...., and ending ...., 19........, (hereinafter called the "period"):

(a) The sole and exclusive right publicly to perform for profit, and to license others publicly to perform for profit, throughout the world any part or all of all the musical and dramatico-musical compositions, published and/or unpublished, which are set forth on Schedule "B" as composed solely by you, and each and all of the musical and dramatico-musical compositions which are hereinafter during the period composed by you;

(b) All your performing rights, which shall include at least non-exclusive rights, publicly to perform for profit, and to license others publicly to perform for profit, any part or all of all of the compositions referred to in Schedule "B" to which subsection "a" of this paragraph is not applicable, and any part or all of all of the musical and dramatico-musical compositions hereinafter composed by you during the period with a collaborator;

You expressly reserve, and there is expressly excluded from the grants in this Paragraph "2", the right to give, or to license, performances of

---

* BMI informed us that their writer and publisher agreements were being revised, however, they were not yet prepared at the time of our printer's deadline.

longer than thirty (30) minutes duration of operas, operettas and musical comedies. The musical and dramatico-musical compositions included within the grants in this Paragraph are hereinafter referred to as the "works;"

(c) The non-exclusive right to record, and cause or permit to be recorded, any part or all of any one or more of the works on electrical transcriptions, wire, tape, film or otherwise, but only (i) for the purpose of performing works publicly for profit by means of radio and television, and (ii) for archive or audition purposes;

(d) The non-exclusive right to adapt, arrange, translate, change and dramatize any part or all of any one or more of the works for performing purposes, including the right to license others so to do.

3. You agree that in each instance that a work is composed by you alone and/or as a collaborator during the period you shall, on or before the date of execution of a grant or license by you or by any collaborator for the publishing or recording of the work, whichever shall first occur, furnish to us a copy of the work, together with a supplement to Schedule "B" setting forth the title of the work and all other information called for by the Schedule.

4. We agree that with respect to each work heretofore or hereafter composed by you for which we obtain and retain exclusive performing rights during the period, including also each such work in which we obtain and retain such exclusive performing rights by reason of your grant hereunder supplemented by one or more grants to us from collaborators to the work or from publishers of the work who are affilated with us, we shall pay to you for the rights granted to us hereunder;

(a) In the event that you are the sole composer of the words and music of the work, royalties equivalent to 50% of the amount of the performance royalties which would be earned by the work during each year of the period as calculated pursuant to our then-current standard practices and procedures, upon the basis of the then-current performance rates generally paid by us to our affiliated, publishers for compositions of the type of the work. It is agreed that, at present, these rates are four cents per performance for each logged local U.S. radio station performance, and six cents per performance per station for each logged U.S. radio network performance;

(b) In the event that there are one or more collaborators in composing the work, royalties equivalent to your pro-rata share, determined on the basis of the number of collaborators, of the 50% referred to in subsection (a) of this Paragraph "4".

The provisions of this Paragraph "4" shall not be effective or applicable with respect to any performance of a work which occurs prior to the date that we receive from you all of the information and material referred to in Paragraph "3" hereof for said work.

5. We agree to pay to you as a minimum payment against the royalties to be earned, pursuant to Paragraph "4" hereof, during each year of the period, not less than ($) dollars for each year of the period, which

sum shall be payable to you in equal quarterly installments on or before the first day of January, April, July and October during each year of the period.

6. A statement showing the number of performances as computed by BMI pursuant to Paragraph "4" hereof, and remittances of payments by BMI to you with respect to same, subject to all proper deductions for advances, shall be furnished by BMI to you at least twice during each full calendar year during the period.

7. (a) You warrant and represent that you are not now party to any contract, either written or oral, pursuant to the provisions of which any person, firm or corporation obtains publishing rights in, or has a first option to obtain publishing rights in, any one or more works which have not yet been composed by you alone and/or with a collaborator.

(b) In each instance, if any, in the future that you become a party to any contract (other than a contract for the writing of part or all of the score for a motion picture or legitimate stage production) either written or oral, with any person, firm or corporation, pursuant to which publishing rights are granted, by way of option or otherwise, for any part of the period, in more than one work which has not yet been composed by you alone and/or as a collaborator, you agree to send us written notice thereof within ten days thereafter. In each instance, if any, that we receive such notice, you grant us options that we in our sole discretion may either:

(1) exclude each work which is subject to the provisions of said contract from the provisions of Paragraph "4" hereof, or

(11) terminate the period of this agreement, effective immediately.

In the event that we elect to exercise either of said options, we shall give you written notice thereof within thirty days after receipt by us from you of the notice referred to in the first sentence of this sub-paragraph (b).

In each instance that you are employed or commissioned by a motion picture producer to write during the period all or part of the score of a motion picture, or by the producer of a revue for the legitimate stage to write during the period all or part of the musical compositions contained therein, we agree to confirm to the producer of the film that such part of the score as is written by you may be performed as part of the exhibition of said film without compensation to us, and to the producer of the revue that your compositions embodied therein may be exhibited on the stage with living artists without compensation to us.

8. You warrant and represent that each and every work, composed by you alone and/or as a collaborator, is original. You agree to indemnify and hold harmless us and our sub-licensees from and against all loss and/or damage resulting from any and all claims of whatsoever name and nature arising from or in connection with the exercise of any one or more of the rights granted by you in this agreement.

9. You make, constitute and appoint us, or our nominee, your true and lawful attorney, irrevocably during the term hereof, in our name or that of our nominee, or in your name, or otherwise, to do all acts, take all

proceedings, execute, acknowledge and deliver any and all instruments, papers, documents, process or pleadings that may be necessary, proper or expedient to restrain infringment of and/or to enforce and protect the rights granted by your hereunder, and to recover damages in respect to or for the infringment or other violation of the said rights, and in our sole judgment to join you and/or others in whose names the copyrights to any of the works may stand; to discontinue, compromise or refer to arbitration, any such actions or proceedings or to make any other disposition of the differences in relation to the premises; provided, however, (a) that any actions or proceedings commenced by us pursuant to the provisions of this paragraph shall be at our sole expense, and (b) that any moneys collected by way of damages or otherwise from any infringment or violation of the aforesaid rights shall be our sole and exclusive property.

10. (a) You grant us an option to extend the period upon the same terms for an additional one (1) year, commencing upon the first day that the period would otherwise expire; provided, however, that the minimum payment referred to in Paragraph "5" hereof shall be for $ for this option year.

(b) In the event that we exercise the option contained in subparagraph "a" of this Paragraph, you grant us an additional option further to extend the period upon the same terms for an additional one (1) year, commencing upon the first day that the period, as theretofore extended, would otherwise expire; provided, however, that the $ minimum payment referred to in Paragraph "5" hereof shall be for $ for this additional option year.

(c) In the event that we exercise the option contained in subparagraph "b" of this Paragraph, you grant us an additional option further to extend the period upon the same terms for an additional one (1) year, commencing upon the first day that the period, as theretofore extended, would otherwise expire; provided, however, that the $ minimum payment referred to in Paragraph "5" hereof shall be for $ for this additional option year.

(d) In the event that we exercise the option contained in subparagraph "c" of this Paragraph, you grant us an additional option further to extend the period upon the same terms for an additional one (1) year commencing upon the first day that the period, as theretofore extended, would otherwise expire; provided, however, that the $ minimum payment referred to in Paragraph "5" hereof shall be for $ for this additional option year.

(e) In the event that we exercise the option contained in subparagraph "d" of this Paragraph, you grant us an additional option further to extend the period upon the same terms for an additional one (1) year, commencing upon the first day that the period, as theretofore extended, would otherwise expire; provided, however, that the $ minimum payment referred to in Paragraph "5" hereof shall be for $ for this additional option year.

11. You warrant and represent that you have the right to enter into this agreement, and that you are not bound by any prior commitments which conflict with your commitments under this agreement.

12. Any controversy or claim arising out of, or relating to this agreement or breach thereof, shall be settled by arbitration, in New York City, in accordance with the laws of the State of New York by three arbitrators to be selected by the American Arbitration Association and said arbitration shall be conducted in accordance with the rules, then obtaining, of said Association, and judgment on the award rendered may be entered in the Supreme Court of the State of New York or in any other Court having jurisdiction thereof.

13. This agreement cannot be changed orally, and shall be interpreted, governed and construed pursuant to the laws of the State of New York.

                          Very truly yours,
                          BROADCAST MUSIC, INC.
                          By ....

ACCEPTED:
....

APPENDIX H

BMI PUBLISHING DEPARTMENT CONTRACT *

AGREEMENT made this   day of   19 ,
between BROADCAST MUSIC, INC., a New York corporation, of 580 Fifth Avenue, New York 19, N.Y., (hereinafter called "PUBLISHER") and

jointly and/or severally (hereinafter called "WRITER").

WITNESSETH:

In consideration of the agreement herein contained and of the sum of $ in hand paid by Publisher to Writer, receipt of which is hereby acknowledged,

the parties agree as follows:

1. Writer hereby sells, assigns, transfers, and delivers to Publisher, its successors and assigns, a certain heretofore unpublished original musical composition, written and/or composed by the above named Writer, now entitled.
including the title, words and music thereof, and the right to secure copyright therein throughout the entire world, and to have and to hold the said copyright and all rights of whatsoever nature thereunder existing.

2. Writer hereby warrants that the said composition is his sole, exclusive and original work, and that he has full right and power to make the within agreement, and that there exists no adverse claim to or in the said composition.

3. In consideration of this agreement, Publisher agrees to pay Writer jointly, in respect of said composition the following:
(a) In respect of regular piano and vocal copies, sold and paid for in the United States of America, a royalty of three cents per copy.
(b) In respect of band parts and orchestrations sold and paid for in the United States of America, a royalty of ten percent (10%) of the list price thereof.
(c) In respect of regular piano and vocal copies, band parts, orchestrations and for the use of said composition in any folio or composite work, sold and paid for in any foreign country, a royalty of fifty percent (50%) of all net sums received by Publisher.
(d) For purposes of royalty statements, if a composition is printed and published in the United States of America, as to copies and rights

---

* BMI informed us that their writer and publisher agreements were being revised, however, they were not yet prepared at the time of our printer's dead line.

BMI PUBLISHING DEPARTMENT CONTRACT

sold in the Dominion of Canada, revenue therefrom shall be considered as of domestic origin.

If, however, the composition is printed by a party other than Publisher in the Dominion of Canada, revenue from sales of copies and rights in Canada shall be considered as having originated in a foreign country.

(e) As to "professional material" not sold or resold, no royalty shall be payable.

(f) An amount equal to fifty percent (50%) of all receipts of Publisher in respect of any licenses issued authorizing the manufacture of parts of instruments serving mechanically to reproduce said composition, or to use said composition in synchronization with sound motion picture; provided, however, that should Publisher manufacture, or cause to be manufactured, parts of instruments serving mechanically to reproduce said composition, Publisher will pay Writer fifty percent (50%) of the statutory recording fee.

(g) Publisher agrees to pay to Writer, as performing royalties, not less than one cent per performance per commercial amplitude modulation United States broadcasting station licensee of Publisher for each full performance of said composition consisting of not less than one full chorus. Such number of performances shall be estimated as accurately as shall be possible from an actual check of performance records of broadcasting stations constituting a representative cross-section of Publisher's licensees; and statements showing the number of performances computed, and accountings with respect to the same, shall be furnished at least semi-annually.

(h) Except as is specifically provided for in the subdivisions of this paragraph 3, no other royalties of any kind shall be paid by Publisher to Writer.

4. It is understood and agreed by and between all of the parties hereto that all sums hereunder payable jointly to Writer shall be divided amongst them respectively as follows:

NAME	SHARE
....	....
....	....
....	....
....	....

5. Publisher shall render Writer, as above, on or before each May 15th covering the three months ending March 31st; each August 15th covering the three months ending June 30th; each November 15th covering the three months ending September 30th; each February 15th covering the three months ending December 31st; hereafter, so long as it shall continue publication or the licensing of any rights in the said composition, royalty statements accompanied by remittance of the amount due.

6. Publisher agrees to publish, or cause to be published, the said

composition in professional copies within six months from the date hereof, and to distribute the same to its broadcast licensees and others in order to encourage the public performance thereof. In the event that Publisher determines that subsequent public demand for such composition has been created, Publisher further agrees to publish such music in saleable form. Should Publisher fail to publish said music in professional form within the period hereinabove set forth, Writer's sole right shall be to demand the return of said composition, whereupon Publisher must within one month after receipt of such notice either publish in professional form, or cause to be published in professional form, the said composition, or at its option, pay Writer $ 100. Upon failure so to publish or to so pay the aforesaid amount, all rights of any and every nature, and the right to secure copyright and/or any copyright secured by Publisher before publication, in and to the said composition, shall revert to and become the property of Writer and shall be reassigned to Writer, and neither party shall be liable to the other on this contract. The payment of the additional sum referred to in this paragraph shall extend the publication date for a period of one year from the date of such payment, and upon such extended date, and the giving by Writer of notice, as hereinabove set forth, all rights shall revert to Writer, as hereinabove set forth, in the event that Publisher does not publish the work in professional form within one month after receipt of such notice.

7. Anything to the contrary notwithstanding, nothing in this agreement contained shall prevent Publisher from authorizing publishers, agents and representatives in countries outside of the United States and Canada (and in Canada if said composition is printed by a party other than Publisher in Canada) from exercising exclusive publication and all other rights in said foreign countries in said composition on the customary royalty basis; and nothing in this agreement shall prevent Publisher from authorizing publishers in the United States from exercising exclusive publication rights and other rights in the United States in said composition, provided Publisher shall pay Writer the royalties herein stipulated. If foreign publication or other rights in said composition are separately conveyed, otherwise than as a part of Publisher's current and/or future catalog, then, but not otherwise, any advance received in respect thereof shall be divided in accordance with paragraph 3 (f) and credited to the account of Writer.

8. Writer may appoint a certified public accountant who shall at any time during business hours have access to all records of Publisher, and of the United States publisher whom Publisher causes to publish said composition relating to said composition for the purpose of verifying royalty statements rendered or which are delinquent under the terms hereof.

9. In the event that Publisher shall fail or refuse, within sixty days after written demand, to furnish, or cause to be furnished, royalty statements described in paragraph 5, or to give Writer access to the records, as set forth in paragraph 8, or in the event that Publisher shall fail to make the payment of any royalties due within thirty days after written demand

therefor, then Writer shall have the option, to be exercised upon ten days' written notice, to cancel this agreement.

Upon such cancellation, all rights of Publisher of any and every nature, and to said composition, shall cease and come to an end and the said rights, including, but not limited to, the right to secure copyright and/or any copyright theretofore secured by Publisher, shall revert to and become the property of, and shall be assigned to Writer. Publisher agrees that it will thereupon execute any and all assignments or other documents which may be necessary or proper to vest the said rights in Writer.

10. Writer hereby consents to such changes, editing and arrangements of said composition, and the setting of words to the music and of music to the words, and the change of the title as Publisher deems desirable. Writer consents to the use of Writer's name and likeness and the title of said composition on the music, recordings, player rolls and in connection with publicity and advertising concerning Publisher and said composition, and agrees that the use of such name, likeness and title may commence prior to publication and may continue for a reasonable period after the termination of this agreement.

11. Written demands and notices other than royalty statements provided for herein shall be sent by registered mail.

12. Any legal action brought by Publisher against any alleged infringer of said composition shall be initiated and prosecuted at its sole expense, and of any recovery made by it as a result thereof, after deduction of the expense of the litigation, a sum equal to fifty percent (50%) shall be paid to Writer.

(a) If a claim is presented against Publisher alleging that the said composition is an infringement upon some other composition, and because thereof Publisher is jeopardized, it shall thereupon serve written notice upon Writer, containing the full details of such claim and thereafter until the claim has been adjudicated or settled shall pay any moneys coming due Writer hereunder in escrow to any bank or trust company to be held pending the outcome of such claim; provided, however, if no suit be filed within twelve months after written notice to Writer by Publisher of the adverse claim, the said bank or trust company shall release and pay to Writer all sums held in escrow, plus any interest which may have been earned thereupon. Such payment shall be without prejudice to the rights of Publisher in event of a subsequent adverse adjudication.

(b) From and after the service of a summons in a suit for infringement filed against Publisher in respect of the said composition, any and all payments hereunder thereafter coming due Writer, shall be paid by Publisher in trust to any bank or trust company until the suit has been finally adjudicated and then be disbursed accordingly, unless Writer shall elect to file an acceptable bond in the sum of such payments in which event the sums due shall be paid to Writer.

13. The parties hereto hereby agree to submit to arbitration in New York City under the rules of the American Arbitration Association and

pursuant to the New York Arbitration Law, any differences arising under this agreement, and hereby agree individually and jointly to abide by and perform any award rendered by the Arbitration and that a judgment of the Supreme Court of the State of New York may be entered upon such award.

14. "Writer", as used herein, shall be deemed to include all composers signing this agreement.

15. This agreement is binding upon the parties hereto and their respective successors in interest and represents the entire understanding between the parties.

16.   identical copies hereof are executed by the parties, the original copy of which shall remain in possession of Publisher and the duplicates in possession of Writer.

IN WITNESS WHEREOF the parties hereto have caused this agreement to be duly executed the day and year first above written.

Witness: BROADCAST MUSIC, INC.

....   BY ....
                                                                        Vice-President

Witness: WRITER .... (L.S.)

....   Address ....

Witness: WRITER .... (L.S.)

....   Address ....

Witness: WRITER .... (L.S.)

....   Address ....

Witness: WRITER .... (L.S.)

....   Address ....

TABLE OF STATUTES AND CONVENTIONS CITED

UNITED STATES

Act of Congress of July 2, 1890, entitled "Act to Protect Trade and Commerce Against Unlawful Restraints and Monopolies," 31–32.

17 U.S.C. (Copyright Act) § 1 (Supp. 1952) —, 17, 18, 19, 22, 23, 45, 85, 96, 97; § 2 —, 7; § 4 —, 6; § 5 —, 6, 22; § 9 —, 9; § 10 —, 6–7, 10, 20; § 12 —, 7, 20; § 13 —, 7, 20; § 14 —, 7, 11; § 16 —, 11–12, § 19 —, 9; § 22 —, 11, 12; § 23 —, 12; § 24 —, 12–13; § 104 —, 88; § 209 —, 11.

U.S. Const., Art. I, sect. 8 —, 5.

EUROPE

8 Ann. c. 19, Great Britain, 78.

Auteurswet 1912 (Netherlands Copyright Law), Article 1 —, 94, 97; Article 12 —, 93, 94, 100; Article 14 —, 93, 94; Article 16 —, 92; Article 17 —, 92; Article 17bis —, 118; Article 25 —, 89–90; Article 30A —, 115, 117–118; Article 38 —, 92; Article 47 —, 91; Article 50(b) —, 94, 97.

Berne Convention, 69, 76, 77, 78; *Berlin Revision*, 69, Article 4 —, 70; *Brussels Revision*, 69, Article 4 —, 70, 72, Article 6 —, 71; *Rome Revision*, 69, Article 4 —, 69–71, 72, 73, Article 5 —, 70–71, 72, Article 6 —, 70–71, 72, Article 6bis —, 90, Article 7 —, 76–77.

Copyright Amendment Act, 1931, Canada, 112.

Copyright Order Confirmation (Mechanical Instruments: Royalties) Act, 1928, Great Britain, 85.

Dramatic and Musical Performers' Protection Act, 1928, Great Britain, 111.

Fine Arts Copyright Act, 1928, Great Britain, 90.

France Constitution, Articles 26–28 —, 91.

Law of 1791, France, 94, 99.

Netherlands Constitution, Article 66 —, 76.

Rome Convention Copyright Order, 1933, Great Britain, 79.

Order in Council, 1915, Great Britain, 79–80.
Statute of Anne (1710), Great Britain, 78.
United Kingdom Copyright Act, 1911, § 1 —, 79, 81, 82, 83, 88, 94, 95, 96; § 2 —, 82, 89; § 3 —, 85–86; § 4 —, 86; § 5 —, 87; § 11 —, 88; § 13 —, 82; § 15 —, 87; § 16, 86; § 17, 81–82, 84; § 18 —, 86; § 19 —, 85, 86, 95; § 21 —, 86; § 35 —, 80, 98.

UNIVERSAL COPYRIGHT CONVENTION

Universal Copyright Convention (1952), Article 2 —, 78; Article 9 —, 77.
—, Appendix Declaration relating to Article XVII —, 78.

TABLE OF CASES CITED

UNITED STATES

Alden-Rochelle, Inc. v. ASCAP, 80 F. Supp. 888 (S.D.N.Y. 1948), 31–32.

Amended Consent Judgment, ASCAP, civil action No. 13–95, entered March 14, 1950 (S.D.N.Y.), 31, 33–34, 37, 54, 56, 60–61, 63, 65, 112, 128–137, 147.

American Tobacco Co. v. Werckmeister, 207 U.S. 284 (1907), 16.

Associated Music Publishers, Inc. v. Debs Memorial Radio Fund, Inc., 141 F. 2d 852 (2d Cir. 1944), 25, 26.

Basevi v. O'Toole Co., Inc., 26 F. Supp. 41 (S.D.N.Y. 1939), 10.

Irving Berlin, Inc. v. Daigle v. Russo, 31 F. 2d 832 (5th Cir. 1929), 26.

BMI and Edward B. Marks Music Corp. v. Deems Taylor, as President of ASCAP, et al., 55 N.Y.S. 2d 94 (Sup. Ct. 1945), 61, 125.

Buck v. Jewell-LaSalle Realty Co., 283 U.S. 191 (1931), 24.

Burrow-Giles Lith. v. Sarony, 111 U.S. 53 (1884), 6.

Caruthers v. R.K.O., 20 F. Supp. 906 (S.D.N.Y. 1937), 8.

Consent Decree, ASCAP, civil action No. 13–95, entered March 4, 1941 (S.D.N.Y.), 32, 41, 43.

Deward & Rich, Inc. v. Bristol Savings & Loan Corp., 120 F. 2d 537 (4th Cir. 1941), 9.

Falk v. Gast, 54 Fed. 890 (2d Cir. 1893), 8.

Famous Music Corporation v. Melz, 28 F. Supp. 767 (W.D. La. 1939), 26.

Ferris v. Frohman, 233 U.S. 424 (1912), 8, 14.

Fitch v. Shubert, 20 F. Supp. 314 (S.D.N.Y. 1937), 13.

Fred Fisher Music Co. v. M. Witmark & Sons, 318 U.S. 643 (1943), 13.

Foreign Consent Judgment, ASCAP, civil action No. 42–245, entered March 14, 1950 (S.D.N.Y.), 124, 138–142.

Golding v. R.K.O., 77 USPQ 415 (Cal. App. 1948), 8.

174 TABLE OF CASES CITED

Heim v. Universal Pictures Co., 154 F. 2d 480 (2d Cir. 1946), 10.
Herbert v. Shanley, 229 Fed. 340 (2d Cir. 1916), 22.
Herbert v. Shanley, 242 U.S. 591 (1917), 23, 25, 26.
Interstate Hotel of Nebraska v. Remick Music Corp., 157 F. 2d 744 (8th Cir. 1946), 26.
Jerome v. Twentieth Century-Fox Film Corp., 67 F. Supp. 736 (S.D.N.Y. 1946), 18.
Leigh v. Barnhart, 96 F. Supp. 194 (D.N.J. 1951), 10.
McCarthy & Fischer v. White, 259 Fed. 364 (S.D.N.Y. 1919), 8, 14.
Modified Consent Decree, BMI, civil action No. 459, entered May 14, 1941 (E.D.Wisc.), 44, 50, 148–153.
National Comics Publications, Inc. v. Fawcett Publications, Inc., 191 F. 2d 594 (2d Cir. 1951), 11.
Patterson v. Century Productions, Inc., 93 F. 2d 489 (2d Cir. 1937), 15.
Photodrama v. Social Uplift Film Corp., 220 Fed. 448 (2d Cir. 1915), 8.
Pushman v. New York Graphic Society, Inc., 287 N.Y. 302 (1942), 8.
Jerome H. Remick & Co. v. American Automobile Accessories Co., 5 F. 2d 411 (6th Cir. 1925), 24, 25.
Shapiro, Bernstein & Co. v. Miracle Record Co., 91 F. Supp. 473 (N.D. Ill. 1950),17, 18, 19, 20, 21, 82.
Uproar Co. v. National Boadcasting Co., 8 F. Supp. 358 (D. Mass. 1934), 14.
U.S. v. ASCAP, civil action No. 13–95, Amended Final Judgment (S.D.N.Y. 1950), 31, 33–34, 37, 54, 56, 60–61, 63, 65, 128–137, 147.
U.S. v. ASCAP, civil action No. 13–95, Consent Decree (S.D.N.Y. 1941) 32, 41, 43.
U.S. v. ASCAP, civil action No. 42–245, Foreign Consent Decree (S.D.N.Y. 1950), 124, 138–142.
U.S. v. ASCAP, E 78–388, S.D.N.Y. (1934), 27, 29, 41, 42.
U.S. v. BMI, civil action No. 459, Modified Consent Decree (E.D.Wisc. 1941), 44, 50, 148–153.
Vargas v. Esquire, 164 F. 2d 522 (7th Cir. 1947), 91.
Washingtonian Pub. Co. v. Pearson, 306 U.S. 30 (1939), 10, 11.
Wheaton v. Peters, 8 Pet. 591 (U.S. 1834), 5, 9.

White v. Kimmell, 193 F. 744 (9th Cir. 1952), 15.

White-Smith Music Publishing Co. v. Apollo Co., 209 U.S. 1 (1908), 10, 17, 20.

Yacoubian v. Carroll, 74 USPQ 257 (S.D. Cal. 1947), 10, 17, 18, 19, 20, 21.

Europe

A.V.R.O. v. BUMA, Hooge Raad, March 4, 1938 (Nederlandsche Jurisprudentie 1938, no. 948, annotated by Prof. P. Scholten), 99.

Boosey v. Whight, 1 Ch. 122 (1900), 83.

Donaldson v. Beckett, 4 Burrows 2303 (K.B. 1769), 5.

Donaldson v. Beckett, 4 Burrows 2408 (H.L. 1774), 5, 79.

Francis, Day & Co. v. Feldman & Co., 2 Ch. 728 (1914) 75.

GEMA v. Tuschinski's Explotatie Maatschappij, Hooge Raad, February 13, 1936 (Nederlandsche Jurisprudentie 1936, no. 443, annotated by Prof. E. M. Meijers), 118.

Gramophone Co. Ltd. v. Carwardine & Co., 1 Ch. 450 (1934), 95.

Halevy v. Rouart-Lerolle, D.P. 1932, 1. 29 note by M. Nast, cited in Mak, Rights Affecting the Manufacture and Use of Gramophone Records 49 (1952); Laurens, *The Idea of Destination in the Turning to Account of Intellectual Works*, 3 Revue Internationale du Droit d'Auteur 40 (April, 1954), 95.

Frans Lehar v. P. Verbeek, Hooge Raad, May 6, 1938 (Nederlandsche Jurisprudentie 1938, No. 635, annotated by Prof. E. M. Meijers), 99.

Sté "Le Chant du Monde" v. Sté Fox Europa et al., Paris Court of Appeals (1st Chamber), Jan. 13, 1953, cited in Inter-Auteurs, no. 112, p. 124 (1953), 92.

Macdonald v. Eyles, 1 Ch. 631 (1921), 102.

Margaret Mitchell (Marsh) v. N.V. Zuid-Hollandsche Boek- en Handelsdrukkerij, Hooge Raad, May 23, 1941 (Nederlandsche Jurisprudentie 1941, no. 931, annotated by Prof. E. M. Meijers), 74, 91.

Messager v. British Broadcasting Co., 2 K.B. 543 (1927), 98.

Monckton v. Gramophone Co., 106 L.T. 84 (1912).

Performing Right Society, Ltd. v. Hammond's Bradford Brewery Co., Ch. 121 (1934), 98, 99.

SACEM v. Kubler, D. 1946. J. 335, cited in Desbois, Le Droit d'Auteur 405 (1950), 99.

Sims v. Marryat, 17 Q.B. 281, (1851) 102.

A. H. S. Ward v. de Handelsvennootschap onder de firma Uitgeversmaatschappij "de Combinatie", Arrondissements Rechtbank, Rotterdam, April 29, 1935; Hooge Raad, June 26, 1936 (Nederlandsche Jurisprudentie 1936, no. 1059, annotated by Prof. E. M. Meijers), 73, 74, 91.

University of London Press, Ltd. v. University Tutorial Press, Ltd., 2 Ch. 601 (1916), 88.

Vereeniging Het Genootschap van Nederlandsche Componisten v. Amersfoortsche Radiocentrale, Hooge Raad, April 30, 1930 (Nederlandsche Jurisprudentie 1931, p. 53, annotated by Prof. E. M. Meijers), 100.

Warne v. Seebohm, 39 Ch. D. 73 (1888), 89.

TABLE OF WORKS CITED

United States

Articles of Association of the American Society of Composers, Authors and Publishers, as in effect June 1, 1950, 35, 36, 37, 40, 54.
ASCAP, The ASCAP Story (1950), 55.
—, Third Copyright Law Symposium (1940), 36.
Ball, The Law of Copyright and Literary Property (1944), 30.
Billboard, December 20, 1952, 59.
—, October 31, 1953, 63.
Broadcasting-Telecasting, October 27, 1952, 28, 44.
Burton, *Business Practices in the Copyright Field*, 7 Copyright Problems Analyzed 87 (1952), 19, 49.
Farmer, *The Perils of (Publisher) Pauline-Or the Peculiar Problems of Book Publishers Featuring Copyright, Defamation and Right of Privacy*, 7 Copyright Problems Analyzed 119 (1952), 75, 76, 81.
Finkelstein, *Public Performance Rights in Music and Performance Societies*, 7 Copyright Problems Analyzed 69 (1952), 29, 55.
—, *The Composer and the Public Interest — Regulation of Performing Right Societies*, 19 Law and Contemporary Problems 275 (1954), 31.
—, *Marketing of the Arts, Anti-Trust Laws and the Arts*, U. of Chicago Law School Conference on the Arts Publishing and the Law (March 5, 1952), 55, 56.
Hearings before Subcommittee on the Judiciary, House of Rep., 82nd Cong., 2nd session, on H.R. 5473, part 2, 28.
Howell, The Copyright Law (3d ed. 1952), 12, 14–15, 20.
Karp, *Copyright Litigation*, 7 Copyright Problems Analyzed 143 (1952), 8.
Klein, *Protective Societies for Authors and Creators*, 1953 Copyright Problems Analyzed 19 (1953), 29, 51.
1 Ladas, The International Protection of Literary and Artistic Property (1938), 73.

2 Ladas, The International Protection of Literary and Artistic Property (1938), 10, 90–91, 92.
McDonald, *Law of Broadcasting*, 7 Copyright Problems Analyzed 31 (1952), 17, 18.
Miller and Mills, *ASCAP-NAB Controversy, The Issues*, 11 Air L.R. 394 (1940), 41, 42, 43.
New York Times, March 7, 1941, 43.
—, March 9, 1941, 44.
—, February 22, 1953, 123.
Reeves, *Superman v. Captain Marvel or, Loss of Literary Property in Comic Strips*, ASCAP Copyright Symposium Number 5, p. 3 (1954), 5.
Schulman, *Author's Rights*, 7 Copyright Problems Analyzed 19 (1952), 7, 8, 9.
Shaw, Lingo of Tin Pan Alley (1950), 49, 51.
Tannenbaum, *Practical Problems in Copyright*, 7 Copyright Problems Analyzed 7 (1952), 8, 15, 85.
Timberg, *The Antitrust Aspects of Merchandising Modern Music: The ASCAP Consent Judgment of 1950*, 19 Law and Contemporary Problems 294 (1954), 65.
Variety, October 17, 1951, 64.
—, February 4, 1953, 46, 64.
—, March 11, 1953, 50, 52, 55, 58, 64.
—, April 8, 1953, 28, 44.
—, July 29, 1953, 45.
—, August 5, 1953, 31.
—, November 11, 1953, 44.
—, December 30, 1953, 32.
—, March 10, 1954, 58.
White, *Musical Copyrights v. the Anti-Trust Laws*, 30 Nebraska L.R. 50 (1950), 42.

Europe

Buma Report for 1953, 120.
Copinger, The Law of Copyright (7th ed. Skone James, 1936), 82.
—, The Law of Copyright (8th ed., Skone James, 1948), 69, 76, 77, 80, 83, 84, 95.
Desbois, Le Droit d'Auteur (1950), 96, 99.
Droit d'Auteur (1954), 69.

DUTCH POPULAR MUSIC, 123.
HIRSCH-BALLIN, COPYRIGHT PROTECTION OF AMERICAN BOOKS IN THE NETHERLANDS (1950), 75.
INTER-AUTEURS, no. 112 (1953), 92.
JAMES, CHARLES F., THE STORY OF THE PERFORMING RIGHT SOCIETY (1951), 101.
Laurens, *The Idea of Destination in the Turning to Account of Intellectual Works*, 3 REVUE INTERNATIONALE DU DROIT D'AUTEUR 36 (April, 1954), 95, 96.
MAK, RIGHTS AFFECTING THE MANUFACTURE AND USE OF GRAMOPHONE RECORDS (1952), 95, 97, 121.
Panhuys, *The Netherlands Constitution and International Law*, 47 AMERICAN JOURNAL OF INTERNATIONAL LAW 537 (1953), 76.
Parès, *The French Conception of Copyright*, 2 REVUE INTERNATIONALE DU DROIT D'AUTEUR (Jan., 1954), 89, 90.
PRS Articles of Association, as amended 25th June 1953, 102, 103, 104, 108.
—, Pamphlet H, 103.
REPORT OF THE COPYRIGHT COMMITTEE TO PARLIAMENT, Cmd 8662 (London, 1952), 73, 82, 90, 99, 110, 112–113.
Tournier, *Judgment of Brussels of May 9, 1953 on the Broadcasting of Gramophone Records*, 1 REVUE INTERNATIONALE DU DROIT D'AUTEUR 10 (Oct., 195.), 96, 97.
Wiessing, *La BUMA*, INTER-AUTEURS, no. 109 (1952), 115.
1 WORLD COPYRIGHT (Pinner ed. 1953), 92, 102.

UNESCO

2 UNESCO Copyright Bulletin nos. 2–3 (1949), 90, 92.
4 UNESCO Copyright Bulletin nos. 1–2 (1951), 5, 91.
5 UNESCO Copyright Bulletin nos. 3–4 (1952), 78.

INDEX

Abandonment of rights, 17; *see also* Dedication to the public.
Abroad: American copyright and works published, 10–12; British, Dutch, French nationals published, 91; *see also* Berne Convention, Universal Copyright Convention.
Ad interim copyright, *see* Copyright — ad interim.
"adherents", 116, 117.
Advertisers, *see* Sponsored broadcasting.
Affiliated broadcasting stations, *see* Broadcasting-networks.
Alien authors: and American copyright, 9–12, 21; and British copyright, 79.
Alterations, 89–91.
American Arbitration Association, 59.
American Book Publishers Council, 75.
American Composers Alliance, 48.
American Performing Right Society, Inc., 48.
American Society of Composers, Authors and Publishers: 27, 36, 41; affiliation with, and BMI, 45–46, 62; annual dues, 37; appeal system, 36, 59; assignments from members, 30, 31, 40, 45, 53–54, 60, 61, 143–146; Board of Appeals, 36; Board of Directors, 34–35, 36, 37, 56; BMI controversy, 40–44, 59, 64; calculation of performances, 38–39; catalog, 42, 56; Classification Committees for royalties, 36; consent decrees, 28, 31–32, 33–34, 37, 41, 43, 54, 55, 59, 60–61, 63, 65, 107, 112, 124, 128–142, 147; consent judgments, *see* ASCAP — consent decrees; domestic royalties, 28, 34, 35; Executive Committee, 34; foreign societies, 39, 94, 138–142; formation of, 27–30; government control — *see* ASCAP-consent decrees; income, 28, 31, 44, 58, 64; Impartial Chairman, 36; licensees, types of, 31; license fees subject to regulation, 34, 55–56; licenses generally, 27, 30, 33, 34, 41, 54–57; licenses not affected by withdrawals from membership, 40; licenses only nondramatic rights, 30–31; licenses to broadcasters, 24–25, 30–31, 32–33, 34, 40–44, 54–57, 59; licenses for motion pictures, 31–32, 33–34; management, 34–35, 56; membership, 29–30, 56, 64, 147; membership requirements, 37, 147; Nominating Committees, 35; Panel, 36; posthumous membership, 29, 34–35; President, 34; program analysis, 38, 39, 53, 58–59; promotional work, 63; publishers and film producers, 56, 64; Relief Fund, 36–37; repertory, 129; reserve fund, 35–36; royalties, 35–36, 37–40, 50–51, 57–58, 59, 60–61, 63, 64, 94, 147; subsidies to standard music, 38, 39, 40; tax benefit, 58; voting rights, 34–35, 36, 147; withdrawal from, 40, 60–61, 62.
AMP, *see* Associated Music Publishers.
Annual dues, ASCAP, 37;.
Antimonopoly law, *see* ASCAP-consent decrees, BMI-consent decree.
Antitrust law, *see* ASCAP-consent decrees, BMI-consent decree.
Application for renewal and extension of copyright, 12, 14.
Arbitration, 59, 120.
Arrangements, copyrighted, 40, 109.
Art gallery, 16.
ASCAP, *see* American Society of Composers, Authors and Publishers.
Assignee, *see* Assignment.
Assignment: of contingent rights and expectancies, 13, 30, 102, 118; of copyright, 9, 10–11, 13, 87–88, 90–91; of publishing rights, 10–11; with reservation of rights, 11; *see also* ASCAP-assignments, BMI-assignments, BUMA-assignments, PRS-assignments.
Associated Music Publishers, 49.
Authorization, *see* Consent.
Authorship, right to claim, 89–91.
Background music, 40.

INDEX

Ball, Horace, 30.
Ballrooms, see Dance halls.
Bands, see Orchestras.
BBC, see British Broadcasting Company.
Beith, Ian Hay 1.
Belgium: phonograph records and publication, 73.
Berlin, Irving, 35.
Berne Convention: 69; Berlin Revision, 69; Brussels Revision, 69; Rome Revision, 69; basic principle, 69–71; Belgian interpretation of publication, 73; broadcasting, 72; British interpretation, 76, 79–81; compliance by members, 76; copies, 72–73; country of origin, definition of, 70; definition of publication, 72; duration of protection, 76–77; Dutch interpretation of publication, 73–75; extent of protection, 71; first publication, importance of place of, 69–72, 77; formalities, 71; French interpretation of publication, 73; gramophone records, 72–73; literary work, 72; member countries, 69; moral right, 90; motion pictures, 72–73; national treatment, concept of, 70–71; non-Union authors, protection of, 70–71, 72, 77, 92; restrictions on non-Union nationals, 70, 71; retaliation against non-Union countries, 71, 77; rights in countries not country of origin, 69–70; rights in country of origin of work, 70–71; simultaneous publication, 70; Universal Copyright Convention, 78; unpublished works, protection of, 69–70, 71, 77; withdrawal, consequences of, 78.
Berne Union, see Berne Convention.
B.I.E.M., see Bureau International de l'Edition Mechanique.
Blanket licenses, see ASCAP-licenses to broadcasters.
Board of Appeals, ASCAP, 36.
Bodenhausen, G. H. C., 117.
Books, see Common law, Copyright, Manufacturing Clause, Manuscript, Registration.
BMI, see Broadcast Music, Inc.
Britico, see British Copyright Protection Co., Ltd.
British Copyright Protection Co., Ltd., 110, 111.
Broadcasting: Britain, 109–110; differences between the United States and Europe, 25–26; 32–33; is a public performance for profit, 24–26, 40–41, 99; mechanical reproduction right and, 95–96, 97, 98, 114; Netherlands, 119; networks, 32–33, 42–44, 46–47, 50, 58–59, 64, 109; nonprofit, 25–26; number of stations in the United States, 32, 40, 58; of a work is not publication, 14, 16, 72; operas, 31, 114; radio-receiving set in public, 24, 99–100; relay station and peformance, 100; right of, 24, 98–99; see also ASCAP, BMI.
Broadcast Music, Inc.: affiliation with, and ASCAP, 45–46, 62; arbitration of disputes with grantors, 59; ASCAP controversy, 40–44, 59, 64; assignments from publishers, 45, 47–48, 52, 53–54, 57, 59, 60, 61–62, 154–160; assignments from writers, 44–48, 49, 51, 52, 53–54, 57, 59, 60, 61–62, 161–170; Board of Directors, 56; catalog, 48, 49, 50, 56; consent decree, 44, 50, 65, 112, 148–153; contractual restrictions, 46, 47, 52, 59; foreign rights, 52–53; formation of, 28, 42, 44; government control, see BMI-consent decree; gross income, 28, 44; guarantee, 53, 57, 63; licenses, 41, 44, 48, 49, 53–55, 56–57, 59; motion pictures, 46, 57; private nature of, 42, 46, 50, 56, 63–64. program analysis, 53, 58–59; promotional work, 63; publishing department, 48–49; royalties, 46, 47, 48, 49, 50–53, 57–58, 59, 61–62, 63–64; subsidies to standard music, 44, 48, 49; termination of affiliation, 62; theatrical productions, 46; warranties from writers and publishers, 48; publisher's contract with BMI writer, 61–62.
BUMA, see Het Bureau Voor Muziek-Auteursrecht.
Bureau International de l'Edition Mechanique, 96, 110, 114, 124.
Bureau Letterkunde van de Stichting tot Exploitatie en Bescherming van Auteursrechten, 123.
Bureau Theaterrechten van de Stichting tot Exploitatie en Bescherming van Auteursrechten, 28, 123.
Burken, Nathan, 29.
Burton, Robert J., 19, 49.
Canada, simultaneous publication in, 73–74, 76.
Canadian Copyright Appeal Board, 112.

182 INDEX

CBS, *see* Columbia Broadcasting System.
Certificate of copyright, *see* Claim of copyright.
Chappells Music, 111.
Children of the author, 12, 37.
Cinematography, *see* Motion Pictures.
CISAC, *see* Confédération Internationale des Sociétés d'Auteur et Compositeurs.
Citizenship of author, 9–10.
Civil suits under the antitrust laws, 31–32, 44, 56.
Claim of copyright, 7, 11, 21.
Classical music, *see* Standard music.
Classification Committee of ASCAP for royalties, 36.
Coin-operated machines, *see* Juke box.
Collaborations, *see* Joint Works.
Colliers, 73.
Columbia Broadcasting System, 42, 64.
Columbia Records, 64.
Commercial exhibition of motion pictures, 14–16.
Commercial broadcasting, *see* Sponsored broadcasting.
Common law protection: by individual states, 5, 6, 7, 8; description of, 8, 2; differences between, and copyright, 21, 22; dramas, 8; duration of, 8–9, 21; extent of, 8, 17, 18, 21, 22; fair use, 8; honor and reputation, 90–91; musical compositions, 8, 16–21; necessity of, 6; performance rights, 8, 18–19, 21, 22; phonograph records, 16–21, 83; purpose of, 9; United States, background of, 5, 6, 7; who may secure, 9, 21; *see also* Copyright, Public domain, Publication.
Competition: in performing rights. 28, 31–32, 65; *see also* ASCAP, BMI.
Composite work, 12.
Compulsory licensing, 18–19, 47, 85, 92, 114.
Congress, 5, 6, 13, 18, 24, 28, 32, 105.
Confédération Internationale des Sociétés d'Auteurs et Compositeurs, 123–124.
Consent: copying without, 7, 111; public performance without, 23, 24, 27, 96, 111; publication without, 7, 111; use without, 7, 22, 96, 111.
Consent decrees, *see* ASCAP-consent decrees, BMI-consent decree.
Consent judgments, *see* ASCAP-consent decrees, BMI-consent decrees
Contingent rights, 13, 30.
Contract to assign, 30.

Conventions, *see* Berne Convention, Universal Copyright Convention.
Copies: and copyright notice, 6–7, 9, 10, 17–20; and exhibition of a film, 84–85; and phonograph records, 17–20, 72–73, 81–84; definition of, 17–20, 84; deposit of, 7, 11, 12, 20, 87; *see also* Sale — as part of publication.
Copying, 7, 88–89, 95.
Copyright: ad interim, 6–7, 11–12; broadcasting, right of, 24, 98–99; differences between, and common law, 21, 22; duration of, in Britain, 79, 81–82, 84, 85–86, 95; duration of, in the Netherlands, 92–93; duration of, in France, 92; duration of, in the United States, 5, 7–8, 11–12, 17, 21, 79; duration of, under Berne Convention, 72, 76–77; fair use, 8; in record manufacturer, 85, 95, 98, 110–113; interpretation of public performance for profit, 24–26; music performing right, 8, 22–24; notice, 6–7, 8–9, 10, 11, 12, 14, 16–21, 49, 71, 87; phonograph records, 18–21, 22–23, 81, 83, 85, 86, 91, 92–93, 94, 95–97, *see also* Copyright — in record manufacturer; protection, extent of, 18, 22; retaining, 7, 9, 10, 11, 17, 20, 21, 84; securing, in The United States, 6–7, 8, 10, 11–12, 19–20, 21, 84; Statutory, Europe generally, 5, 6; statutory, United States generally, 5, 6; subject matter in Britain, 88; subject matter in the Netherlands, 91; subject matter in the United States, 6; voidance of, 7; who may secure, 9–10, 21; *see also* Common law, Public domain, Berne Convention, Unpublished works, Manufacturing clause.
Copyright Office, 7, 11, 12, 20, 21.
Copyrighted arrangements, 40, 52.
"Cornball", 64.
Country of origin, definition of, 70.
Criticism, 89.
"Cue sheet," 106.
Current Performance Fund, *see* ASCAP-royalties.
"Cut-ins," 50–51.
Dance halls, 41, 54–55, 56.
"dance tune," 110.
Date of First Publication, *see* Publication — date of first.
Dedication to the public, 15, 19; *see also* Abandonment.

Deposit of copies, *see* Copies — deposit.
Desbois, Henri, 96.
Destination, relation between, and price, 97;.
Disk Jockey, 59, 64.
Distribution of motion pictures, *see* Motion pictures.
Distribution of phonograph records, *see* Phonograph records.
Distribution to the Public, *see* Public — distribution.
Documentation in the Netherlands for Music, *see* DONEMUS.
Domicile of author, 9, 21.
DONEMUS, 48, 123.
Drama: common law protection of, 8; public performance societies, 27–28; *see also* Dramatic performance — rights and BMI, Public performance.
Dramatic Performance: distinction between, and non-dramatic, 30–31; rights and BMI, 44–45, 46, 53–54, 57; rights reserved by ASCAP members, 30–31, 57.
Dramatico-musical works, PRS definition of, 102–103; *see also* Public performance.
Droit moral, *see* Moral right.
Dual membership, 62.
Dutch: association of men of letters, 116; composers and authors of light music, trade union of, 116; composers of serious music, trade union of, 115; music dealers and publishers association, 115; music performed, amount of, 120.
Dutch Popular Music, 123.
Éditées, 73–74, 75, 76.
Édition, 95.
English language books, *see* Manufacturing clause.
Equitable rights, 7, 61, 102.
European copyright statutes generally, 5, 6.
Exhibition: of motion pictures, 14–16, 72, 102–103; of paintings, 15–16, 91.
Exhibitor, film, 14–16, 31–32, 33–34.
Duration of copyright, *see* Copyright — duration of.
Employer for hire, 13.
Extension of copyright, 12.
Equity, 7, 61.
Exclusive Assignments, 44–45, 47–48, 59.
Exclusive rights, 5, 17, 18, 22, 47–48, 59.

Exhibition, public, 14–16, 21.
Fair dealing, *see* Fair use.
Fair use, 8. 88–89, 92.
Farmer, Arthur E., 75, 76, 81.
Federal Communications Commission, 33.
Federal Court for the Southern District of New York, 34, 54, 55, 59.
Fédération des Sociétés de Droits d'Exécution (performing rights), 124.
Fédération des Sociétés de Droits de Représentation (dramatic rights), 124.
Fédération des Sociétés de Droits de Reproduction Mechanique (mechanical rights), 124.
Fédération des Sociétés de Gens de Lettres (literary rights), 124.
Films, *see* Motion pictures.
Finkelstein, Herman, 29, 55, 63.
First publication, *see* Publication—first.
Folios, 49.
Foreign authors, protection of, in the United States, 9–12; *see also* Berne Convention and Universal Copyright Convention for foreign authors generally.
Foreign origin, 11–12.
Formalities, 7–8, 9, 11–12, 21, 71, 87, 92; *see also* Copies — deposit, Copyright — notice, Registration.
France: Constitution and Berne Convention, 91; moral right, 89–90; publications abroad, 91, 92; phonograph records and publication, 73; unpublished works of non-Union authors, 92.
Fu Manchu 73.
Future works, assignments of, 30, 102, 118.
General publication, 15.
Genootschap van Nederlandsche Componisten, 115.
Gone With The Wind, 74–75.
Government: supervision of broadcasting, 33, 118; and performing right societies, *see* ASCAP — consent decrees, BMI — consent decree, Tribunal, BUMA—government control.
Gramophone records, *see* Phonograph records.
"Grand" performing right, 31; *see also* Dramatic performance, Dramatico-musical compositions.
Great Britain; Berne Convention, 76.
Hay, Ian 1.

INDEX

Heirs of author, 9, 87, 92.
Herbert, Victor, 25, 29.
Het Bureau Voor Muziek-Auteursrecht: "adherents", 116, 117; assignments from adherents, 118–119; Board of Directors (General Council), 116–117; catalog, 115, 116; cultural activities, 123; Executive Committee, 117, 118; expenses, 122; Directeur (General Manager), 117; formation of, 115; Government Commissioner (*Regerings-Commissaris*), 117–118; government control, 115–118; licenses, 119, 122; management, 116–118; membership, 115, 116; membership requirements, 116; President, 117; programs, 119–120, 122; royalties, 120–122.
Hilversum I and II, 119.
Hirsch-Ballin, E. D., 75.
Holmes, Justice Oliver Wendell, 25, 26.
"home movies", 85.
Howell, Herbert A., 14, 20.
Impartial Chairman, ASCAP, 36.
Implied license, 24.
Import of foreign works into the United States, *see* Manufacturing clause.
"Independent" broadcasting station, *see* "Local" broadcasting station.
Infringement: proceedings, deposit and registration in, 7, 11, 20; willful, 88; must be substantial, 88–89.
Interim fee, 34.
"Intermediary," performing right, *see* Performing Right Societies.
International copyright, *see* Foreign authors, Berne Convention, Universal Copyright Convention.
International Copyright Union, *see* Berne Convention.
International Union for the Protection of Literary and Artistic Works, *see* Berne Convention.
Issuance to the public, *see* Public — distribution.
James, Charles F., 100–101.
Johnson, Thor, 123.
Joint venture, 61.
Joint works, 37–38, 48, 59.
Juke box: exception, reason for, 23–24; licensing in Britain, 105; performance is not for profit, 22–24, 94.
Karp, Joseph D., 8.
Kefauver, Senator Estes, 105.
Ladas, Stephen P., 10, 90–91.
Leasing of motion pictures, 15, 16.
Library of Congress, 7.

Libel of author through alterations, 91.
Licenses: from ASCAP members individually, 31; implied, 24; *see also* ASCAP — licenses, BMI-licenses.
Limited publication, 15.
Listener license, *see* Tax.
Literary property right, *see* Common law protection-description of.
Literary works: public performance of, 23, 72; *see also* Books, Manufacturing Clause, Manuscript, Publication, Common Law, Copyright.
"Local" broadcasting Station, 32–33, *see also* Broadcasting — networks.
Mak, W., 97, 121.
Manufacturing clause, 11–12, 71, 87.
Manuscript, 5, 7, 8, 9, 15, 16, 84, 87.
E. B. Marks Music Corp., 40, 61.
McDonald, Joseph A., 18.
MCPS, *see* Mechanical Copyright Protection Society.
Mechanical contrivances, *see* Mechanical rights, Phonograph records.
Mechanical Copyright Protection Society, 110, 111.
Mechanical reproduction, right of, *see* Mechanical rights.
Mechanical rights, 11, 17, 18, 33–34, 83–84, 85, 93, 94, 95–96; *see also* Phonograph records, Motion pictures — sound track.
Membership in two societies, 62.
Metro-Goldwyn-Mayer, 64.
M-G-M, *see* Metro-Goldwyn-Mayer.
Miller, Neville, 41, 43.
Mills, E. C., 42.
Monopoly by performing right societies, 28, 31–32, 112–113, 116, 124; *see also* ASCAP-consent decrees, BMI-consent decree.
Moral right, 89–91.
Motion pictures: and BMI, 46; and European societies, 107; distribution of, 14–16, 72–73, 91; exhibition of, 14-16, 33–34, 46, 72, 107; performance right, definition of, 129; registration of, 7; sound track part of mechanical right, 16, 18; restrictions on licensing sound track of, 33–34, 107; sound track, right to license, distinct from performing right, 26, 56–57.
Motion picture producers: with affiliated music publishing companies, 35, 56, 64; licenses from ASCAP, 33–34, 35, 56–57, 107.
Motion picture theatres, licenses from ASCAP, 31–34, 107.

Multiplications, 93.
Music: common law protection of, 8, 17–21, 22; registration of, 7; novelty, 49; right to vend sheet, distinct from performing right, 26; sheet, affect of broadcasting on sale of, 43; sheet, manufacturing clause not applicable to, 11–12; sheet, royalties, 29; statutory provision, 6; see also, Background music, Musical comedies, Phonograph records, Public performance, Standard music.
Music publisher, see ASCAP, BMI.
Musical comedies, 45, 46, 54, 57.
Musicians' Union (Britain), 110–113.
MUZAK, 31, 33.
NAB, see National Association of Broadcasters.
National Association of Broadcasters, 41, 42, 44.
National Ballroom Operators Association, 41, 54–55.
National Broadcasting Co., 42.
National treatment, principle of, 70–71, 78.
Nationality of author, 9, 21, 69–72, 79–80, 91.
NBC, see National Broadcasting Company.
Nederlandse Vereniging van Letterkundigen, 116.
Netherlands: Constitution and Berne Convention, 76; Minister of Justice, 115–118; publication, definition of, 73–75; publications abroad, 91, 92; unpublished works of non-Union authors, 92.
Networks, see Broadcasting – networks
Newspaper summary, 89.
Next of kin of author, 12.
Noncommercial exhibition of motion pictures, 14–16.
Non-dramatic: formation of societies for, public performance of music, 27–28, 44–45; public performance of literary works, 23; performances, distinction between, and dramatic, 30–31; see also ASCAP — assignments, BMI — assignments, HUMA — assignments PRS — assignments.
Non-exclusive: assignments to ASCAP, 31, 54, 59; rights and BMI, 47–48, 59; see also Compulsory licensing.
Non-existing works, assignments of, 30, 102.
Nonprofit broadcasting, 25–26. performing right society, definition of, 29; public performance of music, see Public performance — nonprofit.
Nonresident alien authors, 9, 21.
Non-sponsored broadcasts, 26.
Non-Union authors, see Berne Convention.
Non-Union countries, see Berne Convention.
Notice, copyright, see Copyright-notice.
Novelty compositions, 49.
Onze Lichte Muziek, 123.
Openbaarmaking, 93.
Opera, 31, 45, 54, 57.
Orchestras, 55, 63–64.
Orders in Council, 76, 79–80.
Originality, meaning of, 88.
Our Light Music, 123.
Owned and operated stations, 33.
Painting, public exhibition of a, 15–16, 91.
Panel, ASCAP, 36.
Parés, Philippe, 89, 90.
Parliament, 83–84.
Paternity, right of, 89–91.
"payolas," 50–51.
Per Program licenses, see ASCAP Licenses to Broadcasters.
Percentage-of-receipts license, 32, 41, 42, 43–44.
Performance, see Public Performance.
Performing right fees, 27, 55–56, see also ASCAP-licenses, BMI-licenses, BUMA-licenses, PRS-licenses, SACEM-licenses.
Performing right, PRS definition of, 102.
Performing right societies: formation of the French society (SACEM), 27–28; government control of, see ASCAP-consent decrees, BMI-consent decrees, BUMA-government control Canadian Copyright Appeal Board; reason for and function of, 27–28, 124; reciprocal contracts, 124; reserving rights for, 11; see also ASCAP, BMI, BUMA, PRS, SACEM.
Performing Right Society, Ltd.: associate memberhsip, 101–102; British Broadcasting Company, dispute with, 112; exclusive assignments of present and future non-dramatic rights, 102–104; extent of operations 103; formation of, 100–101; Directors, 101; General Council, 101; General Manager, 101; income and

expense, 104–105, 106; licenses, 104, 105, 112; licenseees, 104, 107; management, 101; membership, 101; President, 101; programs, 105–106, 107; royalties, 105, 106, 107–108, 109–110; Tribunal for disputes with users, 112–113; warranties from members, 103; voting, 101–102, 108.
Period of Protection, see Copyright-duration of.
Periodicals, manufacturing clause applicable to, 11–12.
"performers' right", 111.
Permission, see Consent.
Perpetual protection, 8–9, 21, 81–84.
Personality, right of, 89–91.
Petit droit, 27, 30.
Phonographic Performance, Ltd., 110–113.
Phonograph records: compulsory license and statutory royalties, 18–19, 47, 85, 114; manufacturers copyright in, 85, 95, 98; not copies, 17–20, 72–73, 81–84; right to vend, distinct from performing right, 26, 95–96, 97; performance part of publication right, 94, 95–97, 98, 114; sale and distribution of, and publication, 16–21, 72–73, 81–84, 91, 92–93, 95–96, 97; affect of broadcasting on, 43, 64, 110, see also Copyright — in phonograph records.
"Policing" public performances, 27.
Posthumous Publication, see Publication — posthumously.
Power of attorney, 104, 118–119.
PPL, see Phonographic Performance, Ltd.
Presidential proclamation, see Proclamation.
Private Performance, 25; see also Public Performance.
Private: study, 89; use, 96.
Proclamation, Presidential, 10, 21.
Profit: public performance of music for, see Public performance of music for profit.
Prompt deposit, failure of, 7.
PRS, see Performing Right Society, Ltd.
Public: distribution and publication, 6–9, 14–21, 72–76, 80, 81–84, 91, 92–93, 97; exhibition, 14–16; making work known to the, 5, 14, 82, 94, 100; see also Publication, Sale.
Public Performance: and motion pictures, 14–16, 21, 33–34, 46, 72–73, 84, 91, 107; broadcasting is a, 24–26, 98–99; Dutch dramatic society, 28; by *radio distributie*, 100; by radio-receiving set, 24, 99–100; French dramatic society, 27; of a drama is not publication, 14, 16, 21, 72, 81, 91; of dramatico-musical compositions, 22, 23, 30–31, 46, 57, 81, 91, 115; of music for profit, 8, 18, 22–26, 40–41; of music is not a publication, 14, 16, 18–19, 21, 72, 81, 82, 91; nonprofit, of music, 22–24, 25–26, 95; of records and publication right, 95–96, 111, 114; right recognized in France, 27; rights in common law drama, 8; rights in common law music, 8, 21, 22; rights in copyrighted drama, 22, 23; rights in record manufacturer, 85, 95, 110–113; rights, necessity of collective action, 27–28; right of, merged with mechanical right, 33–34; see also Performing right societies, ASCAP, BMI, Broad-casting.
Publication: abroad, 10–12, 69–71, 78, 79–80, 91; Berne protection of non-Union authors, 70, 71, 72; broadcasting, 14, 72; copyright notice, 6–7, 8–9, 10, 14, 16–21; definition of, 7–8, 14–16, 72–76, 80, 81, 82, 84, 91, 92; first, date of, 7–8, 11–12, 14–16, 80–81; first, place of, 5, 9, 10, 11–12, 14–16, 69–72, 80–81, 91, 92; first, right of, 8; general, 15; includes mechanical reproduction, 95–97; includes performances by records, 95–97, 98; limited, 15; motion pictures, 14–16, 72–73, 84–85, 91; phonograph records, 16–21, 72–73, 81–84, 91, 92–93; posthumously, 12, 92–93; retaining copyright, 9, 72; securing copyright, 6–9, 10, 11–12, 21, 70–76, 78, 80–81; termination of common law protection, 8, 16–21, 79; unauthorized, 7; see also Copies, Public, Sale, Simultaneous publication.
Public domain: boundary between, and common law, 8–9, 14–21; boundary between, and copyright, 8–9, 12, 14, 17–18, 20.
Published works, see Copies, Public, Publication.
Publisher, music, see ASCAP, BMI.
RCA Victor Records, 64.

Radio-diffusion, see *Radio distributie*.
Radio distributie, 31, 33, 100.
Radio Program Foundation, 41–42, 48.
Radio receiving set: in public is a performance, 24, 99–100; license necessary for public performance for profit, 24–25, 99.
Radio Tax, see Tax.
Radio Union, 119.
Radio, see Broadcasting.
Rate regulation, 34, 55–56.
Reciprocity, 10.
Records, see Phonograph records.
Regerings-Commissaris, 117–118.
Register of Copyrights, 7.
Registration: and infringement proceedings, 7; Britain does not require, 86–87; for renewal and extension of copyright, 12; of published works, 7, 11–12, 17; see also Unpublished works.
Regulation of performing right societies, see ASCAP—consent decrees, BMI-consent decree, Tribunal, BUMA-government control.
Relay station, see *Radio distributie*.
Relief Fund, ASCAP, 36–37.
Renewal of Copyright, 12–14, 87.
REPORT OF THE COPYRIGHT COMMITTEE TO PARLIAMENT, 73, 82, 90, 99, 110, 112–113.
Republication in the United States, 10.
Rescission of copyright contracts, 125.
Research, 89.
Reservation of rights, 11, 15.
Restrictions on protection, see Copies — deposit of, Formalities, Manufacturing clause, Berne Convention—restrictions.
Reversionary interest, 87.
Review, 89.
G. Ricordi & Co. of Milan, 42, 45, 48, 54.
Royalties, see ASCAP, BMI, BUMA, PRS, SACEM, and Statutory royalties.
S.A.C.D., see Société des Auteurs et Compositeurs Dramatiques.
SACEM, see Société des Auteurs, Compositeurs et Éditeurs de Musique.
Sale: as part of publication, 6–9, 14–21, 72–76, 80, 81, 84–85, 91; of copies and copyright notice, 6–7, 9; of copyright, 13, 29; see also Assignment of copyright.
Scenario, 15.

S.D.R.M., see Société pour l'Administration du Droit de Reproduction Méchanique des Auteurs, Compositeurs et Éditeurs.
SEBA, see Bureau Theaterrechten van de Stichting tot Exploitatie en Bescherming van Auteursrechten; Bureau Letterkunde van de Stichting tot Exploitatie en Bescherming van Auteursrechten.
"Serious" music, see Standard music.
SESAC, Inc., 28.
Shaw, Arnold, 51.
Sheet music, see Music.
Sherman Act, 31.
"Signature tune," 109–110.
Simultaneous publication, 70, 80–81.
Skone James, F. E., 76, 77, 80, 82–83, 84, 95.
"Small" performing rights, 30, 129.
Société des Auteurs, Compositeurs et Éditeurs de Musique: formation of, 27–28; broadcasting revenue, 114; juke boxes, 113; monopoly, 113; non-dramatic performing rights (*petit droits*), 113, 114; operating in the Netherlands, 115–116; programs, 113–114; royalties from ASCAP, 113–114; royalty distribution, 114.
Société des Auteurs et Compositeurs Dramatiques, 27, 114.
Société des Gens de Lettres, 114.
Société pour l'Administration du Droit de Reproduction Mécanique des Auteurs, Compositeurs et Éditeurs, 114.
Society of European Stage Authors and Composers, 28.
Songwriters' Protective Association, 51, 60.
Sound track, motion picture, see Motion Pictures.
Source licensing, 33–34, 42–44.
SPA, see Songwriters' Protective Association.
Specific performance, 30.
Sponsored broadcasting, commercially, 25–26, 32, 42, 43–44.
Standard music, 34, 35, 38, 39, 40, 41, 44, 45, 48, 49, 101, 110, 120–122.
States: statutes regulating ASCAP, 31; individual, and common law, 5, 6, 7, 8.
Statutory: copyright, see Copyright-statutory; performance fees, see Rate regulation; royalties, 18–19, 47, 85, 114.

STEMRA, see Stichting tot Exploitatie van Mechanische Reproductie Rechten der Auteurs.
Stichting tot Exploitatie van Mechanische Reproductie Rechten der Auteurs, 123.
Subject of foreign nation, 9–10.
Sub-publishing, 108, 121.
Sustainer programs, 26, 32.
Synchronization right, see Motion Pictures-sound track.
Tannenbaum, Samuel W., 15, 85.
Tax: on radio receiving set owners, 32, 104, 114, 119; benefit through ASCAP, 58.
Television: distinction between dramatic and non-dramatic performances, 30–31; see also Broadcasting.
Term of copyright, see Copyright, duration of.
Termination of affiliation with performing societies, 40, 60–62.
"Tie-ins," 64.
"Time," 32.
Timberg, Sigmund, 64–65.
Tournier, Alphonse, 96, 97.
Transmission, see Broadcasting.
Tribunal, 112–113.
Twentieth Century-Fox Films, 64.
Uitvoering, 100.
Unauthorized, see Consent.
Uniform songwriters' contract, 60, 63.
United Kingdom: and United States, 5, 79, 80; unpublished works, 8; works first published elsewhere, 5.
United States: statutory copyright generally, 5–14; and United Kingdom, 5, 79, 80.
Universal Copyright Convention, 77–78.
Unpublished works: advantages of not registering, 18; Berne Convention, 69–72, 77; broadcasting, 14, 16, 72; distribution and exhibition of motion pictures, 14–16, 72–73; phonograph recordings, 16–21, 72–73, 81–84; British protection of, 79, 81–84, 86–87; American protection of, 7–8, 9, 22; registration of, 6–8, 9, 17–21, 86–87; United States generally, 5, 6–7; Europe generally, 5, 77; Universal Copyright Convention, 78; see also Public Performance, Publication.
Use: creator's right at common law, 8; relation between, and price, 97.
Users: ASCAP's definition of, 54, 129; see also Motion Pictures, Broadcasting, ASCAP-licenses, BMI-licenses, BUMA-licenses, PRS-licenses.
Vereniging van Muziekhandelaren en -Uitgevers in Nederland, 115.
Vereniging Woord- en Toondichters der Lichte Muziek, 116.
Victor, see RCA Victor Records.
Voidance of copyright, 7.
Ward, A. H. S., 73–74.
Warner Bros., 64.
Warranties, 48.
Widow of the author, 12, 37.
Widower of author, 12, 37.
Wiessing, C. A., 115.
Will, absence of author's, and renewal of copyright, 12.
"Wired Music," see MUZAK.
Withdrawal: from performing right society, 40, 60–62, 125; from Berne Union, 78.
Withholding work from the public, 86, 96.
Writer: meaning of, as used in this book, 30.
Zavin, Theodora, 45.